THE SOCIAL AND POLITICAL
DOCTRINES OF
CONTEMPORARY EUROPE

The

SOCIAL AND POLITICAL DOCTRINES OF CONTEMPORARY EUROPE

BY

MICHAEL OAKESHOTT

WITH A FOREWORD BY

ERNEST BARKER

American Edition
WITH FIVE PREFACES BY
FREDERIC A. OGG

CAMBRIDGE: AT THE UNIVERSITY PRESS
NEW YORK: THE MACMILLAN COMPANY
1945

First Edition *1939*
Second Edition *1941*
American Edition *1942*

Reprinted January, 1944
Reprinted March, 1945

PRINTED IN THE UNITED STATES OF AMERICA

FOREWORD TO FIRST EDITION

The last twenty-one years have been fruitful in fresh statements of social and political doctrine. Some of the most notable statements have been made either *ex cathedra* or by persons who afterwards came to occupy the chair. In the autumn of 1917 Lenin issued his pamphlet on *The State and Revolution*, stating the doctrine of Marxianism in the form to which he afterwards sought to give effect. In 1925 there appeared the first volume, and in 1927 the second, of Herr Hitler's *Mein Kampf.* In 1931 there was issued the Encyclical of Pius XI, *Quadragesimo Anno*, which restated and expanded the Catholic doctrine of economic society. In 1932 Signor Mussolini contributed to the new Italian Encyclopaedia an essay on *La Dottrina del Fascismo*. These are classical documents of four schools of contemporary European thought—the Communist, the National Socialist, the Catholic and the Fascist. No similar document has appeared to restate the doctrine of another school—that of Liberal or Parliamentary Democracy—which stands by the side of the other four. Here the foundations were laid, and the fundamental statements made, in the nineteenth century. But age is no proof of obsolescence; and the doctrine of Parliamentary Democracy is a living and vigorous member of the contemporary body of European thought.

In the course of last year I suggested to Mr Oakeshott (and he has generously and quickly acted on my suggestion) that he should collect a volume which would illustrate, in authentic and original texts, the tenets of the main schools. He has drawn me into consultation; and we have discussed together the scheme of the volume. But it is he who has done the work; and I have only served in the office of a consultant. I cannot but hope that the result of the work will commend itself to the reader. He will find ready to his use (often in new translations) not only the core and essence of contemporary statements of doctrine, but also—and this more especially in regard to the doctrines of Communism and Catholicism—the gist of the previous expositions which are expanded or developed in these contemporary statements. He will find that the doctrine of Parliamentary Democracy has not been forgotten: he will also find that the new doctrines of Fascism and National Socialism have been illustrated not only by statements of their theory, but also by legislative texts which throw further light on that theory.

A work of this nature cannot but be of service, perhaps in schools as well as in universities, but particularly in universities. The subject of social and political theory is professed in our universities under different titles—here "political philosophy", there "the theory of the Modern State", and here again "the principles of politics". The difficulty of the student is to come to grips with contemporary theory in any authentic expression. It is not to be found in any work of the study, or in any single language: it appears in the utterances and pronouncements of the leaders of States and parties and Churches (for political science seems to have risen from the study to the tribune): it appears in Latin, German and Italian—not to speak of Russian. A book which seeks to harvest these riches, and to harvest them in the scholarly temper of objective and unprejudiced understanding, cannot but offer to the student a welcome food for thought.

But we are all students—enforced students—to-day, in the debate and clash of doctrines which whirls around us and affects all our lives. The spate of books on social and political issues is a measure of the general interest and the general concern. Forty years ago I could keep abreast of the political literature which concerned my times: to-day it is a hopeless task. All the more reason that the general reader and the ordinary citizen should turn to a book which brings him face to face with the fundamental issues, as they are stated by those who, in word and action, have given them form and motion. Commentaries always matter; but the texts themselves are vital. Every citizen, I cannot but feel, has some measure of duty to study these texts, and will derive advantage from their study. He will be a better citizen of his own country, and a better member of the society of Europe—which still exists, in spite of all these differences of doctrine. I would therefore commend this book for study in far wider circles than those of the university; and I venture to hope that it may reach study-groups of working men and women, and penetrate into every forum of discussion. For it is not only politics that some of these doctrines touch. It is also the whole social order: it is the principles of morals and religion: it is life itself.

Doctrines are not everything; and it is easy to magnify their influence. They matter, and they matter profoundly; but their translation into effect, and their actual achievement, also matter. Laws and institutions, and the practical operation of laws and institutions, have to be studied a well as doctrines. Indeed the study of the operation of doctrines is a necessary part of the understanding of doctrines; and sometimes it may even be found (as perhaps in the case of Italian Fascism) that the operation of a doctrine preceded its enunciation. The fact remains that ideas, when once they have been enunciated in a form of authority, possess a dynamic force. The reader who studies the ideas expressed in this book will gain, at the least, some understanding of the forces which are working on men's minds in contemporary Europe. If he can go farther, and discover *how* they work and *what* they produce, his gain will be all the greater. But he will already have gained a great deal if he has grasped the great *idées-forces* which are active around and about him.

ERNEST BARKER

5 *November* 1938

NOTE ON SECOND EDITION, 1941

The last two passages have been added to the section entitled *National Socialism* (on pp. 224 and 226); and, in an Appendix (pp. 232 ff.), two additions to the section entitled *Representative Democracy*. A Subject Index has also been added.

NOTE ON AMERICAN EDITION, 1942

An increasing demand for this book in the United States, particularly for use in courses on contemporary government, has provided the occasion for an American edition. Advantage has been taken of this opportunity for the inclusion of a preface to each of the five sections, by Professor Frederic A. Ogg of the University of Wisconsin; these prefaces are specifically addressed to readers in the United States, and will be found particularly useful by instructors and students using the book in college work.

June 1942

CONTENTS

INTRODUCTION

Contemporary Europe presents the spectator with a remarkable variety of social and political doctrines; indeed it is improbable that this collection of communities has ever before shown such fertility of invention in this field. Of course it is some centuries now since Western Europe could be said to subscribe to and live under a single and universal conception of man, society and government, and during the last couple of centuries thinkers with fresh views on these matters have not been wanting; a variety of social and political doctrines is not in itself a novelty. What is remarkable about contemporary Europe is the number and variety of the social and political doctrines that have acquired some sort of realization in practice, that have communities actually living under them. The unity, in this respect, which Europe in the past enjoyed can be exaggerated, and its present lack of unity in doctrine is to some extent due merely to the egregious habit of modern communities of compounding for their policies, ambitions and experiments by elevating them into principles We live in an age of self-conscious communities. Even the crudest of the regimes of contemporary Europe, the regime which, admittedly, owes least to a systematically thought-out doctrine, the Fascist regime in Italy, appears to value self-righteousness enough to join with the others in claiming a doctrine of its own. Opportunism has suffered the emasculation of being converted into a principle; we have lost not only the candour of Machiavelli but also even the candour of the *Anti-Machiavel*. But it is a loss not to be regretted without qualification. It is evidence, at least, that nobody now expects a hearing who does not exhibit some anxiety to act on principle, who is not prepared to explain his conduct in some terms other than those of mere personal inclination. It is an advantage, also, to anyone who wishes to understand the various regimes of contemporary Europe, to be provided with some statement of the doctrines on which they rely: it absolves him, in part, from the necessity of deducing the doctrine for himself from the policies and actions of the regime, deductions which are more likely to be ingenious than sound, which might be disclaimed and which would certainly be resented. Moreover, this variety of social and political doctrine is not to be explained as merely the product of a fashion which has become a craze. It denotes a deep and natural dissatisfaction with the social and political doctrine, broadly to be called Liberalism, which if it did not capture, at least fascinated Western Europe since before 1789: a natural dissatisfaction, because this doctrine had become as nearly established as any such doctrine could be, and had, in consequence, become boring, and all its profundity could not rescue it from the fate which pursues whatever becomes intellectually boring. In short, this variety of social and political doctrine may be seen as the self-assertion of elements in our civilization which the established doctrine, even in its most profound statements, never fully recognized or adequately expressed. And if the self-assertion is fumbling—even the most enlightened despotisms breed incapacity in their subjects, and the intellectual dominance of Liberalism was hardly short of a despotism. There is much to regret in the modern world: what is not dangerously old appears to be dangerously new, and there are many who will be inclined to dismiss its social and political doctrines as, all of them, remarkable contributions to the history of human folly. This, however, is to be unduly severe; these doctrines are all we have, each of them is an expression of something in our civilization, in some cases of what were better forgotten, in others of what to our loss we have failed to remember, and in all of what we cannot merely ignore. And we cannot merely regret them without regretting our civilization—a fruitless, if heroic, act.

The object of this book is to provide the relevant material for beginning a study of the social and political doctrines of contemporary Europe. These doctrines I have taken to be five in number—Representative Democracy, Catholicism, Communism, Fascism and National Socialism; and in each case I have attempted to collect the best available statements—sometimes official, always authoritative—of the more important elements which compose the doctrine. I have thought it better to select substantial passages, rather than to make the book an anthology of aphorisms and brief statements; and unless an indication to the contrary is given, the passages quoted are complete. I am responsible, also, for most of the headings which appear above the different passages.

The limits of my design are deliberate and severe, and I will point them out at once. First, the book deals only with those social and political doctrines of modern Europe which have found some actual realization, which are represented in the life and order of some national community. Within this limitation my selection is, I believe, tolerably complete. There are, perhaps, communities which do not conform to any one of these doctrines, though they are rare; but there is none which does not embody either a strong tendency towards one or other of these doctrines exclusively, or a mixture of two or more of them. Secondly, it deals solely with the doctrines themselves, the intellectual constructions on which the various regimes of contemporary Europe rely, and not with the actual laws, institutions, machinery of government and working of those regimes. Sometimes I have used the more general provisions of a law, or the outline of an institution, to illustrate a doctrine, but in no case have I attempted to give a complete account of any law or institution, and much less to give any account at all of the actual working of a regime. Indeed, for my purpose, a law which was promulgated but never put into effective operation might be as good evidence as one which had, in its working, already begun to change the life of the community. This is not a handbook of contemporary European constitutional law or practice, but of the doctrines and intellectual systems adduced to explain or excuse the policies and conduct of governments and communities in Europe to-day. Thirdly, no attempt is made here to provide material for the study of the public or the back-stairs origin or history of these doctrines and their respective regimes. Each of them belongs to some current of tradition, often of national tradition, in our civilization, and it may be true that some of these regimes owe their origin and continuance to the influence of some sinister interest which does not appear in the doctrine itself—these are questions for the historian of modern Europe; I leave them alone. And further, even if we believe that all such doctrines are (in some way) the products of the social conditions in which they appear, that they are merely expressions of the passion for self-preservation of some community, it does not follow that an examination of the doctrines themselves is without interest or relevance, or that to provide materials for such an examination is to assert (by implication) that these doctrines are independent of the social circumstances of their construction. Fourthly, each of these doctrines has what may be called a universal aspect, each makes some claim to universal, if temporary, application: Fascism does not represent itself as appropriate for Italy alone, "the Europe of to-morrow will be Fascist"; and Communism is not thought of as a notion of society and government relevant solely to Russia. And it is upon this universal aspect that I have laid my emphasis. Many of the pronouncements of those who speak for the various regimes are of ephemeral significance, many are pardonable rhetorical exaggerations, many merely *ruses de guerre*, and for these reasons I have neglected them. Where I have quoted from a social or political programme I have done so because it represents more than a policy, because it represents the fundamental doctrine of the regime. What I have aimed at is to give, in each case, the fairest and most authoritative statement of the doctrine concerned. And lastly, I have provided no commentary on these doctrines; to do so adequately would require space and learning neither of which I command. And indeed, so many commentaries exist already that, rather than to add to them, it appeared more useful to provide a book of documents to be used in conjunction with them.[1]

In short, this book is for those who are interested in ideas; and those who are not, need not trouble to turn its pages. It is a common opinion to-day that what is important about a social and political doctrine is its emotive value, and our attention is constantly directed to this rather than to the doctrine itself as an intellectual construction. And this opinion may be true. But anyone subject to the fascination of ideas will not need to be persuaded that these doctrines are, as doctrines, interesting and important. Each of them is not merely a political doctrine, a doctrine about the nature of the state and the ends of government, but also a social doctrine, a conception of society and of the place and function of the individual in society. If what we had to deal with was a collection of merely political creeds we might be excused the tedium of considering them closely; their significance would be limited and their importance small. But what we are presented with in contemporary European thought is at least five separate and distinct ways of conceiving the fundamental character of society, and, by implication, five separate and distinct ways of conceiving the nature and earthly destiny of man. Five is, perhaps, four too many for a single civilization if it is to be harmonious with itself; but, while it is, I think, possible to see that they are not so separate and distinct as they would like to represent themselves, it would be foolish to attribute to our civilization a unity which it has lost, merely on the ground that these doctrines are to some small extent complementary. At least they are distinct enough to merit separate consideration, and influential and profound enough to repay close study.

---

[1] The lists of books at the end of each section contain a brief selection from the more recent commentaries (where possible in English), and are in no sense intended to be bibliographies of the doctrines themselves.

There is, however, one danger that the intellectual critic of political doctrines should avoid. He is apt to think that the value of a regime or of a condition or an ideal of society depends upon the coherence with which the doctrine associated with it is expressed. He observes a system of reasons adduced to explain the practice of a regime, and he is apt to conclude that because it leaves something to be desired the regime itself stands condemned. He is ready to dismiss Fascism because of the obvious confusion of Mussolini's mind, or Communism because of the obscurity, ambiguity and dogmatism of the Marxian analysis. And this tendency may lead him astray. The value of a regime, fortunately, does not depend upon the intellectual competence of its apologists; indeed, in most cases, practice is more coherent than doctrine and its superiority should be recognized. Nevertheless, when a regime chooses to rationalize its practice, chooses to issue an official statement of the social and political doctrine upon which it relies—and this is so with most of the regimes of contemporary Europe—the coherence of such a statement becomes a matter of importance; and if it can be convicted of intellectual confusion, that is not a fault to be brushed aside as insignificant. What the intellectual critic of a doctrine has to say is certainly relevant, though it is not all that can be said and is unlikely to affect the course of affairs.

The social and political doctrines or creeds of modern Europe have an intellectual content which can be examined and judged, but from one standpoint at least they are all, though not equally, disappointing. They are not in the strict sense philosophies, and it would be a mistake to be disappointed because they are not what they do not pretend to be. But to each of them is attached a body of philosophical ideas which, in the view of their exponents, is appropriate to them; or perhaps it would be truer to say that the exponents of these social and political doctrines have not been able to deny themselves excursions into philosophical thought. And these excursions are remarkably unsatisfactory. It is not, perhaps, to be expected that these social and political thinkers should be profound or critical philosophers, and it is only to be expected that when they attempt philosophical analysis or criticism they are quickly out of sight of anything like dry land; but when we are led on a philosophical excursion it is difficult to avoid hoping for something better than what we are shown here. In this respect the Catholic social and political doctrine stands far above any of the others, for it at least has the help of a profound philosophical thinker, St Thomas Aquinas, and is not dependent for its philosophy on some vague leaning towards a half understood and wholly confused pragmatism which would give no better support if it were more fully understood. The philosophy attached to Representative Democracy is, perhaps, a little better than that on which some other of these social and political doctrines depend but it is not a philosophy that anyone could accept nowadays without a radical restatement which has yet to be provided. But here again, it would be a mistake to dismiss these social and political doctrines on account of the inadequacy of the philosophical ideas or systems with which their apologists have chosen to ally them. It is relevant to point out the confusion of ideas which goes under the title of the Marxian theory of knowledge, or to remark upon the inadequate philosophical foundation of Mill's individualism, but the doctrines of neither Communism nor Democracy will altogether succumb to attacks from this direction. And the most useful service the philosophic critic can perform is that of freeing these social and political doctrines from the encumbrance of these largely parasitic philosophical and pseudo-philosophical ideas.

The general contents of this symposium is, I think, what anyone acquainted with the subject would look to find. But perhaps a word of explanation will be expected for placing first Representative Democracy, or even for its inclusion at all. To call Representative Democracy into our debate will appear to some to be calling in a Rip van Winkle of social and political doctrine who cannot understand what the others are saying and who has not the wit to learn, and whose sleep has been all the more profound because it has been the waking slumber of dogmatic repose. Moreover, the characteristic simple-mindedness of the Representative Democratic doctrine makes it appear in the modern world as a fool among knaves. With Catholicism, it will be felt, the case is different; it at least does not suffer from the peculiar deadness of last year's fashion. Catholic social and political doctrine might (by the ignorant) be considered a harmless museum piece; but the corpse of liberty (we have it on good authority) stinks. There are, however, adequate reasons for considering the social and political doctrine of Representative Democracy among the doctrines of contemporary European thought, and they are not connected with any hypothetical resurrection which it might experience: we need not trespass into the future.[1] First, it is

[1] I neglect the untenable view that Representative Democracy is merely a method of government, implying no specific doctrine of the nature of society and the individual citizen.

impossible to understand either Communism, Fascism or National Socialism without first understanding the doctrine of Representative Democracy; though when it is understood, it is difficult to understand some, though not all, of the criticisms which these newer doctrines advance against it. Each of these newer doctrines is an express reaction from the Democratic doctrine as a whole or from some specific elements of it. It is the parent of these ungracious children. But secondly, while each of these rejects what it takes to be the characteristic doctrine of Representative Democracy, so great is its influence over them that each finds it necessary to make some compromise. Sometimes the compromise is merely verbal, as when the Fascist suggests that democracy can and should be understood in such a way that Fascism will appear the truest and most genuine democracy. Sometimes it is tactical and seems to be designed to have the effect of watering down a doctrine otherwise too intoxicating for any save its apostles. But, in one degree or another, the Democratic doctrine, or elements of it, lives on in these other doctrines (in Communism which represents itself as an extension of the democratic ideal, and even in Fascism and National Socialism which represent themselves as, fundamentally, a denial of that ideal), and they owe it a debt which they have not yet found a way either of hiding or of liquidating successfully. An authoritarian regime, no doubt, can "liquidate" the liberal supporters which, for one reason or another, helped to bring it into being; but no modern authoritarian doctrine can liquidate its debt to the doctrine of Democracy. And thirdly, of course, the social and political doctrine of Representative Democracy is that under which the majority of civilized mankind still live.

Nevertheless, I cannot conceal the difficulty I have had in choosing my passages for Representative Democracy. The name I do not attempt to defend; it is a choice largely of convenience. The obvious choice of "Liberal Democracy" I rejected because the doctrine I wanted to represent is not to be confused with the crude and negative individualism which is apt to be associated with Liberalism; it is something both older and younger than Liberalism, something of which Liberalism was an expression but an incomplete expression. Liberalism in that sense is perhaps dead; the doctrine of Representative Democracy has survived that death. And again, Liberalism in England is apt still to be understood as the creed of a party and to be contrasted with Conservatism and Socialism; whereas the doctrine I wished to find some statement of, the doctrine of Representative or Parliamentary Democracy, is a tradition expressed, so far as this country is concerned, in the spirit of our laws rather than in the programme of any one party. Nevertheless, it is a Liberal doctrine. Ignorant people are still to be found writing as if the history of Liberalism were merely the history of the rise and dominance of a peculiarly narrow brand of individualism; and if their ignorance were not dangerous it might be ignored. But, while the other doctrines which we have to consider are moderately precise and systematic (though the price they pay, in most cases, is a remarkable rigidity, and their system is mostly on the surface), the social and political beliefs of Representative Democracy are more in the nature of a tradition and a tendency than a well-knit doctrine, and are, in consequence, more difficult to state precisely and completely. I do not wish to suggest (what I do not believe) that this doctrine of Representative Democracy is the final deliverance of the human mind on questions of society and government (that it is, what Mussolini and others accuse it of asserting itself to be, "outside history"),[1] but it has the advantage of all the others in that it has shown itself capable of changing without perishing in the process, and it has the advantage (denied to all others save Catholicism) of not being the hasty product of a generation but of belonging to a long and impressive tradition of thought. It contains, I believe, a more comprehensive expression of our civilization than any of the others (though it is by no means either a complete or a satisfactory expression as it stands), and its adaptability is a sign of vitality rather than mere vagueness. It has not yet thrown off altogether the doctrine of individualism which was once its core, and consequently I have thought it right to include J. S. Mill's classic statement of that doctrine. But it has long since modified its individualism, which was always a tendency rather than a principle, and consequently Mill's doctrine requires to be supplemented by the kind of view which appears in the passage printed from T. H. Green. For the rest, it is impossible to make of it an entirely coherent doctrine, and I have represented it by what is admittedly a miscellaneous collection of passages each illus-

[1] This is the commonest of accusations made against the doctrine of Representative Democracy, and there is some shadow of truth in it. But if we neglect the wilder statements of this and the other doctrines, it would appear that it is not Democracy which is peculiarly "insensible of mortality and desperately mortal" but these others which represent themselves as reactions against democratic principles. They all involve a social and political life planned to last indefinitely (National Socialism is given a life of 2000 years by Hitler), and what could be more pretentious?

trating some important element. And if the doctrine as a whole appears a little dusty, I can only hope that I have not made it appear more dusty than it certainly is. At all events, if I have succeeded in conveying what I believe to be its central principles—that a society must not be so unified as to abolish vital and valuable differences, nor so extravagantly diversified as to make an intelligently co-ordinated and civilized social life impossible, and that the imposition of a universal plan of life on a society is at once stupid and immoral—I shall have done what I intended to do.

The selections for the other parts of the book need no defence; they are, in the main, the obvious selections and, in most cases, no alternative to them exists. Each section might have been made larger than it is, but I doubt if in so doing I should have added anything but matters of detail to the general outline of the doctrines. And, in any case, what I have aimed at throughout is to provide the relevant material for anyone anxious to make a beginning on the study of these doctrines, rather than a complete corpus of authorities.

The social and political doctrine of Catholicism is included, in the first place, because of its inherent merits. As a doctrine it is closer-knit and more systematic than any of the other current doctrines. Its strength lies in its coherence and its rigidity. In virtue of the one it is an example from which modern social and political thought has much to learn; in virtue of the other it appears in the modern world to some extent as a stranger, and the criticism Catholicism offers of other doctrines is less convincing than its statement of its own. It is, also, the repository of an element of profound importance in the European tradition; it is the only contemporary representative of a genuine Natural Law theory, and it is evidence that this theory is not yet dead. If this doctrine is a stranger in the modern world, it is certainly not an exotic doctrine: authoritarian without the capriciousness of the other authoritarian doctrines, it reminds us of an inheritance we have neglected. No greater or more instructive contrast[1] could exist than that between the Liberal Democratic conception of government (so admirably expressed in the passage taken from Abraham Lincoln) and the Catholic doctrine as it appears in the Encyclical *Immortale Dei* of Leo XIII; and yet both of these views belong to our civilization. And, so far as this country is concerned, I venture to suggest that many of

---

[1] Except, perhaps, the contrast between the Catholic and the Fascist of National Socialist conceptions of authority.

the principles which belong to the historic doctrine of Conservatism are to be found in this Catholic doctrine. The inclusion of this doctrine is justified, further, on the ground that it is the social and political doctrine which, when I began to write this Introduction, was embodied in the Constitution of the Republic of Austria. It has found a home also in contemporary Ireland and in Portugal.

It is the custom of some writers to-day to recur to an earlier tradition and speak of the doctrine which I have called Communism as the doctrine of Socialism. But since there is still more than one kind of Socialism, I have thought it less ambiguous to use the other title. From some points of view the social and political doctrine of Communism is the most remarkable that the contemporary world has to show. It has its connexions with the past, and, as a doctrine, it is certainly not what some of its professors pretend—related to the past only by reaction. But it proposes a type of society, and indeed a type of man, more unlike what the world has hitherto seen than any of the other doctrines. It has suffered grievously from those who have undertaken to expound it, but it has managed to survive their attentions. It contains the most radical criticism that the Liberal Democratic doctrine has yet had to face; but, at the same time, it appears to preserve largely unchanged the most questionable element of Liberal Democracy, what may be called its moral ideal: "the plausible ethics of productivity". It is the most complicated of all the doctrines we have to consider, but it is never tired of proclaiming its simplicity; it makes a vast display of philosophical ideas, but it is full of self-contradictions; it is encumbered with a quaint mediaeval jargon, but it has become the creed of millions. It is, I believe, among the new doctrines, the one from which we have most to learn, but it is the doctrine which stands most in need of radical restatement.

Of course, it is not strictly accurate to take the present regime in Russia as an example of Communist society, for it does not pretend to be more than the first stage in the process of liquidating capitalist society; it is not Communism but the Dictatorship of the Proletariat. Nevertheless, the change from this society to one genuinely communistic is not, according to the doctrine, so revolutionary a change as that required to overthrow Capitalism, and if and when Communism is established in Russia we need not expect it to involve a social order radically different from what at present prevails. The main principles of the new social order are already established; it remains for them to create the new type of man presupposed in Communism. The Russian Constitution of 1936 is, consequently, a document of the first importance. It relies, of course, on the Marxian doctrine of Communism, but it comes nearer to making a real advance upon that doctrine than any other statement I have met. And a close study of it will dispose of the superficial view (which was never even plausible) that the distinction between Communism and the other authoritarian doctrines is of negligible importance.

Of all the current social and political doctrines that of Fascism is the most difficult to assess. Perhaps it is more than an elaborate and verbose expression of the spirit of *fregarsene*, but how much more it is difficult to say. It asserts as fundamental principles what anyone might be excused for believing for a short time and in unfortunate circumstances: few can desire war more than anything else, but it is understandable that some people after a period of peace or humiliation should be persuaded that life without *la gloire* is an ignoble thing. But it is impossible to dismiss Fascism as merely the doctrine of a community morbidly anxious to assert its superiority. The Fascist criticism of Liberal Democracy is far too acute to be merely ignored. Much of that criticism, it is true, is beside the mark because it is directed against a doctrine which nobody has believed in for fifty years. And when Fascism shies from the fallacy of individualism—an individual who is independent of his society—it does nothing more significant than to bog itself in the ditch, wildly embracing the opposite fallacy of a society which is independent of its members. But the attack on the moral ideal of Liberal Democracy is, I think, well-founded; that was always the weakest part of the doctrine. But again, when Fascism comes to put something in its place we are given nothing better than what was rejected but under a new and more flashy name. There may be something more inspiring in the materialism of Fascism, the materialism of an army and conquest, the materialism of a preference for methods of violence, than in the duller materialism of Liberal Democracy, but it is certainly not less materialistic. It is sheer obfuscation of the mind to call the one ideal material and the other spiritual. Fascism, like the other doctrines, has its parade of philosophic ideas, but, in spite of this, it remains a doctrine of cryptic statements and crude assertions, and even those most sympathetic to the regime as it exists in Italy cannot consider the present statement of the doctrine altogether satisfactory.

National Socialism in Germany is the youngest of the new regimes

in Europe, and more than any of the others it came into being in order
to put a specific policy in operation. It is a regime of nationalism more
fierce even than the Fascist; it is socialistic only in the sense of being a
planned society. But, like the others, it claims a universal character; it
has a message for the world as well as for Germany, and it relies upon
an elaborate doctrine, not only of government but also of society. It is
an authoritarian doctrine, but its affinity to Fascism is more on the
surface than at the centre; and National Socialism has the advantage of
Fascism in the possession of a doctrine incomparably more coherent.
Nevertheless, it is surprising that so empirical a doctrine should have
come out of Germany. It has little to show of the imaginative power of
the Marxian doctrine, and little of the reasoning of the Catholic. Its
memento audere semper is merely a programme of power masquerading as
a social ideal. This doctrine, in form and content, can be seen in many
respects to exhibit the temperament of the community in which it prevails
(this indeed is what is claimed for it), and to belong to a tradition in
German social and political thought. Not many of the tenets of National
Socialism are new, but they are held to-day with an unrivalled self-
consciousness and an unmatched solemnity. Even those who are
inspired by the doctrine must find it difficult to admire its tone of self-
righteousness. Its opposition to Representative Democracy is fundamental, and not based merely upon the alleged defects of democratic
political arrangements. Its doctrines of Race and Blood and of Leadership
separate it firmly from every other current doctrine. But it has not been
able to discard Liberalism altogether: it asserts "complete liberty of
creed and conscience", even if it follows up the assertion with provisions which make that liberty unrecognizable—provisions, I mean,
in its doctrine and not merely in practice. And its moral ideal is as
crudely materialistic (though this is denied) as that of Liberal Democracy at its worst.[1] Indeed, there is not much in our past that we
would gladly forget which is not represented and reasserted in this
doctrine.

---

[1] With regard to the moral ideals represented in these doctrines, the fundamental
cleavage appears to me to lie neither between those which offer a spiritual ideal
and those which offer a material ideal, nor in the actual content of the moral ideals
themselves, but between those which hand over to the arbitrary will of a society's
self-appointed leaders the planning of its entire life, and those which not only
refuse to hand over the destiny of a society to any set of officials but also consider
the whole notion of planning the destiny of a society to be both stupid and
immoral. On the one side are the three modern authoritarian doctrines, Com-

The reader will not have mistaken this introduction for a comprehensive survey of the social and political doctrines of contemporary Europe; it is no more than it pretends to be, a preface to a collection of material from which he can make his own judgement. It is, perhaps, idle to direct his attention to any particular conclusion, but to me the most remarkable conclusion is the comparatively small amount of damage which the doctrine of Representative Democracy has suffered from this bombardment. One would have thought it possible, if not easy, to convict so muddled a theory of some fresh defect. And yet, when we consider the net result of this criticism, it is difficult to see that anything relevant has been said against the doctrine which, for example, Matthew Arnold did not say half a century ago, and said much better. The debt of the modern authoritarian doctrines to Liberalism is impossible to conceal, and anyone anxious to extract the true metal of the Liberal doctrine from the base ore from which it has never yet been successfully separated, will look hopefully to modern authoritarianism for relevant and constructive criticisms. But he will look in vain. Each, perhaps, offers something, and some of these doctrines more than others; but the total of their relevant criticisms is absurdly small. Indeed, modern scepticism as to the efficacy of thought is unambiguously reflected in most of these doctrines. They do not trouble to hide their tendency to descend from reasoned statements to mere assertions and from thought to febrile activity as a substitute for thought. None of them can be taken as a model of intellectual clarity, and all are ambiguous or deficient at the most important point. The social and political doctrines of contemporary Europe are striking mainly in virtue of their defects as doctrines and their remarkable success in subjugating whole communities.

munism, Fascism and National Socialism; on the other Catholicism and Liberalism. To the Liberal and the Catholic mind alike the notion that men can authoritatively plan and impose a way of life upon a society appears to be a piece of pretentious ignorance; it can be entertained only by men who have no respect for human beings and are willing to make them the means to the realization of their own ambitions. Nevertheless, it belongs to both Fascism and National Socialism to represent themselves as offering a great spiritual ideal as a challenge to the materialism of Liberalism and Communism. And no one can deny that Liberalism and Communism are both materialistic doctrines. But nothing of this materialism is lost in the new authoritarian doctrines, except the name. They have the advantage over Marxism because they are newer and could profit by its mistakes; but they have learnt nothing significant except that a materialistic doctrine can be made palatable in the contemporary world only by making it appear something other than it is.

I

REPRESENTATIVE DEMOCRACY

In the first section of this book (together with the Appendix), Mr Oakeshott presents selected readings on a form of polity combining two basic elements—democracy and representation. Etymologically, "democracy" means government by the people—if not by all of the people, at any rate by the many. The ancient world made some approach to this political form: all adult male citizens had seats in the Athenian *ecclesia* of the fifth century B.C.; two hundred years later, landless men and freedmen were found voting in the *comitia*, or plebeian assembly, at Rome. From political rights, under these régimes, were excluded, however, all slaves and other non-citizens, comprising the bulk of the population; and not until the nineteenth century was far advanced did democracy, conceived as resting on manhood (and eventually universal) suffrage, become a reality in any considerable portions of the world.

In the meantime, the representative element had been added. To be sure, the principle of representation was not unknown to the Greeks and Romans. The democracy developed among these peoples was, however, in all cases *direct* rather than *representative*; that is to say, it entailed a meeting together, in primary assembly, of all of the politically eligible, in the fashion perpetuated to our own day in some small communities, including certain Swiss cantons and many New England towns. For obvious reasons, the people of a large state cannot be convoked in this manner; even if it were otherwise, they could not transact business *en masse*. Therefore when—first of all in countries lying on both sides of the Pyrenees, then in England, and presently in France—the development of nation-wide parliaments is first encountered, such gatherings are found organized on the pattern of representative, rather than direct, or "pure", democracy; in other words, voters arranged in groups—by geographical areas or according to professions or other "functional" affiliation—chose from their ranks some restricted number to attend parliamentary meetings and there speak for them. Representative democracy became an accepted, and by the early twentieth century a widespread, form of polity—the form which no less keen a student of political phenomena than Woodrow Wilson believed to be "about universally to prevail".

In his effort to bring together classic statements evincing the genius of representative democracy in its most basic aspects, Mr

Oakeshott has drawn chiefly upon six writers—three of them English, one French, one American, and one (Paine) who, born in England but identified almost equally with England and America, was more of an international figure than any of the others. In the initial extract, comprising the first three or four pages of a hundred-page essay, *On Liberty*, devoted to examining and defending freedom of thought and expression, John Stuart Mill, chief English liberal philosopher of mid-nineteenth-century England, gives, as Mr Oakeshott remarks, "a statement, as brief as it is brilliant, of the liberal view of history". In four other selections (one of them in the Appendix), Mill shows how individuality, while still a precious asset, has of necessity been curbed by the development of social controls; (2) discusses the most fundamental of all political questions, namely, the point at which one's innate right to freedom of action ceases and the right of society (mainly through the instrumentality of the state) to assert its regulative authority begins; (3) shows why, despite all its shortcomings, representative government is ideally the best form; and (4) explains why the well-being of free institutions requires that different nationalities have their own separate governments.

In §2, "The Love of Freedom", the masterful French political interpreter of a hundred years ago, Alexis de Tocqueville, contends that the passion for liberty, where it exists, is so much a part of the very nature of man that it is useless to attempt to describe it for such as cannot feel it. In §7, William Cobbett, early nineteenth-century English radical and pioneer in political journalism, sets forth his reasons for holding that, of all human rights in society, the "great right of all" is that of taking part in the making of law. Law, in this view, is not incompatible with liberty; rather, it is a necessary condition of and safeguard for liberty; and in the passage from *Liberal Legislation and Freedom of Contract*, by the Oxford professor and philosopher of two generations ago, Thomas H. Green, the relation between the two, in the democratic state, is explained with rare lucidity.

To the references listed on page 42 may be added: E. M. Sait, *Democracy* (1929); *ibid., Political Institutions: A Preface* (1938); F. W. Coker, *Recent Political Thought* (1934), Parts II–III; W. S. Carpenter, *Democracy and Representation* (1925); T. V. Smith, *The Democratic Way of Life* (1926); *The Federalist* (1788).

I

The social and political doctrine of Representative Democracy is a tradition of ideas rather than a fully coherent system, and in this section I have tried to illustrate some of the more important elements of that tradition. In English thought the tradition has drawn life from a great variety of sources; it has succeeded to more than one inheritance. Aristocratic constitutionalism, Nonconformity and Radicalism each contributed something. But as it exists in the contemporary world it is not to be identified with these or any other of its sources. It is not, of course, the exclusive product of English minds, but since the best that has been written in English on the subject is as good as anything to be found elsewhere, the bulk of my selections are from English writers. And since it belongs to the character of this doctrine to be a little behind the times (I know of no contemporary classic statement of the doctrine), the bulk of my selections are from nineteenth-century writers.

The first passage, on the history of Liberty, is included because in no case is it truer than in the case of Representative Democracy that the tendency of a doctrine is well seen in its conception of the past course of events, and the opening paragraphs of J. S. Mill's essay *On Liberty* give a statement, as brief as it is brilliant, of the Liberal view of history.

For each passage in this selection others, by other writers, might have been substituted, but the result would have been the same. The apparent omission of any statement of the doctrine of Property belonging to Representative Democracy perhaps needs justification. My defence is that while the concept of property which belongs to this social doctrine is of the first importance, it is, in this doctrine, in the nature of a deduction from a more fundamental concept, the concept of the individual; and in this respect the democratic conception of property differs from that which belongs to the Catholic theory. A genetic treatment of this doctrine might show the conception of individuality springing from the conception and institution of property; but, as I have said elsewhere, I am not concerned with questions of genesis, and there can be no doubt that in the logical structure of this doctrine the conception of property is subordinate.

The passage to which I have given the title *Democracy and Dictatorship* requires an explanation. Centuries of struggle against despotism has embedded in the doctrine of Liberalism the belief that the enemy of liberty is the single tyrant, the despot, and against this enemy all the forces of the liberal doctrine have been directed. Its fear has been, always, the reappearance of absolute monarchy. And this fear, preventing it from recognizing and guarding against other forms of anti-Liberalism, has put it out of touch with the contemporary world. Liberalism was found to be without appropriate doctrinal weapons for combating what has turned out to be the real danger. This defect is illustrated in the passage I have quoted from Abraham Lincoln, a passage which I should not have included if it did not represent something fundamental in the Liberal democratic doctrine: its peculiarly erroneous view of the nature and causes of dictatorship in the modern world.

§ 1. THE HISTORY OF LIBERTY

JOHN STUART MILL

The struggle between Liberty and Authority is the most conspicuous feature in the portions of history with which we are earliest familiar, particularly in that of Greece, Rome, and England. But in old times this contest was between subjects, or some classes of subjects, and the Government. By liberty, was meant protection against the tyranny of the political rulers. The rulers were conceived (except in some of the popular governments of Greece) as in a necessarily antagonistic position to the people whom they ruled. They consisted of a governing One, or a governing tribe or caste, who derived their authority from inheritance or conquest, who, at all events, did not hold it at the pleasure of the governed, and whose supremacy men did not venture, perhaps did not desire, to contest, whatever precautions might be taken against its oppressive exercise. Their power was regarded as necessary, but also as highly dangerous; as a weapon which they would attempt to use against their subjects, no less than against external enemies. To prevent the weaker members of the community from being preyed upon by innumerable vultures, it was needful that there should be an animal of prey stronger than the rest, commissioned to keep them down. But as the king of the vultures would be no less bent upon preying on the flock than any of the minor harpies, it was indispensable to be in a perpetual attitude of defence against his beak and claws. The aim, therefore, of patriots was to set limits to the power which the ruler should be suffered to exercise over the community; and this limitation was what they meant by liberty. It was attempted in two ways. First, by obtaining a recognition of certain immunities, called political liberties or rights, which it was to be regarded as a breach of duty in the ruler to infringe, and which if he did infringe, specific resistance, or general rebellion, was held to be justifiable. A second, and generally a later expedient, was the establishment of constitutional checks, by which the consent of the community, or of a body of some sort, supposed to represent its interests, was made a necessary condition to some of the more important acts of the governing power. To the first of these modes of limitation, the ruling power, in most European countries, was compelled, more or less, to submit. It was not so with the second; and, to attain this, or when already in some degree possessed, to attain it more completely, became everywhere the principal object of the lovers of liberty. And so long as mankind were content to combat one enemy by another, and to be ruled by a master, on condition of being guaranteed more or less efficaciously against his tyranny, they did not carry their aspirations beyond this point.

A time, however, came, in the progress of human affairs, when men ceased to think it a necessity of nature that their governors should be an independent power, opposed in interest to themselves. It appeared to them much better that the various magistrates of the State should be their tenants or delegates, revocable at their pleasure. In that way alone, it seemed, could they have complete security that the powers of government would never be abused to their disadvantage. By degrees this new demand for elective and temporary rulers became the prominent object of the exertions of the popular party, wherever any such party existed; and superseded, to a considerable extent, the previous efforts to limit the power of rulers. As the struggle proceeded for making the ruling power emanate from the periodical choice of the ruled, some persons began to think that too much importance had been attached to the limitation of the power itself. *That* (it might seem) was a resource against rulers whose interests were habitually opposed to those of the people. What was now wanted was, that the rulers should be identified with the people; that their interest and will should be the interest and will of the nation. The nation did not need to be protected against its own will. There was no fear of its tyrannizing over itself. Let the rulers be effectually responsible to it, promptly removable by it, and it could afford to trust them with power of which it could itself dictate the use to be made. Their power was but the nation's own power, concentrated, and in a form convenient for exercise. This mode of thought, or rather perhaps of feeling, was common among the last generation of European Liberalism, in the Continental section of which it still apparently predominates. Those who admit any limit to what a government may do, except in the case of such governments as they think ought not to exist, stand out as brilliant exceptions among the political thinkers of the Continent. A similar tone of sentiment might by this time have been prevalent in our own country, if the circumstances which for a time encouraged it, had continued unaltered.

But, in political and philosophical theories, as well as in persons, success discloses faults and infirmities which failure might have concealed from observation. The notion, that the people have no need to limit their power over themselves, might seem axiomatic, when popular government was a thing only dreamed about, or read of as having existed at some distant period of the past. Neither was that notion necessarily disturbed by such temporary aberrations as those of the French Revolution, the worst of which were the work of a usurping few, and which, in any case, belonged, not to the permanent working of popular institutions, but to a sudden and convulsive outbreak against monarchical and aristocratic despotism. In time, however, a democratic republic came to occupy a large portion of the earth's surface, and made itself felt as one of the most powerful members of the community of nations; and elective and responsible government became subject to the observations and criticisms which wait upon a great existing fact. It was now perceived that such phrases as "self-government", and "the power of the people over themselves", do not express the true state of the case. The "people" who exercise the power are not always the same people with those over whom it is exercised; and the "self-government" spoken of is not the government of each by himself, but of each by all the rest. The will of the people, moreover, practically means the will of the most numerous or the most active *part* of the people; the majority, or those who succeed in making themselves accepted as the majority; the people, consequently *may* desire to oppress a part of their number; and precautions are as much needed against this as against any other abuse of power. The limitation, therefore, of the power of government over individuals loses none of its importance when the holders of power are regularly accountable to the community, that is, to the strongest party therein. This view of things, recommending itself equally to the intelligence of thinkers and to the inclination of those important classes in European society to whose real or supposed interests democracy is adverse, has had no difficulty in establishing itself; and in political speculations "the tyranny of the majority" is now generally included among the evils against which society requires to be on its guard.

Like other tyrannies, the tyranny of the majority was at first, and is still vulgarly, held in dread, chiefly as operating through the acts of the public authorities. But reflecting persons perceived that when society is itself the tyrant—society collectively over the separate individuals who compose it—its means of tyrannizing are not restricted to the acts which it may do by the hands of its political functionaries. Society can and does execute its own mandates: and if it issues wrong mandates instead of right, or any mandates at all in things with which it ought not to meddle, it practises a social tyranny more formidable than many kinds of political oppression, since, though not usually upheld by such extreme penalties, it leaves fewer means of escape, penetrating much more deeply into the details of life, and enslaving the soul itself. Protection, therefore, against the tyranny of the magistrate is not enough: there needs protection also against the tyranny of the prevailing opinion and feeling; against the tendency of society to impose, by other means than civil penalties, its own ideas and practices as rules of conduct on those who dissent from them; to fetter the development, and, if possible, prevent the formation, of any individuality not in harmony with its ways, and compels all characters to fashion themselves upon the model of its own. There is a limit to the legitimate interference of collective opinion with individual independence: and to find that limit, and maintain it against encroachment, is as indispensable to a good condition of human affairs, as protection against political despotism.

From *On Liberty* (1859)

§ 2. THE LOVE OF FREEDOM

DE TOCQUEVILLE

I have often asked myself what is the source of that passion for political freedom which in all ages has been the fruitful mother of the greatest things which mankind has achieved—and in what feelings that passion strikes root and finds its nourishment.

. It is evident that when nations are ill-directed they soon conceive the wish to govern themselves; but this love of independence, which springs up only under the influence of certain transient evils produced by despotism, is never lasting; it passes away with the accident that gave rise to it; and what seemed to be the love of freedom was no more than the hatred of a master. That which nations made to be free really hate is the curse of dependence.

Nor do I believe that the true love of freedom ever arises from the consideration of material benefits, which often rather obscures it. It is true that in the long run freedom brings to those who know how to keep it, ease, comfort and often wealth; but there are times at which it disturbs for a season the possession of these blessings; there are often times when despotism alone can confer the enjoyment of them. The men who value freedom only for such things as these are not men who ever long preserve it.

That which at all times has won the hearts of a few for the cause of freedom, is its own attractions, its own *charme*, independent of its material benefits: the pleasure of being able to speak, to act, to breathe, without restriction, under the sole government of God and the laws. He who seeks in freedom something other than this is born for slavery.

There are nations which have indefatigably pursued freedom through every sort of peril and hardship. They loved it, not for its material benefits; they regarded freedom itself as a gift so precious and so necessary that no other could console them for the loss of that which consoles them for the loss of everything else. Others grow weary of freedom in the midst of their prosperity; they allow it to be snatched away from them without resistance, lest they should sacrifice by an effort that well-being which it has bestowed upon them. For them to remain free, nothing is wanting but a true taste for freedom. I attempt no analysis of that great emotion for those who cannot feel it. It enters of its own accord into the generous hearts God has prepared to receive it; it fills them, it inspires them; but to the meaner minds which have never felt it, it is past finding out.

From L'Ancien Régime et la Révolution (1856)

§ 3. INDIVIDUALITY

JOHN STUART MILL

It is desirable that in things which do not primarily concern others, individuality should assert itself. Where, not the person's own character, but the traditions or customs of other people are the rule of conduct, there is wanting one of the principal ingredients of human happiness, and quite the chief ingredient of individual and social progress.

In maintaining this principle, the greatest difficulty to be encountered does not lie in the appreciation of means towards an acknowledged end, but in the indifference of persons in general to the end itself. If it were felt that the free development of individuality is one of the leading essentials of well-being; that it is not only a co-ordinate element with all that is designated by the terms civilization, instruction, education, culture, but is itself a necessary part and condition of all those things; there would be no danger that liberty should be undervalued, and the adjustment of the boundaries between it and social control would present no extraordinary difficulty. But the evil is, that individual spontaneity is hardly recognized by the common modes of thinking as having any intrinsic worth, or deserving any regard on its own account. The majority, being satisfied with the ways of mankind as they now are (for it is they who make them what they are), cannot comprehend why those ways should not be good enough for everybody; and what is more, spontaneity forms no part of the ideal of the majority of moral and social reformers, but is rather looked on with jealousy, as a troublesome and perhaps rebellious obstruction to the general acceptance of what these reformers, in their own judgement, think would be best for mankind. Few persons, out of Germany, even comprehend the meaning of the doctrine which Wilhelm von Humboldt, so eminent both as a *savant* and as a politician, made the text of a treatise—that "the end of man, or that which is prescribed by the eternal or immutable dictates of reason, and not suggested by vague and transient desires, is the highest and most harmonious development of his powers to a complete and consistent whole"; that, therefore, the object "towards which every human being must ceaselessly direct his efforts, and on which especially those who design to influence their fellow-men must ever keep their eyes, is the individuality of power and development"; that for this there are two requisites, "freedom, and variety of situations"; and that from the union of these arise "individual vigour and manifold diversity", which combine themselves in "originality".[1]

Little, however, as people are accustomed to a doctrine like that of von Humboldt, and surprising as it may be to them to find so high a value attached to individuality, the question, one must nevertheless think, can only be one of degree. No one's idea of excellence in conduct is that people should do absolutely nothing but copy one another. No one would assert that people ought not to put into their mode of life, and into the conduct of their concerns, any impress whatever of their own judgement, or of their own individual character. On the other hand, it would be absurd to pretend that people ought to live as if nothing whatever had been known in the world before they came into it; as if experience had as yet done nothing towards showing that one mode of existence, or of conduct, is preferable to another. Nobody denies that people should be so taught and trained in youth as to know and benefit by the ascertained results of human experience. But it is the privilege and proper condition of a human being, arrived at the maturity of his faculties, to use and interpret experience in his own way. It is for him to find out what part of recorded experience is properly applicable to his own circumstances and character. The traditions and customs of other people are, to a certain extent, evidence of what their experience has taught *them*; presumptive evidence, and as such, have a claim to his deference: but, in the first place, their experience may be too narrow; or they may not have interpreted it rightly. Secondly, their interpretation of experience may be correct, but unsuitable to him. Customs are made for customary circumstances and customary characters; and his circumstances or his character may be uncustomary. Thirdly, though the customs be both good as customs, and suitable to him, yet to conform to custom, merely *as* custom, does not educate or develop in him any of the qualities which are the distinctive endowment of a human being. The human faculties of perception, judgement,

---

[1] *The Sphere and Duties of Government*, from the German of Baron Wilhelm von Humboldt, pp. 11–13.

discriminative feeling, mental activity, and even moral preference, are exercised only in making a choice. He who does anything because it is the custom makes no choice. He gains no practice either in discerning or in desiring what is best. The mental and moral, like the muscular powers, are improved only by being used. The faculties are called into no exercise by doing a thing merely because others do it, no more than by believing a thing only because others believe it. If the grounds of an opinion are not conclusive to the person's own reason, his reason cannot be strengthened, but is likely to be weakened, by his adopting it: and if the inducements to an act are not such as are consentaneous to his own feelings and character (where affection, or the rights of others, are not concerned) it is so much done towards rendering his feelings and character inert and torpid, instead of active and energetic. . . .

But society has now fairly got the better of individuality; and the danger which threatens human nature is not the excess, but the deficiency, of personal impulses and preferences. Things are vastly changed since the passions of those who were strong by station or by personal endowment were in a state of habitual rebellion against laws and ordinances, and required to be rigorously chained up to enable the persons within their reach to enjoy any particle of security. In our times, from the highest class of society down to the lowest, every one lives as under the eye of a hostile and dreaded censorship. Not only in what concerns others, but in what concerns only themselves, the individual or the family do not ask themselves—what do I prefer? or, what would suit my character and disposition? or, what would allow the best and highest in me to have fair play, and enable it to grow and thrive? They ask themselves, what is suitable to my position? what is usually done by persons of my station and pecuniary circumstances? or (worse still) what is usually done by persons of a station and circumstances superior to mine? I do not mean that they choose what is customary in preference to what suits their own inclination. It does not occur to them to have any inclination, except for what is customary. Thus the mind itself is bowed to the yoke: even in what people do for pleasure, conformity is the first thing thought of; they like in crowds; they exercise choice only among things commonly done: peculiarity of taste, eccentricity of conduct, are shunned equally with crimes: until by dint of not following their own nature they have no nature to follow: their human capacities are withered and starved: they become incapable of any strong wishes or native pleasures, and are generally without either opinions or feelings of home growth, or properly their own. Now is this, or is it not, the desirable condition of human nature?

From *On Liberty*

§ 4. THE LIMITS OF SOCIAL AUTHORITY

JOHN STUART MILL

What, then, is the rightful limit to the sovereignty of the individual over himself? Where does the authority of society begin? How much of human life should be assigned to individuality, and how much to society?

Each will receive its proper share, if each has that which more particularly concerns it. To individuality should belong the part of life in which it is chiefly the individual that is interested; to society, the part which chiefly interests society.

Though society is not founded on a contract, and though no good purpose is answered by inventing a contract in order to deduce social obligations from it, every one who receives the protection of society owes a return for the benefit, and the fact of living in society renders it indispensable that each should be bound to observe a certain line of conduct towards the rest. This conduct consists, first, in not injuring the interests of one another; or rather interests, which, either by express legal provision or by tacit understanding, ought to be considered as rights; and secondly, in each person's bearing his share (to be fixed on some equitable principle) of the labours and sacrifices incurred for defending the society or its members from injury and molestation. These conditions society is justified in enforcing, at all costs to those who endeavour to withhold fulfilment. Nor is this all that society may do. The acts of an individual may be hurtful to others, or wanting in due consideration for their welfare, without going to the length of violating any of their constituted rights. The offender may then be justly punished by opinion, though not by law. As soon as any part of a person's conduct affects prejudicially the interests of others, society has jurisdiction over it, and the question whether the general welfare will or will not be promoted by interfering with it, becomes open to discussion. But there is no room for entertaining any such question when a person's conduct affects the interests of no persons besides himself, or needs not affect them unless they like (all the persons concerned being of full age, and the ordinary amount of understanding). In all such cases, there should be perfect freedom, legal and social, to do the action and stand the consequences.

It would be a great misunderstanding of this doctrine to suppose that it is one of selfish indifference, which pretends that human beings have no business with each other's conduct in life, and that they should not concern themselves about the well-doing or well-being of one another, unless their own interest is involved. Instead of any diminution, there is need of a great increase of disinterested exertion to promote the good of others. But disinterested benevolence can find other instruments to persuade people to their good than whips and scourges, either of the literal or the metaphorical sort. I am the last person to undervalue the self-regarding virtues; they are only second in importance, if even second, to the social. It is equally the business of education to cultivate both. But even education works by conviction and persuasion as well as by compulsion, and it is by the former only that, when the period of education is passed, the self-regarding virtues should be inculcated. Human beings owe to each other help to distinguish the better from the worse, and encouragement to choose the former and avoid the latter. They should be for ever stimulating each other to increased exercise of their higher faculties, and increased direction of their feelings and aims towards wise instead of foolish, elevating instead of degrading, objects and contemplations. But neither one person, nor any number of persons, is warranted in saying to another human creature of ripe years, that he shall not do with his life for his own benefit what he chooses to do with it. He is the person most interested in his own well-being: the interest which any other person, except in cases of strong personal attachment, can have in it, is trifling, compared with that which he himself has; the interest which society has in him individually (except as to his conduct to others) is fractional, and altogether indirect; while with respect to his own feelings and circumstances, the most ordinary man or woman has means of knowledge immeasurably surpassing those that can be possessed by any one else. The interference of society to overrule his judgement and purposes in what only regards himself must be grounded on general presumptions; which may be altogether wrong, and even if right, are as likely as not to be misapplied to individual cases, by persons no better acquainted with the circumstances of such cases than those are who look at them merely from without. In this department, therefore, of human affairs, Individuality has its proper field of action. In the conduct of human beings towards one another it is necessary that general rules should for the most part be observed, in order that people may know what they have to expect: but in each person's own concerns his individual spontaneity is entitled to free exercise. Considerations to aid his judgement, exhortations to strengthen his will, may be offered to him, even obtruded on him, by others: but he himself is the final judge. All errors which he is likely to commit against advice and warning are far outweighed by the evil of allowing others to constrain him to what they deem his good. . . .

The distinction here pointed out between the part of a person's life which concerns only himself, and that which concerns others, many persons will refuse to admit. How (it may be asked) can any part of the conduct of a member of society be a matter of indifference to the other members? No person is an entirely isolated being; it is impossible for a person to do anything seriously or permanently hurtful to himself, without mischief reaching at least to his near connections, and often far beyond them. If he injures his property, he does harm to those who directly or indirectly derived support from it, and usually diminishes, by a greater or less amount, the general resources of the community. If he deteriorates his bodily or mental faculties, he not only brings evil upon all who depended on him for any portion of their happiness, but disqualifies himself for rendering the services which he owes to his fellow-creatures generally; perhaps becomes a burthen on their affection or benevolence; and if such conduct were very frequent, hardly any offence that is committed would detract more from the general sum of good. Finally, if by his vices or follies a person does no direct harm to others, he is nevertheless (it may be said) injurious by his example; and ought to be compelled to control himself, for the sake of those whom the sight or knowledge of his conduct might corrupt or mislead.

And even (it will be added) if the consequences of misconduct could be confined to the vicious or thoughtless individual, ought society to abandon to their own guidance those who are manifestly unfit for it? If protection against themselves is confessedly due to children and persons under age, is not society equally bound to afford it to persons of mature years who are equally incapable of self-government? If gambling, or drunkenness, or incontinence, or idleness, or uncleanliness, are as injurious to happiness, and as great a hindrance to improvement, as many or most of the acts prohibited by law, why (it may be asked) should not law, so far as is consistent with practicability and social convenience, endeavour to repress these also? And as a supplement to the unavoidable imperfections of law, ought not opinion at least to organize a powerful police against these vices, and visit rigidly with social penalties those who are known to practise them? There is no question here (it may be said) about restricting individuality, or impeding the trial of new and original experiments in living. The only things it is sought to prevent are things which have been tried and condemned from the beginning of the world until now; things which experience has shown not to be useful or suitable to any person's individuality. There must be some length of time and amount of experience after which a moral or prudential truth may be regarded as established: and it is merely desired to prevent generation after generation from falling over the same precipice which has been fatal to their predecessors.

I fully admit that the mischief which a person does to himself may seriously affect, both through their sympathies and their interests, those nearly connected with him and, in a minor degree, society at large. When, by conduct of this sort, a person is led to violate a distinct and assignable obligation to any other person or persons, the case is taken out of the self-regarding class, and becomes amenable to moral disapprobation in the proper sense of the term. If, for example, a man, through intemperance or extravagance, becomes unable to pay his debts, or, having undertaken the moral responsibility of a family, becomes from the same cause incapable of supporting or educating them, he is deservedly reprobated, and might be justly punished; but it is for the breach of duty to his family or creditors, not for the extravagance. If the resources which ought to have been devoted to them, had been diverted from them for the most prudent investment, the moral culpability would have been the same. George Barnwell murdered his uncle to get money for his mistress, but if he had done it to set himself up in business, he would equally have been hanged. Again, in the frequent case of a man who causes grief to his family by addiction to bad habits, he deserves reproach for his unkindness or ingratitude; but so he may for cultivating habits not in themselves vicious, if they are painful to those with whom he passes his life, or who from personal ties are dependent on him for their comfort. Whoever fails in the consideration generally due to the interests and feelings of others, not being compelled by some more imperative duty, or justified by allowable self-preference, is a subject of moral disapprobation for that failure, but not for the cause of it, nor for the errors, merely personal to himself, which may have remotely led to it. In like manner, when a person disables himself, by conduct purely self-regarding, from the performance of some definite duty incumbent on him to the public, he is guilty of a social offence. No person ought to be punished simply for being drunk; but a soldier or a policeman should be punished for being drunk on duty. Whenever, in short, there is a definite damage, or a definite risk of damage, either to an individual or to the public, the case is taken out of the province of liberty, and placed in that of morality or law.

But with regard to the merely contingent, or, as it may be called, constructive injury which a person causes to society, by conduct which neither violates any specific duty to the public, nor occasions perceptible hurt to any assignable individual except himself; the inconvenience is one which society can afford to bear, for the sake of the greater good of human freedom. If grown persons are to be punished for not taking proper care of themselves, I would rather it were for their own sake, than under pretence of preventing them from impairing their capacity or rendering to society benefits which society does not pretend it has a right to exact. But I cannot consent to argue the point as if society had no means of bringing its weaker members up to its ordinary standard of rational conduct, except waiting till they do something irrational, and then punishing them, legally or morally, for it. Society has had absolute power over them during all the early portion of their existence: it has had the whole period of childhood and nonage in which to try whether it could make them capable of rational conduct in life. The existing generation is master both of the training and the entire circumstances of the generation to come; it cannot indeed make them perfectly wise and good, because it is itself so lamentably deficient in goodness and wisdom; and its best efforts are not always, in individual cases, its most successful ones; but it is perfectly well able to make the rising generation, as a whole, as good as, and a little better than, itself. If society lets any considerable number of its members grow up mere children, incapable of being acted on by rational consideration of distant motives, society has itself to blame for the consequences. Armed not only with all the powers of education, but with the ascendancy which the authority of a received opinion always exercises over the minds who are least fitted to judge for themselves; and aided by the *natural* penalties which cannot be prevented from falling on those who incur the distaste or the contempt of those who know them; let not society pretend that it needs, besides all this, the power to issue commands and enforce obedience in the personal concerns of individuals, in which, on all principles of justice and policy, the decision ought to rest with those who are to abide the consequences. Nor is there anything which tends more to discredit and frustrate the better means of influencing conduct than a resort to the worse. If there be among those whom it is attempted to coerce into prudence or temperance any of the material of which vigorous and independent characters are made, they will infallibly rebel against the yoke. No such person will ever feel that others have a right to control him in his concerns, such as they have to prevent him from injuring them in theirs; and it easily comes to be considered a mark of spirit and courage to fly in the face of such usurped authority, and do with ostentation the exact opposite of what it enjoins; as in the fashion of grossness which succeeded, in the time of Charles II, to the fanatical moral intolerance of the Puritans. With respect to what is said of the necessity of protecting society from the bad example set to others by the vicious or the self-indulgent; it is true that bad example may have a pernicious effect, especially the example of doing wrong to others with impunity to the wrong-doer. But we are now speaking of conduct which, while it does no wrong to others, is supposed to do great harm to the agent himself: and I do not see how those who believe this can think otherwise than that the example, on the whole, must be more salutary than hurtful, since, if it displays the misconduct, it displays also the painful or degrading consequences which, if the conduct is justly censured, must be supposed to be in all or most cases attendant on it.

But the strongest of all the arguments against the interference of the public with purely personal conduct is that, when it does interfere, the odds are that it interferes wrongly, and in the wrong place. On questions of social morality, of duty to others, the opinion of the public, that is, of an overruling majority, though often wrong, is likely to be still oftener right; because on such questions they are only required to judge of their own interests; of the manner in which some mode of conduct, if allowed to be practised, would affect themselves. But the opinion of a similar majority, imposed as a law on the minority, on questions of self-regarding conduct, is quite as likely to be wrong as right; for in these cases public opinion means, at the best, some people's opinion of what is good or bad for other people; while very often it does not even mean that; the public, with the most perfect indifference, passing over the pleasure or convenience of those whose conduct they censure, and considering only their own preference. There are many who consider as an injury to themselves any conduct which they have a distaste for, and resent it as an outrage to their feelings; as a religious bigot, when charged with disregarding the religious feelings of others, has been known to retort that they disregard his feelings, by persisting in their abominable worship or creed. But there is no parity between the feeling of a person for his own opinion, and the feeling of another who is offended at his holding it; no more than between the desire of a thief to take a purse, and the desire of the right owner to keep it. And a person's taste is as much his own peculiar concern as his opinion or his purse. It is easy for any one to imagine an ideal public which leaves the freedom and choice of individuals in all uncertain matters undisturbed, and only requires them to abstain from modes of conduct which universal experience has condemned. But where has there been seen a public which set any such limit to its censorship? or when does the public trouble itself about universal experience? In its interferences with personal conduct it is seldom thinking of anything but the enormity of acting or feeling differently from itself; and this standard of judgement, thinly disguised, is held up to mankind as the dictate of religion and philosophy, by nine-tenths of all moralists and speculative writers. These teach that things are right because they are right; because we feel them to be so. They tell us to search in our own minds and hearts for laws of conduct binding on ourselves and on all others. What can the poor public do but apply these instructions, and make their own personal feelings of good and evil, if they are tolerably unanimous in them, obligatory on all the world?

From *On Liberty*

§5. THE NATURE OF GOVERNMENT

(i)

ABRAHAM LINCOLN

Government is a combination of the people of a country to effect certain objects by joint effort. The best framed and best administered governments are necessarily expensive; while by errors in frame and maladministration most of them are more onerous than they need be, and some of them very oppressive. Why, then, should we have government? Why not each individual take to himself the whole fruit of his labour, without having any of it taxed away, in services, corn or money? Why not take just so much land as he can cultivate with his own hands, without buying it of anyone?

The legitimate object of government is "to do for the people what needs to be done, but which they cannot, by individual effort, do at all, or do so well, for themselves". There are many such things—some of them exist independently of the injustice of the world. Making and maintaining roads, bridges, and the like; providing for the helpless young and afflicted; common schools; and disposing of deceased men's property, are instances.

But a far larger class of objects springs from the injustice of men. If one people will make war upon another, it is a necessity with that other to unite and co-operate for defence. Hence the military department. If some men will kill, or beat, or constrain others, or despoil them of property, by force, fraud, or noncompliance with contracts, it is a common object with peaceful and just men to prevent it. Hence the criminal and civil departments.

(1834)

(ii)

THOMAS PAINE

What is government more than the management of the affairs of a Nation? It is not, and from its nature cannot be, the property of any particular man or family, but of the whole community, at whose expense it is supported; and though by force or contrivance it has been usurped into an inheritance, the usurpation cannot alter the right of things. Sovereignty, as a matter of right, appertains to the Nation only, and not to any individual; and a Nation has at all times an inherent indefeasible right to abolish any form of government it finds inconvenient, and establish such as accords with its interest, disposition and happiness. The romantic and barbarous distinction of men with kings and subjects, though it may suit the condition of courtiers, cannot that of citizens; and is exploded by the principle upon which Governments are now founded. Every citizen is a member of the Sovereignty, and, as such, can acknowledge no personal subjection; and his obedience can be only to the laws. . . .

[There is] a system of principles as universal as truth and the existence of man, and combining moral with political happiness and national prosperity.

1. *Men are born and always continue free, and equal in respect of their rights. Civil distinctions, therefore, can be founded only on public utility.*

2. *The end of all political associations is the preservation of the natural and imprescriptible rights of man; and those rights are liberty, property, security, and resistance of oppression.*

3. *The Nation is essentially the source of all sovereignty; nor can any* INDIVIDUAL, *or* ANY BODY OF MEN, *be entitled to any authority which is not expressly derived from it.*

In these principles there is nothing to throw a Nation into confusion by inflaming ambition. They are calculated to call forth wisdom and abilities, and to exercise them for the public good, and not for the emolument or aggrandizement of particular descriptions of men or families.

From *The Rights of Man* (1791)

§6. THAT THE IDEALLY BEST FORM OF GOVERNMENT IS REPRESENTATIVE GOVERNMENT

JOHN STUART MILL

It has long (perhaps throughout the entire duration of British freedom) been a common saying, that if a good despot could be ensured, despotic monarchy would be the best form of government. I look upon this as a radical and most pernicious misconception of what good government is; which, until it can be got rid of, will fatally vitiate all our speculations on government.

The supposition is, that absolute power, in the hands of an eminent individual, would ensure a virtuous and intelligent performance of all the duties of government. Good laws would be established and enforced, bad laws would be reformed; the best men would be placed in all situations of trust; justice would be as well administered, the public burthens would be as light and as judiciously imposed, every branch of administration would be as purely and as intelligently conducted, as the circumstances of the country and its degree of intellectual and moral cultivation would admit. I am willing, for the sake of the argument, to concede all this; but I must point out how great the concession is; how much more is needed to produce even an approximation to these results than is conveyed in the simple expression, a good despot. Their realization would in fact imply, not merely a good monarch, but an all-seeing one. He must be at all times informed correctly, in considerable detail, of the conduct and working of every branch of administration, in every district of the country, and must be able, in the twenty-four hours per day which are all that is granted to a king as to the humblest labourer, to give an effective share of attention and superintendence to all parts of this vast field; or he must at least be capable of discerning and choosing out, from among the mass of his subjects, not only a large abundance of honest and able men, fit to conduct every branch of public administration under supervision and control, but also the small number of men of eminent virtues and talents who can be trusted not only to do without that supervision, but to exercise it themselves over others. So extraordinary are the faculties and energies required for performing this task in any supportable manner, that the good despot whom we are supposing can hardly be imagined as consenting to undertake it, unless as a refuge from intolerable evils, and a transitional preparation for something beyond. But the argument can do without even this immense item in the account. Suppose the difficulty vanquished. What should we then have? One man of superhuman mental activity managing the entire affairs of a mentally passive people. Their passivity is implied in the very idea of absolute power. The nation as a whole, and every individual composing it, are without any potential voice in their own destiny. They exercise no will in respect to their collective interests. All is decided for them by a will not their own, which it is legally a crime for them to disobey. What sort of human beings can be formed under such a regimen? What development can either their thinking or their active faculties attain under it? On matters of pure theory they might perhaps be allowed to speculate, so long as their speculations either did not approach politics, or had not the remotest connection with its practice. On practical affairs they could at most be only suffered to suggest; and even under the most moderate of despots, none but persons of already admitted or reputed superiority could hope that their suggestions would be known to, much less regarded by, those who had the management of affairs. A person must have a very unusual taste for intellectual exercise in and for itself, who will put himself to the trouble of thought when it is to have no outward effect, or qualify himself for functions which he has no chance of being allowed to exercise. The only sufficient incitement to mental exertion, in any but a few minds in a generation, is the prospect of some practical use to be made

of its results. It does not follow that the nation will be wholly destitute
of intellectual power. The common business of life, which must
necessarily be performed by each individual or family for themselves,
will call forth some amount of intelligence and practical ability, within
a certain narrow range of ideas. There may be a select class of *savants*,
who cultivate science with a view to its physical uses, or for the pleasure
of the pursuit. There will be a bureaucracy, and persons in training for
the bureaucracy, who will be taught at least some empirical maxims of
government and public administration. There may be, and often has
been, a systematic organization of the best mental power in the country
in some special direction (commonly military) to promote the grandeur
of the despot. But the public at large remain without information and
without interest on all the greater matters of practice; or, if they have
any knowledge of them, it is but a *dilettante* knowledge, like that which
people have of the mechanical arts who have never handled a tool. Nor
is it only in their intelligence that they suffer. Their moral capacities
are equally stunted. Wherever the sphere of action of human beings is
artificially circumscribed, their sentiments are narrowed and dwarfed
in the same proportion. The food of feeling is action: even domestic
affection lives upon voluntary good offices. Let a person have nothing
to do for his country, and he will not care for it. It has been said of old,
that in a despotism there is at most but one patriot, the despot himself;
and the saying rests on a just appreciation of the effects of absolute
subjection, even to a good and wise master. Religion remains: and here
at least, it may be thought, is an agency that may be relied on for
lifting men's eyes and minds above the dust at their feet. But religion,
even supposing it to escape perversion for the purposes of despotism,
ceases in these circumstances to be a social concern, and narrows into
a personal affair between an individual and his Maker, in which the
issue at stake is but his private salvation. Religion in this shape is quite
consistent with the most selfish and contracted egoism, and identifies
the votary as little in feeling with the rest of his kind as sensuality itself.

A good despotism means a government in which, so far as depends
on the despot, there is no positive oppression by officers of state, but in
which all the collective interests of the people are managed for them, all
the thinking that has relation to collective interests done for them, and
in which their minds are formed by, and consenting to, this abdication
of their own energies. Leaving things to the government, like leaving
them to Providence, is synonymous with caring nothing about them,

and accepting their results, when disagreeable, as visitations of Nature. With the exception, therefore, of a few studious men who take an intellectual interest in speculation for its own sake, the intelligence and sentiments of the whole people are given up to the material interests, and, when these are provided for, to the amusement and ornamentation, of private life. But to say this is to say, if the whole testimony of history is worth anything, that the era of national decline has arrived: that is, if the nation had ever attained anything to decline from. If it has never risen above the condition of an Oriental people, in that condition it continues to stagnate. But if, like Greece or Rome, it had realized anything higher, through the energy, patriotism, and enlargement of mind, which as national qualities are the fruits solely of freedom, it relapses in a few generations into the Oriental state. And that state does not mean stupid tranquillity, with security against change for the worse; it often means being overrun, conquered, and reduced to domestic slavery, either by a stronger despot, or by the nearest barbarous people who retain along with their savage rudeness the energies of freedom.

Such are not merely the natural tendencies, but the inherent necessities of despotic government; from which there is no outlet, unless in so far as the despotism consents not to be despotism; in so far as the supposed good despot abstains from exercising his power, and, though holding it in reserve, allows the general business of government to go on as if the people really governed themselves. However little probable it may be, we may imagine a despot observing many of the rules and restraints of constitutional government. He might allow such freedom of the press and of discussion as would enable a public opinion to form and express itself on national affairs. He might suffer local interests to be managed, without the interference of authority, by the people themselves. He might even surround himself with a council or councils of government, freely chosen by the whole or some portion of the nation; retaining in his own hands the power of taxation, and the supreme legislative as well as executive authority. Were he to act thus, and so far abdicate as a despot, he would do away with a considerable part of the evils characteristic of despotism. Political activity and capacity for public affairs would no longer be prevented from growing up in the body of the nation; and a public opinion would form itself not the mere echo of the government. But such improvement would be the beginning of new difficulties. This public opinion, independent of the monarch's dictation, must be either with him or against him; if not the one, it will be the other. All governments must displease many persons, and these having now regular organs, and being able to express their sentiments, opinions adverse to the measures of government would often be expressed. What is the monarch to do when these unfavourable opinions happen to be in the majority? Is he to alter his course? Is he to defer to the nation? If so, he is no longer a despot, but a constitutional king; an organ or first minister of the people, distinguished only by being irremovable. If not, he must either put down opposition by his despotic power, or there will arise a permanent antagonism between the people and one man, which can have but one possible ending. Not even a religious principle of passive obedience and "right divine" would long ward off the natural consequences of such a position. The monarch would have to succumb, and conform to the conditions of constitutional royalty, or give place to some one who would. The despotism, being thus chiefly nominal, would possess few of the advantages supposed to belong to absolute monarchy; while it would realize in a very imperfect degree those of a free government; since however great an amount of liberty the citizens might practically enjoy, they could never forget that they held it on sufferance, and by a concession which under the existing constitution of the state might at any moment be resumed; that they were legally slaves, though of a prudent, or indulgent, master.

It is not much to be wondered at if impatient or disappointed reformers, groaning under the impediments opposed to the most salutary public improvements by the ignorance, the indifference, the intractableness, the perverse obstinacy of a people, and the corrupt combinations of selfish private interests armed with the powerful weapons afforded by free institutions, should at times sigh for a strong hand to bear down all these obstacles, and compel a recalcitrant people to be better governed. But (setting aside the fact, that for one despot who now and then reforms an abuse, there are ninety-nine who do nothing but create them) those who look in any such direction for the realization of their hopes leave out of the idea of good government its principal element, the improvement of the people themselves. One of the benefits of freedom is that under it the ruler cannot pass by the people's minds, and amend their affairs for them without amending them. If it were possible for the people to be well governed in spite of themselves, their good government would last no longer than the freedom of a people usually lasts who have been liberated by foreign arms without their own co-operation. It is true, a despot may educate the people; and to do so really, would be the best apology for his despotism. But any education which aims at making human beings other than machines, in the long run makes them claim to have the control of their own actions. The leaders of French philosophy in the eighteenth century had been educated by the Jesuits. Even Jesuit education, it seems, was sufficiently real to call forth the appetite for freedom. Whatever invigorates the faculties, in however small a measure, creates an increased desire for their more unimpeded exercise; and a popular education is a failure, if it educates the people for any state but that which it will certainly induce them to desire, and most probably to demand.

I am far from condemning, in cases of extreme exigency, the assumption of absolute power in the form of a temporary dictatorship. Free nations have, in times of old, conferred such power by their own choice, as a necessary medicine for diseases of the body politic which could not be got rid of by less violent means. But its acceptance, even for a time strictly limited, can only be excused, if, like Solon or Pittacus, the dictator employs the whole power he assumes in removing the obstacles which debar the nation from the enjoyment of freedom. A good despotism is an altogether false ideal, which practically (except as a means to some temporary purpose) becomes the most senseless and dangerous of chimeras. Evil for evil, a good despotism, in a country at all advanced in civilization, is more noxious than a bad one; for it is far more relaxing and enervating to the thoughts, feelings, and energies of the people. The despotism of Augustus prepared the Romans for Tiberius. If the whole tone of their character had not first been prostrated by nearly two generations of that mild slavery, they would probably have had spirit enough left to rebel against the more odious one.

There is no difficulty in showing that the ideally best form of government is that in which the sovereignty, or supreme controlling power in the last resort, is vested in the entire aggregate of the community; every citizen not only having a voice in the exercise of that ultimate sovereignty, but being, at least occasionally, called on to take an actual part in the government, by the personal discharge of some public function, local or general.

To test this proposition, it has to be examined in reference to the two branches into which the inquiry into the goodness of a government con-

veniently divides itself, namely, how far it promotes the good management of the affairs of society by means of the existing faculties, moral,
intellectual, and active, of its various members, and what is its effect in
improving or deteriorating those faculties.

The ideally best form of government, it is scarcely necessary to say,
does not mean one which is practicable or eligible in all states of
civilization, but the one which, in the circumstances in which it is
practicable and eligible, is attended with the greatest amount of beneficial consequences, immediate and prospective. A completely popular
government is the only polity which can make out any claim to this
character. It is pre-eminent in both the departments between which the
excellence of a political constitution is divided. It is both more favourable to present good government, and promotes a better and higher
form of national character, than any other polity whatsoever.

Its superiority in reference to present well-being rests upon two
principles, of as universal truth and applicability as any general propositions which can be laid down respecting human affairs. The first is,
that the rights and interests of every or any person are only secure from
being disregarded when the person interested is himself able, and
habitually disposed, to stand up for them. The second is, that the
general prosperity attains a greater height, and is more widely diffused,
in proportion to the amount and variety of the personal energies
enlisted in promoting it.

Putting these two propositions into a shape more special to their
present application; human beings are only secure from evil at the
hands of others in proportion as they have the power of being, and are,
self-*protecting*; and they only achieve a high degree of success in their
struggle with Nature in proportion as they are self-*dependent*, relying
on what they themselves can do, either separately or in concert, rather
than on what others do for them.

The former proposition—that each is the only safe guardian of his
own rights and interests—is one of those elementary maxims of prudence, which every person, capable of conducting his own affairs,
implicitly acts upon, wherever he himself is interested. Many, indeed,
have a great dislike to it as a political doctrine, and are fond of holding
it up to obloquy, as a doctrine of universal selfishness. To which we
may answer, that whenever it ceases to be true that mankind, as a rule,
prefer themselves to others, and those nearest to them to those more
remote from that moment Communism is not only practicable, but the

only defensible form of society; and will, when that time arrives, be assuredly carried into effect. For my own part, not believing in universal selfishness, I have no difficulty in admitting that Communism would even now be practicable among the *élite* of mankind, and may become so among the rest. But as this opinion is anything but popular with those defenders of existing institutions who find fault with the doctrine of the general predominance of self-interest, I am inclined to think they do in reality believe that most men consider themselves before other people. It is not, however, necessary to affirm even thus much in order to support the claim of all to participate in the sovereign power. We need not suppose that when power resides in an exclusive class, that class will knowingly and deliberately sacrifice the other classes to themselves: it suffices that, in the absence of its natural defenders, the interest of the excluded is always in danger of being overlooked; and, when looked at, is seen with very different eyes from those of the persons whom it directly concerns. In this country, for example, what are called the working classes may be considered as excluded from all direct participation in the government. I do not believe that the classes who do participate in it have in general any intention of sacrificing the working classes to themselves. They once had that intention; witness the persevering attempts so long made to keep down wages by law. But in the present day their ordinary disposition is the very opposite: they willingly make considerable sacrifices, especially of their pecuniary interest, for the benefit of the working classes, and err rather by too lavish and indiscriminating beneficence; nor do I believe that any rulers in history have been actuated by a more sincere desire to do their duty towards the poorer portion of their countrymen. Yet does Parliament, or almost any of the members composing it, ever for an instant look at any question with the eyes of a working man? When a subject arises in which the labourers as such have an interest, is it regarded from any point of view but that of the employers of labour? I do not say that the working men's view of these questions is in general nearer to the truth than the other: but it is sometimes quite as near; and in any case it ought to be respectfully listened to, instead of being, as it is, not merely turned away from, but ignored. . . .

It is an adherent condition of human affairs that no intention, however sincere, of protecting the interests of others can make it safe or salutary to tie up their own hands. Still more obviously true is it, that by their own hands only can any positive and durable improvement of their circumstances in life be worked out. Through the joint influence of these two principles, all free communities have both been more exempt from social injustice and crime, and have attained more brilliant prosperity, than any others, or than they themselves after they lost their freedom. Contrast the free states of the world, while their freedom lasted, with the contemporary subjects of monarchical or oligarchical despotism: the Greek cities with the Persian satrapies; the Italian republics and the free towns of Flanders and Germany, with the feudal monarchies of Europe; Switzerland, Holland, and England, with Austria or ante-revolutionary France. Their superior prosperity was too obvious ever to have been gainsaid: while their superiority in good government and social relations is proved by the prosperity, and is manifest besides in every page of history. If we compare, not one age with another, but the different governments which co-existed in the same age, no amount of disorder which exaggeration itself can pretend to have existed amidst the publicity of the free states can be compared for a moment with the contemptuous trampling upon the mass of the people which pervaded the whole life of the monarchical countries, or the disgusting individual tyranny which was of more than daily occurrence under the systems of plunder which they called fiscal arrangements, and in the secrecy of their frightful courts of justice.

It must be acknowledged that the benefits of freedom, so far as they have hitherto been enjoyed, were obtained by the extension of its privileges to a part only of the community; and that a government in which they are extended impartially to all is a desideratum still un-realized. But though every approach to this has an independent value, and in many cases more than an approach could not, in the existing state of general improvement, be made, the participation of all in these benefits is the ideally perfect conception of free government. In pro-portion as any, no matter who, are excluded from it, the interests of the excluded are left without the guarantee accorded to the rest, and they themselves have less scope and encouragement than they might other-wise have to that exertion of their energies for the good of themselves and of the community, to which the general prosperity is always proportioned.

Thus stands the case as regards present well-being; the good management of the affairs of the existing generation. If we now pass to the influence of the form of government upon character, we shall find the superiority of popular government over every other to be, if possible, still more decided and indisputable.

This question really depends upon a still more fundamental one, viz., which of two common types of character, for the general good of humanity, it is most desirable should predominate—the active, or the passive type; that which struggles against evils, or that which endures them; that which bends to circumstances, or that which endeavours to make circumstances bend to itself.

The commonplaces of moralists, and the general sympathies of mankind, are in favour of the passive type. Energetic characters may be admired, but the acquiescent and submissive are those which most men personally prefer. The passiveness of our neighbours increases our sense of security, and plays into the hands of our wilfulness. Passive characters, if we do not happen to need their activity, seem an obstruction the less in our own path. A contented character is not a dangerous rival. Yet nothing is more certain than that improvement in human affairs is wholly the work of the uncontented characters; and, moreover, that it is much easier for an active mind to acquire the virtues of patience than for a passive one to assume those of energy....

The only government which can fully satisfy all the exigencies of the social state is one in which the whole people participate; that any participation, even in the smallest public function, is useful; that the participation should everywhere be as great as the general degree of improvement of the community will allow; and that nothing less can be ultimately desirable than the admission of all to a share in the sovereign power of the state. But since all cannot, in a community exceeding a single small town, participate personally in any but some very minor portions of the public business, it follows that the ideal type of a perfect government must be representative.

From *Considerations on Representative Government* (1861)

§7. THE RIGHT TO TAKE PART IN MAKING LAWS

WILLIAM COBBETT

Now, then, in order to act well our part, as citizens, or members of the community, we ought clearly to understand what our rights are; for, on our enjoyment of these depend our duties, rights going before duties, as value received goes before payment. I know well, that just the contrary of this is taught in our political schools, where we are told that our first duty is to obey the laws; and it is not many years ago, that Horsley, Bishop of Rochester, told us, that the people had nothing to do with the laws but to obey them. The truth is, however, that the citizen's first duty is to maintain his rights, as it is the purchaser's first duty to receive the thing for which he has contracted.

Our rights in society are numerous; the right of enjoying life and property; the right of exerting our physical and mental powers in an innocent manner; but, the great right of all, and without which there is, in fact, no right, is, the right of taking a part in the making of the laws by which we are governed. This right is founded in that law of nature spoken of above; it springs out of the very principle of civil society; for what compact, what agreement, what common assent, can possibly be imagined by which men would give up all the rights of nature, all the free enjoyment of their bodies and their minds, in order to subject themselves to rules and laws, in the making of which they should have nothing to say, and which should be enforced upon them without their assent? The great right, therefore, of every man, the right of rights, is the right of having a share in the making of the laws, to which the good of the whole makes it his duty to submit.

With regard to the means of enabling every man to enjoy this share, they have been different, in different countries, and, in the same countries, at different times. Generally it has been, and in great communities it must be, by the choosing of a few to speak and act in behalf of the many: and, as there will hardly ever be perfect unanimity amongst men assembled for any purpose whatever, where fact and argument are to decide the question, the decision is left to the majority, the compact being that the decision of the majority shall be that of the whole. Minors are excluded from this right, because the law considers them as infants, because it makes the parent answerable for civil damages committed by them, and because of their legal incapacity to make any compact. Women are excluded because husbands are answerable in law for their wives, as to their civil damages, and because the very nature of their sex makes the exercise of this right incompatible with the harmony and happiness of society. Men stained with indelible crimes are excluded, because they have forfeited their right by violating the laws, to which their assent has been given. Insane persons are excluded, because they are dead in the eye of the law, because the law demands no duty at their hands, because they cannot violate the law, because the law cannot affect them; and, therefore, they ought to have no hand in making it.

But, with these exceptions, where is the ground whereon to maintain that any man ought to be deprived of this right, which he derives directly from the law of nature, and which springs, as I said before, out of the same source with civil society itself? Am I told, that property ought to confer this right? Property sprang from labour, and not labour from property; so that if there were to be a distinction here, it ought to give the preference to labour. All men are equal by nature; nobody denies that they ought to be equal in the eye of the law; but, how are they to be thus equal if the law begin by suffering some to enjoy this right and refusing the enjoyment to others? It is the duty of every man to defend his country against an enemy, a duty imposed by the law of nature as well as by that of civil society, and without the recognition of this duty, there could exist no independent nation, and no civil society. Yet, how are you to maintain that this is the duty of every man, if you deny to some men the enjoyment of a share in the making of the laws? The poor man has a body and a soul as well as the rich man; like the latter, he has parents, wife, and children; a bullet or a sword is as deadly to him as to the rich man; there are hearts to ache and tears to flow for him as well as for the squire or the lord or the loan-monger; yet, notwithstanding this equality, he is to risk all, and, if he escape, he is still to be denied an equality of rights! If, in such a state of things, the artisan, or labourer, when called out to fight in defence of his country, were to answer: "Why should I risk my life? I have no possession but my labour; no enemy will take that from me; you, the rich, possess all the land and all its products; you make what laws you please without my participation or assent; you punish me at your pleasure; you say that my want of property excludes me from the right of having a share in the making of the laws; you say that the property that I have in my labour is nothing worth; on what ground, then, do you call on me to risk my life?" If, in such a case, such questions were put, the answer is very difficult to be imagined.

In cases of civil commotion, the matter comes still more home to us. On what ground is the rich man to call the artisan from his shop, or the labourer from the field, to join the sheriff's posse or the militia, if he refuse to the labourer and artisan the right of sharing in the making of the laws? Why are they to risk their lives here? To uphold the laws, and to protect property. What! laws, in the making of, or assenting to, which they have been allowed to have no share? Property, of which they are said to possess none? What! compel men to come forth and risk their lives for the protection of property; and then, in the same breath, tell them, that they are not allowed to share in the making of the laws, because, and only because, they have no property! Not because they have committed any crime; not because they are idle or profligate; not because they are vicious in any way; but solely because they have no property; and yet, at the same time, compel them to come forth and risk their lives for the protection of property!

But, the paupers? Ought they to share in the making of the laws? And why not? What is a pauper; what is one of the men to whom this degrading appellation is applied? A very poor man; a man who is, from some cause or other, unable to supply himself with food and raiment without aid from the parish rates. And, is that circumstance alone to deprive him of his right, a right of which he stands more in need than any other man? Perhaps he has, for many years of his life, contributed directly to those rates; and ten thousand to one he has, by his labour, contributed to them indirectly. The aid which, under such circumstances, he receives, is his right; he receives it not as an alms: he is no mendicant; he begs not; he comes to receive that which the laws of the country award him in lieu of the larger portion assigned him by the law of nature. Pray mark that, and let it be deeply engraven on your memory. The audacious and merciless Malthus (a parson of the Church Establishment) recommended, some years ago, the passing of a law to put an end to the giving of parish relief, though he recommended no law to put an end to the enormous taxes payed by poor people. In his book he said, that the poor should be left to the law of nature, which, in case of their having nothing to buy food with, doomed them to starve. They would ask nothing better than to be left to the law of nature; that law which knows nothing about buying food or anything else; that law which bids the hungry and the naked take food and raiment wherever you find it best and nearest at hand; that law which awards all possessions to the strongest; that law the operations of which would clear out the London meat-markets and the drapers' and jewellers' shops in about half an hour: to this law the parson wished the Parliament to leave the poorest of the working-people; but, if the Parliament had done it, it would have been quickly seen that this law was far from "dooming them to be starved".

Nor is the deepest poverty without its useful effects in society. To the practice of the virtues of abstinence, sobriety, care, frugality, industry, and even honesty and amiable manners and acquirement of talent, the two great motives are to get upwards in riches or fame, and to avoid going downwards to poverty, the last of which is the most powerful of the two. It is, therefore, not with contempt, but with compassion, that we should look on those, whose state is one of the decrees of nature, from whose sad example we profit, and to whom, in return, we ought to make compensation by every indulgent and kind act in our power, and particularly by a defence of their rights. To those who labour, we, that labour not with our hands, owe all that we eat, drink and wear; all that shades us by day, and that shelters us by night; all the means of enjoying health and pleasure; and, therefore, if we possess talent for the task, we are ungrateful or cowardly, or both, if we omit any effort within our power to prevent them from being slaves; and, disguise the matter how we may, a slave, a real slave, every man is, who has no share in making the laws which he is compelled to obey. . . .

If the right to have a share in making the laws were only a feather; if it were a fanciful thing; if it were only a speculative theory; if it were but an abstract principle; on any of these suppositions, it might be considered as of little importance. But it is none of these; it is a practical matter; the want of it not only is, but must of necessity be, felt by every man who lives under that want. If it were proposed to the shopkeepers in a town, that a rich man or two, living in the neighbourhood, should have power to send, whenever they pleased, and take away as much as they pleased of the money of the shopkeepers, and apply it to what uses they please: what an outcry the shopkeepers would make! And yet, what would this be more than taxes imposed on those who have no voice in choosing the persons who impose them? Who lets another man put his hand into his purse when he pleases? Who, that has the power to help himself, surrenders his goods or his money to the will of another? Has it not always been, and must it not always be, true, that, if your property be at the absolute disposal of others, your ruin is certain? And if this be, of necessity, the case amongst individuals and parts of the community, it must be the case with regard to the whole community.

From *Advice to Young Men and Women, Advice to a Citizen* (1829)

§8. LIBERTY AND LAW

T. H. GREEN

We shall probably all agree that freedom, rightly understood, is the greatest of blessings; that its attainment is the true end of all our efforts as citizens. But when we thus speak of freedom, we should consider carefully what we mean by it. We do not mean merely freedom from restraint or compulsion. We do not mean merely freedom to do as we like irrespectively of what it is that we like. We do not mean a freedom that can be enjoyed by one man or one set of men at the cost of a loss of freedom to others. When we speak of freedom as something to be so highly prized, we mean a positive power or capacity of doing or enjoying something worth doing or enjoying, and that, too, something that we do or enjoy in common with others. We mean by it a power which each man exercises through the help or security given him by his fellow-men, and which he in turn helps to secure for them. When we measure the progress of a society by its growth in freedom, we measure it by the increasing development and exercise on the whole of those powers of contributing to social good with which we believe the members of the society to be endowed; in short, by the greater power on the part of the citizens as a body to make the most and best of themselves. Thus, though of course there can be no freedom among men who act not willingly but under compulsion, yet on the other hand the mere removal of compulsion, the mere enabling a man to do as he likes, is in itself no contribution to true freedom. In one sense no man is so well able to do as he likes as the wandering savage. He has no master. There is no one to say him nay. Yet we do not count him really free, because the freedom of savagery is not strength, but weakness. The actual powers of the noblest savage do not admit of comparison with those of the humblest citizen of a law-abiding state. He is not the slave of man, but he is the slave of nature. Of compulsion by natural necessity he has plenty of experience, though of restraint by society none at all. Nor can he deliver himself from that compulsion except by submitting to this restraint. So to submit is the first step in true freedom, because the first step towards the full exercise of the faculties with which man is endowed. But we rightly refuse to recognize the highest development on the part of an exceptional individual or exceptional class, as an advance towards the true freedom of man, if it is founded on a refusal of the same opportunity to other men. The powers of the human mind have probably never attained such force and keenness, the proof of what society can do for the individual has never been so strikingly exhibited, as among the small groups of men who possessed civil privileges in the small republics of antiquity. The whole framework of our political ideas, to say nothing of our philosophy, is derived from them. But in them this extraordinary efflorescence of the privileged class was accompanied by the slavery of the multitude. That slavery was the condition on which it depended, and for that reason it was doomed to decay. There is no clearer ordinance of that supreme reason, often dark to us, which governs the course of men's affairs, than that no body of men should in the long run be able to strengthen itself at the cost of others' weakness. The civilization and freedom of the ancient world were shortlived because they were partial and exceptional. If the ideal of true freedom is the maximum of power for all members of human society alike to make the best of themselves, we are right in refusing to ascribe the glory of freedom to a state in which the apparent elevation of the few is founded on the degradation of the many, and in ranking modern society, founded as it is on free industry, with all its confusion and ignorant licence and waste of effort, above the most splendid of ancient republics.

If I have given a true account of that freedom which forms the goal of social effort, we shall see that freedom of contract, freedom of all the forms of doing what one will with one's own, is valuable only as a means to an end. That end is what I call freedom in the positive sense: in other words, the liberation of the powers of all men equally for contributions to a common good. No one has a right to do what he will with his own in such a way as to contravene this end. It is only through the guarantee which society gives him that he has property at all, or, strictly speaking, any right to his possessions. This guarantee is founded on a sense of common interest. Every one has an interest in securing to every one else the free use and enjoyment and disposal of his possessions, so long as that freedom on the part of one does not interfere with a like freedom on the part of others, because such freedom contributes to that equal development of the faculties of all which is the highest good for all. This is the true and the only justification of rights of property. Rights of property, however, have been and are claimed which cannot thus be justified. We are all now agreed that men cannot rightly be the property of men. The institution of property being only justifiable as a means to the free exercise of the social capabilities of all, there can be no true right to property of a kind which debars one class of men from such free exercise altogether. We condemn slavery no less when it arises out of a voluntary agreement on the part of the enslaved person. A contract by which any one agreed for a certain consideration to become the slave of another we should reckon a void contract. Here, then, is a limitation upon freedom of contract which we all recognize as rightful. No contract is valid in which human persons, willingly or unwillingly, are dealt with as commodities, because such contracts of necessity defeat the end for which alone society enforces contracts at all.

Are there no other contracts which, less obviously perhaps but really, are open to the same objection? In the first place, let us consider contracts affecting labour. Labour, the economist tells us, is a commodity exchangeable like other commodities. This is in a certain sense true, but it is a commodity which attaches in a peculiar manner to the person of man. Hence restrictions may need to be placed on the sale of this commodity which would be unnecessary in other cases, in order to prevent labour from being sold under conditions which make it impossible for the person selling it ever to become a free contributor to social good in any form. This is most plainly the case when a man bargains to work under conditions fatal to health, in an unventilated factory. Every injury to the health of the individual is, so far as it goes, a public injury. It is an impediment to the general freedom; so much deduction from our power, as members of society, to make the best of ourselves. Society is, therefore, plainly within its right when it limits freedom of contract for the sale of labour, so far as is done by our laws for the sanitary regulations of factories, workshops, and mines. It is equally within its right in prohibiting the labour of women and young persons beyond certain hours. If they work beyond those hours, the result is demonstrably physical deterioration; which, as demonstrably, carries with it a lowering of the moral forces of society. For the sake of that general freedom of its members to make the best of themselves, which it is the object of civil society to secure, a prohibition should be put by law, which is the deliberate voice of society, on all such contracts of service as in a general way yield such a result. The purchase or hire of unwholesome dwellings is properly forbidden on the same principle. Its application to compulsory education may not be quite so obvious, but it will appear on a little reflection. Without a command of certain elementary arts and knowledge, the individual in modern society is as effectually crippled as by the loss of a limb or a broken constitution. He is not free to develop his faculties. With a view to securing such freedom among its members it is as certainly within the province of the state to prevent children from growing up in that kind of ignorance which practically excludes them from a free career in life, as it is within its province to require the sort of building and drainage necessary for public health.

Our modern legislation then with reference to labour, and education, and health, involving as it does manifold interference with freedom of contract, is justified on the ground that it is the business of the state, not indeed directly to promote moral goodness, for that, from the very nature of moral goodness, it cannot do, but to maintain the conditions without which a free exercise of the human faculties is impossible. It does not indeed follow that it is advisable for the state to do all which it is justified in doing. We are often warned now-a-days against the danger of over-legislation; or, as I heard it put in a speech of the present home secretary in the days when he was sowing his political wild oats, of "grandmotherly government". There may be good ground for the warning, but at any rate we should be quite clear what we mean by it. The outcry against state interference is often raised by men whose real objection is not to state interference but to centralization, to the constant aggression of the central executive upon local authorities. As I have already pointed out, compulsion at the discretion of some elected municipal board proceeds just as much from the state as does compulsion exercised by a government office in London. No doubt, much needless friction is avoided, much is gained in the way of elasticity and adjustment to circumstances, by the independent local administration of general laws; and most of us would agree that of late there has been a dangerous tendency to override municipal discretion by the hard and fast rules of London "departments". But centralization is one thing: over-legislation, or the improper exercise of the power of the state, quite another. It is one question whether of late the central government has been unduly trenching on local government, and another question whether the law of the state, either as administered by central or by provincial authorities, has been unduly interfering with the discretion of individuals. We may object most strongly to advancing centralization, and yet wish that the law should put rather more than less restraint on those liberties of the individual which are a social nuisance. But there are some political speculators whose objection is not merely to centralization, but to the extended action of the law altogether. They think that the individual ought to be left much more to himself than has of late been the case. Might not our people, they ask, have been trusted to learn in time for themselves to eschew unhealthy dwellings, to refuse dangerous and degrading employment, to get their children the schooling necessary for making their way in the world? Would they not for their own comfort, if not from more chivalrous feeling, keep their wives and daughters from overwork? Or, failing this, ought not women, like men, to learn to protect themselves? Might not all the rules, in short, which legislation of the kind we have been discussing is intended to attain, have been attained without it; not so quickly, perhaps, but without tampering so dangerously with the independence and self-reliance of the people?

Now, we shall probably all agree that a society in which the public health was duly protected, and necessary education duly provided for, by the spontaneous action of individuals, was in a higher condition than one in which the compulsion of law was needed to secure those ends. But we must take men as we find them. Until such a condition of society is reached, it is the business of the state to take the best security it can for the young citizens' growing up in such health and with so much knowledge as is necessary for their real freedom. In so doing it need not at all interfere with the independence and self-reliance of those whom it requires to do what they would otherwise do for themselves. The man who, of his own right feeling, saves his wife from overwork and sends his children to school, suffers no moral degradation from a law which, if he did not do this for himself, would seek to make him do it. Such a man does not feel the law as constraint at all. To him it is simply a powerful friend. It gives him security for that being done efficiently which, with the best wishes, he might have much trouble in getting done efficiently if left to himself. No doubt it relieves him from some of the responsibility which would otherwise fall to him as head of a family, but, if he is what we are supposing him to be, in proportion as he is relieved of responsibilities in one direction he will assume them in another. The security which the state gives him for the safe housing and sufficient schooling of his family will only make him the more careful for their well-being in other respects, which he is left to look after for himself. We need have no fear, then, of such legislation having an ill-effect on those who, without the law, would have seen to that being done, though probably less efficiently, which the law requires to be done. But it was not their case that the laws we are considering were especially meant to meet. It was the overworked women, the ill-housed and untaught families, for whose benefit they were intended. And the question is whether without these laws the suffering classes could have been delivered quickly or slowly from the condition they were in. Could the enlightened self-interest or bene-volence of individuals, working under a system of unlimited freedom of contract, have ever brought them into a state compatible with the free development of the human faculties? No one considering the facts can have any doubt as to the answer to this question. Left to itself, or to the operation of casual benevolence, a degraded population perpetu-ates and increases itself. Read any of the authorized accounts, given before royal or parliamentary commissions, of the state of the labourers, especially of the women and children, as they were in our great in-dustries before the law was first brought to bear on them, and before freedom of contract was first interfered with in them. Ask yourself what chance there was of a generation, born and bred under such conditions, ever contracting itself out of them. Given a certain standard of moral and material well-being, people may be trusted not to sell their labour, or the labour of their children, on terms which would not allow that standard to be maintained. But with large masses of our population, until the laws we have been considering took effect, there was no such standard. There was nothing on their part, in the way either of self-respect or established demand for comforts, to prevent them from working and living, or from putting their children to work and live, in a way in which no one who is to be a healthy and free citizen can work and live. No doubt there were many high-minded employers who did their best for their work-people before the days of state-interference, but they could not prevent less scrupulous hirers of labour from hiring it on the cheapest terms. It is true that cheap labour is in the long run dear labour, but it is so only in the long run, and eager traders do not think of the long run. If labour is to be had under conditions incompatible with the health or decent housing or education of the labourer, there will always be plenty of people to buy it under those conditions, careless of the burden in the shape of rates and taxes which they may be laying up for posterity. Either the standard of well-being on the part of the sellers of labour must prevent them from selling their labour under those conditions, or the law must prevent it.

With a population such as ours was forty years ago, and still largely is, the law must prevent it and continue the prevention for some generations, before the sellers will be in a state to prevent it for themselves.

From *Liberal Legislation and Freedom of Contract* (1880)

§9. DEMOCRACY AND DICTATORSHIP

ABRAHAM LINCOLN

That our government should have been maintained in its original form from its establishment until now, is not much to be wondered at. It had many props to support it through that period, which are now decayed or crumbled away. Through that period it was felt by all to be an undecided experiment; now it is understood to be a successful one. Then, all that sought celebrity and fame and distinction expected to find them in the success of it. Their ambition aspired to display before an admiring world a practical demonstration of the truth of a proposition which had hitherto been considered at best as no better than problematical—namely, the capability of a people to govern themselves. If they succeeded they were to be immortalized; their names were to be transferred to counties, and cities, and rivers, and mountains; and to be revered and sung, toasted through all time. If they failed, they were to be called knaves, and fools, and fanatics for a fleeting hour; then to sink and be forgotten. They succeeded. The experiment is successful, and thousands have won their deathless names in making it so. But the game is caught; and I believe it is true that with the catching end the pleasures of the chase. This field of glory is harvested, and the crop is already appropriated. But new reapers will arise, and they too will seek a field. It is to deny what the history of the world tells us is true, to suppose that men of ambition and talents will not continue to spring up among us. And when they do, they will as naturally seek the gratification of their ruling passion as others have done before them. The question then is, Can that gratification be found in supporting and maintaining an edifice that has been erected by others? Most certainly it cannot. Many great and good men, sufficiently qualified for any task they should undertake, may even be found whose ambitions would aspire to nothing beyond a seat in Congress, a gubernatorial or a presidential chair; but such belong not to the family of the lion, or the tribe of the eagle. What! think you these places would satisfy an

Alexander, a Caesar, or a Napoleon? Never! Towering genius disdains a beaten path. It seeks regions hitherto unexplored. It sees no distinction in adding story to story upon the monuments of fame erected to the memory of others. It denies that it is glory enough to serve under any chief. It scorns to tread in the footsteps of any predecessor, however illustrious. It thirsts and burns for distinction; and if possible, it will have it, whether at the expense of emancipating slaves or enslaving freemen. Is it unreasonable, then, to expect that some man possessed of the loftiest genius, coupled with ambition sufficient to push it to the utmost stretch, will at some time spring up among us? And when such an one does, it will require the people to be united with each other, attached to the government and laws, and generally intelligent, to successfully frustrate his designs....

I think the authors of that notable instrument[1] intended to include *all* men, but they did not intend to declare all men equal *in all respects*.... They define with tolerable distinctness in what respects they did consider all men created equal—equal with "certain inalienable rights, among which are life, liberty, and the pursuit of happiness". This they said, and this they meant. They did not mean to assert the obvious untruth that all were then actually enjoying that equality, nor yet that they were about to confer it immediately upon them. In fact, they had no power to confer such a boon. They meant simply to declare the right, so that enforcement of it might follow as fast as circumstances should permit.

They meant to set up a standard maxim for free society, which shall be familiar to all, and revered by all; constantly looked to, constantly laboured for, and even though never perfectly attained, constantly approximated, and thereby constantly spreading and deepening its influence and augmenting the happiness and value of life to all people ... everywhere. The assertion that "all men are created equal" was of no practical use in effecting our separation from Great Britain; it was placed in the Declaration not for that, but for future use. Its authors meant it to be...a stumbling block to all those who in after times might seek to turn a free people back into the hateful paths of despotism. They knew the proneness of prosperity to breed tyrants, and they meant when such should appear in this fair land and commence their vocation, they should find left for them at least one hard nut to crack.

(1837, 1857)

[1] The Declaration of Independence.

BOOK LIST

G. DE RUGGIERO. *European Liberalism* (1927)

A. D. LINDSAY. *The Essentials of Democracy* (1929)

L. WOOLF. *After the Deluge* (1931)

J. S. FULTON and C. R. MORRIS. *In Defence of Democracy* (1935)

R. BASSETT. *The Essentials of Parliamentary Democracy* (1935)

W. LIPPMAN. *The Good Society* (1937)

C. H. McILWAIN. *Constitutionalism and the Changing World* (1939)

II

CATHOLICISM

In his introduction, Mr Oakeshott observes that each of the five doctrines dealt with in this book "is not merely a political doctrine, a doctrine about the nature of the state and the ends of government, but also a social doctrine, a conception of society and of the place and function of the individual in society" (p. xiv). This is preëminently true of the doctrine set forth in the ensuing section. The extracts presented—all save the final one taken from papal encyclicals and letters—have to do not only with the origins, nature, and functions of the state, but with the family, with private associations (such as trade unions), with labor, with the institution of private property, with individual liberties, and in short, either explicitly or by implication, with every basic aspect of social relationship and obligation. There is also a unity and coherence which no one can claim for the doctrine dealt with in the preceding section. One reason for this is that the entire body of Catholic doctrine derives in exceptional degree from formulation by a single towering authority, the prince of scholastic philosophers and theologians, St Thomas Aquinas. A second reason lies in the fact that, whereas there is no single authoritative expounder of democratic doctrine, Catholic doctrine is enunciated, interpreted, and applied to practical situations through a single channel—the Vatican—whose every pronouncement on social matters is received by all Catholics with respect, if not as dogma. If a third reason were to be added, it would be the obvious unifying effect of viewing all human life and conduct from the single vantage point of religion.

A helpful approach to the passages presented will be supplied by listing at the outset some of the fundamental questions to which one may expect here to find answers—from the viewpoint, that is, of persons for whom the Catholic doctrine holds the sum-total of truth about the social (including political) relationships of man. Here are a few of them: (1) What is the ultimate reason for the social nature of man? (2) Why must every civilized community have some ruling authority? (3) From what source is such authority derived, and what principles must be observed by those who exercise it? (4) What freedom is allowable to men in selecting the forms or institutions through which they shall be governed? (5) What shall be the relation between ecclesiastical and civil authority? (6) What is the obligation of the individual toward each of these authorities? (7) What is the relation of man-made law to natural, or divine, law? (8) In how far is the state justified in regulating family life, and also the formation of groups and associations for economic or other purposes? (9) What are the bases and limits of freedom for the individual? (10) Is there any right of revolt against constituted authority, i.e., any right of revolution? (11) Is there a right of private property, and if so, what is its source and its justification? (12) Is labor a mere "chattel", or, as our Supreme Court would say, a "commodity"? (13) What is the obligation of employers with respect to a "just" wage, and what principles should govern in determining such a wage?

To all of these, and many similar, questions, the Catholic doctrine offers coherent, categorical, *ex cathedra*, answers. Representative Democracy has answers to them, too,—but secular answers, sometimes hesitant, and often discordant. In the Catholic view, for example, the source of all civil authority (although not necessarily of the organs through which such authority is exercised) is divine ordinance. From the side of secular Democracy come various conflicting theories on the point, among them the social contract interpretation of Jean Jacques Rousseau, which to the Catholic mind is abhorrent. One may profitably read the sonorous passages that follow, not merely as a means of obtaining an objective knowledge of the essentials of one of the five great rival doctrines dealt with in this book, but with a view to measuring the subjective appeal of a body of opinion which has at least the satisfying aspects of unity and consistency. In the case of the extracts from the constitution of Eire, it will be instructive to read with a main purpose of identifying those provisions and meanings which can reasonably be attributed to the Catholic environment in which the instrument took form and operates.

C. C. Marshall, *The Roman Catholic Church in the Modern State* (new ed., 1931), will be found an interesting and temperate discussion of a subject often precipitating lively controversy. Cf. H. J. Laski, *Authority in the Modern State* (1919). On Thomas Aquinas, see P. Wicksteed, *Dante and Aquinas* (1913); and on the constitution of Eire, J. G. S. MacNeill, *Studies in the Constitution of the Irish Free State* (Dublin, 1925).

II

The social and political doctrine of Catholicism is a doctrine in terms of Natural Law; it belongs, that is, to the most ancient of the Western European traditions of social and political thought. So far as Catholicism is concerned this tradition received a definitive statement in the philosophy of St Thomas Aquinas. But in modern times an admirable restatement of it was made in Leo XIII's remarkable series of Encyclical Letters, the most important of which are: *Arcanum* (1880), *Diuturnum* (1881), *Immortale Dei* (1885), *Libertas* (1888), and *Rerum Novarum* (1891). More recently, the present Pope, Pius XI, has contributed to the exposition of this doctrine a number of letters to different national branches of the Church, and two Encyclicals, *Quadragesimo Anno* (1931) and *Divini Redemptoris* (1937). I have gone to the pronouncements of Leo XIII and Pius XI for the statement of this doctrine, and I have quoted from all these Encyclicals with the exception of *Divini Redemptoris*, directed against Communism, which seemed to provide nothing that was not available elsewhere and to display no very profound appreciation of the doctrine of Communism.

The regimes in contemporary Europe which have been profoundly influenced by the Catholic doctrine are those which prevail in Ireland and Portugal, and until recently that which existed in Austria. Consequently I have included some parts of the new Irish Constitution (1937), and I have made some reference to Portugal in the list of books for this section.

§ 1. THE NATURE AND END OF THE CHRISTIAN STATE

It is no difficult matter to determine what would be the form and character of the State if it were governed according to the principles of Christian philosophy. Man's natural instinct is to live in civil society: for he cannot attain in solitude the necessary means of life, nor the

45

development of his mental and moral faculties; and therefore, by a
Divine provision, he is born for a domestic and civil union and association with men, by which alone the needs of life can be adequately
supplied. But as no society can hold together unless someone be over
all, directing all by the same efficacious impulse to a common object,
every civilized community stands in need of a ruling authority; and
this authority, no less than society itself, originates in nature, and therefore has for its author God Himself. From this it follows that there
can be no public power except from God. For God alone is the true
and supreme Lord of the world; all things whatsoever must be subject
to Him and must serve Him; so that whoever possess the right of
governing have it from no other source but from God, the supreme
Ruler of all. "There is no power but from God." The right of ruling,
however, is not necessarily joined with any special form of government:
it may assume either one form or another, provided that it be such as to
ensure the general welfare. But whatever be the form of government,
rulers must be mindful of God, the supreme Ruler of the world, and
must set Him before themselves as an example and a law in their
administration. For as, in things that are visible, God has produced
secondary causes, wherein the Divine nature and action can in some
way be perceived, and which conduce to the end to which the course of
the world is directed; so in civil society He has willed that there should
be a ruling authority, and that they who hold it should be, as it were,
an image of the Divine power and providence over mankind. The rule,
therefore, must be just; and not that of a master, but like that of a
father; for the power of God over man is most just and joined with a
paternal goodness: and it must be carried on for the good of the citizens,
because those who rule over others have authority only for the welfare
of the State. Moreover the civil authority must not be subservient to
the advantages of one or of a few, for it was established for the common
good of all. But if those who are in authority rule unjustly; if they err
through arrogance or pride; if their measures be injurious to the
people; let them know that hereafter an account must be rendered to
God, and the stricter in proportion to the sacredness of their office or
the greatness of their dignity. "The mighty shall be mightily tor-
mented." Thus, indeed, will the majesty of the law meet with honourable and willing reverence from the people; for when once they are
convinced that rulers hold authority from God, they will feel that it is a
matter of justice and duty to be obedient to them, and to show to

them respect and fidelity with somewhat of the affection of children to their parents. "Let every soul be subject to higher powers." Indeed to condemn lawful authority, in whomsoever vested, is as unlawful as to resist the Divine will; and whoever resists that, rushes wilfully to destruction. "He that resisteth the power, resisteth the ordinance of God; and they that resist purchase to themselves damnation." Wherefore to cast aside obedience, and by popular violence to incite the country to sedition, is treason, not only against man, but against God.

The State, being thus constituted, is clearly bound to satisfy its many and great duties towards God by the public profession of religion. Nature and reason which bind every individual religiously to worship God, because we belong to Him, and must return to Him from Whom we came, bind the civil community by the same law. For men living together in society are no less under the power of God than individuals are; and society, no less than individuals, owes gratitude to God, its author, its preserver, and the beneficent source of the innumerable blessings it has received. Therefore, as no one may neglect his duties towards God; and as it is the first duty of every one to embrace religion both in mind and heart—not such a religion as each may choose, but that one which God commands, and which by certain and undoubted marks is proved to be the only true one; in like manner States cannot without crime act as though God did not exist, or cast off the care of religion as alien to them or useless, or out of several kinds of religion adopt whichever they please; but they are absolutely bound to the worship of God in the way that He has shown to be His will. Therefore among rulers the Name of God must be holy; and one of their first duties must be to favour religion, to protect it, to cover it with the authority of the laws, and not to institute or decree anything incompatible with its security. They owe this also to the people over whom they rule. For we are all by birth and adoption destined to enjoy, after this frail and short life, a supreme and final good in heaven; and to this end all effort should be referred. And because upon this depends the full and perfect happiness of men, therefore the attainment of this end is of all conceivable interests the most important. Hence civil society, which has been established for the common welfare, must, while guarding the prosperity of the community, so look to the interests of its individual members as not to impede in any way, but to facilitate as far as possible, the attainment of that supreme and unchangeable good which they look for. For this, attention must especially be paid to the most careful and inviolate preservation of religion, by the practice of which man is united to God.

God has divided the charge of the human race between two powers, the ecclesiastical and the civil, the one being set over divine and the other over human things. Each is supreme in its kind: each has fixed limits within which it is contained, and those limits are defined by the nature and special object of each; so that there is, as it were, a circle marked out, within which each acts by its own right. But, inasmuch as each has authority over the same subjects, and it might come to pass that one and the same thing, though in different respects, yet still the same thing, might pertain to the jurisdiction and judgement of both, therefore God, Who foreseeth all things and Who has established these two powers, has in due order arranged the course of each in right relation to the other. "For the powers that are, are ordained of God." If it were not so, contentions and conflicts would often arise; and not unfrequently man would hesitate in anxiety and doubt, like a traveller with two roads before him, not knowing what course to follow; with two powers commanding contrary things, which he could not disobey without neglect of duty. But it would be most repugnant to think this of the wisdom and goodness of God; for even in physical things, though they are of a far lower order, He has so combined the forces and causes of nature with a sort of wonderful harmony, that none of them is a hindrance to the rest, and all of them most fitly and aptly work together for the great end of the universe. There must, therefore, between these two powers be a certain orderly connexion, which may be compared to the union of the soul and body in man. The nature and extent of that connexion can be determined only, as We have said, by having regard to the nature of each power, and taking account of the relative excellence and nobility of their purpose; for one of them has for its proximate and chief object the comforts of this mortal life, the other the everlasting joys of heaven. Whatever, therefore, in human things is in any way sacred; whatever pertains to the salvation of souls or to the worship of God, either in its own nature, or by reason of the end to which it is referred; all this is subject to the power and judgement of the Church: but all other things, contained in the civil and political order, are rightly subject to the civil authority; for Jesus Christ has commanded that what is Caesar's shall be rendered to Caesar, and what belongs to God shall be rendered to God. There are times, however when another method of concord is available for peace and liberty We mean when rulers and the Roman Pontiff come to an understanding concerning any particular matter. At such times the Church gives singular proof of her maternal love, by the greatest possible kindness and indulgence.

Such then, as We have briefly indicated, is the Christian organization of civil society: no rash or fanciful fiction, but deduced from the highest and truest principles, which are confirmed by natural reason itself.

In such a conformation of the State there is nothing that can be thought unworthy of the dignity of rulers, or unbecoming; and so far is it from lessening the rights of sovereignty, that it adds to it stability and grandeur. For, if it be fully considered, this conformation has a great perfection, which all others lack; and from it various excellent results would follow, if each part would keep its place and discharge fully the office and work to which it is appointed. In truth, in the constitution of the State such as We have described, Divine and human things are properly divided; the rights of citizens are assured, and defended by Divine, natural, and human law; and the duties of every one are wisely marked out, and their fulfilment is well insured. In their uncertain and laborious journey to the everlasting city, all men see that they have safe guides and helpers on their way; and they know also that they have others whose business it is to protect them and their property, and to obtain or secure for them all other things that are essential for this life. Domestic society acquires that firmness and solidity which it needs, in the sanctity of marriage one and indissoluble; the rights and duties of husband and wife are regulated with wise justice and equity; due honour is secured to the woman; the authority of the man is conformed to the example of the authority of God; the power of the father is tempered by a due regard for the dignity of the wife and offspring; and the best possible provision is made for the guardianship, for the welfare, and for the education of the children. In the political and civil affairs the laws aim at the common good, and are not determined by the deceptive wishes and judgements of the multitude, but by truth and justice; the authority of rulers is vested with a sacredness more than human, and is restrained from deviating from justice and overstepping the limits of power; and the obedience of citizens is rendered with honour and dignity, because it is not the servitude of man to man, but obedience to the will of God exercising His sovereignty

by means of men. And this being recognized and admitted, it is felt to
be just that the dignity of rulers should be respected, that the public
authority should be constantly and faithfully obeyed, that no act of
sedition should be committed, and that the civil order of the State
should be kept intact.

That fatal and deplorable passion for innovation which was aroused
in the sixteenth century, first threw the Christian religion into confusion,
and then, by natural sequence, passed on to philosophy, and thence
pervaded all ranks of society. From this source, as it were, issued those
later maxims of unbridled liberty which, in the midst of the terrible
disturbances of the last century, were excogitated and proclaimed as
the principles and foundations of that new jurisprudence, previously
unknown, which, in many points, is out of harmony, not only with the
Christian law, but with the natural law also. Amongst these principles
the chief one is that which proclaims that all men, as by race and nature
they are alike, are also equal in their life; that each is so far master of
himself as in no way to come under the authority of another; that he is
free to think on every subject as he likes, and to act as he pleases; that
no man has any right to rule over others. In a society founded upon
these principles, government is only the will of the people, which, as it
is under the power of itself alone, so is alone its own ruler. It chooses,
nevertheless, those to whom it shall entrust itself; but in such a way that
it transfers to them, not so much the right, as the office of governing,
which is to be exercised in its name. The authority of God is passed
over in silence, as if either there were no God, or He cared nothing for
human society; as if men, either as individuals or in society, owed
nothing to God; or as if there could be a government of which the
whole cause, and power, and authority, do not reside in God Himself.
In this way, as is evident, a State becomes nothing but a multitude,
mistress and governor of itself. And since the people is said to contain
in itself the source of all rights and of all power, it follows that the State
does not deem itself bound by any kind of duty towards God; that it
makes no public profession of religion; that it does not hold itself
bound to inquire which of the many religions is the only true one, nor
to prefer one religion to the rest, and to show it special favour; but
rather to give equal rights to all religions, to the end that the public
order shall not incur injury from any of them. It is a part of this theory
that all questions concerning religion are to be referred to private

judgement; that every one is allowed to follow whatever religion he prefers, or none at all if he approves of none. Hence these consequences naturally arise: the judgement of each conscience is without regard to law; the freest opinions are expressed as to the practice or neglect of Divine worship; and there is unbounded license for men to think what they like, and to publish what they think.

Such foundations of the State being laid, which at this time are in general favour, it easily appears into what an unjust position the Church is driven. When the conduct of affairs is in accordance with doctrines of this kind, to the Catholic religion is assigned only a position equal or inferior to that of alien societies; no regard is paid to ecclesiastical laws; and The Church, which by the command and mandate of Jesus Christ, ought to teach all nations, finds herself forbidden in any way to deal with the public instruction of the people. As for matters which are of mixed jurisdiction, the rulers of the civil power lay down the law at their own pleasure, and in this matter haughtily set aside the most sacred laws of the Church. Wherefore they bring under their own jurisdiction the marriages of Christians, deciding even as to the marriage bond, and as to the unity and indissolubility of marriage. They lay their hands on the goods of the clergy, denying that the Church can hold property. Finally, they so act with regard to the Church that, rejecting altogether her claim to the nature and rights of a perfect society, they hold her to be in no way different from other societies in the State; and on that account, if she possesses any right or legal means of acting, she is said to hold it by the concession and favour of the government. If in any State the Church, with the approval of the civil laws, retains her own right, and an agreement has been publicly made between the two powers, men begin to cry out that the affairs of the Church must be severed from those of the State, wishing thereby to violate with impunity their pledged faith, and to have unchecked control over all things.

From Encyclical *Immortale Dei* (1885)

When it is a question of deciding what persons are to govern public affairs, that decision may in certain cases be left to the choice and preferences of the majority, without Catholic doctrine opposing the slightest obstacle to it. For though this choice determines the individual person of the sovereign, it does not confer the rights of sovereignty; it is not the constitution of authority which is thus decided, but the person who is to exercise that authority. Neither are the different political systems of any concern; there is nothing that prevents the Church from approving government by one man or government by several, so long as the government is a just one, assiduous in the common good. So that, saving established rights, communities are not forbidden to adopt whatever political regime seems best adapted to their own genius, or to their traditions and their customs.

If one wishes to determine from what source is derived the power of the State, the Church teaches, with reason, that it must be looked for in God. This is what she has found expressly set forth in the Holy Scriptures and in the monuments of Christian antiquity. Moreover, it is impossible to conceive a doctrine more agreeable to reason, more favourable to the interests of sovereigns and of nations. . . .

Those who would attribute the origin of civil society to a free contract, must perforce assign the same origin to authority; in that case, they say that each individual has yielded up some part of his rights and that all have voluntarily placed themselves under the power of the one in whom are vested their individual rights. But the error, a considerable one, of these philosophers consists in not seeing what is nevertheless evident; it is, that men do not live savage and solitary; it is that, prior to any resolution of their wills, their natural condition is to live in society. Add to this, that the pact on which this argument is based is an invention and a myth; and that, even were it real, it could never invest political sovereignty with the same degree of strength, dignity and stability which both the safety of the State and the interests of the citizens require. Authority can enjoy that dignity and that stability only so long as God is understood to be the source, august and sacred, from which it derives.

This doctrine not only is the truest, but it is impossible to conceive a more beneficial one. For indeed, if the authority of those who rule derives from the power of God Himself, then immediately, and for that very reason, it acquires a more than human dignity; it is not that dignity, compounded of absurdity and impiety, of which the Roman emperors dreamed when they awarded themselves divine honours, but a real and tangible dignity communicated to a man as a gift and a token of heavenly liberality. Henceforth, subjects are bound to obey their princes as they would God, not so much from the fear of punishment as out of respect to majesty; not in a sentiment of servility, but under the inspiration of conscience. And authority, thus stayed in its due place, will find itself much strengthened; for the citizens, finding themselves compelled by duty, will necessarily feel that disobedience and revolt are forbidden them, persuaded as they will be, from true principles, that to resist the power of the State is to oppose the Divine will, to refuse to honour the sovereign is to refuse to honour God. . . .

Within a State which takes refuge beneath these tutelary principles, there no longer exist pretexts for the motivation of seditions, nor passions to set them ablaze: everything is secure, the dignity and the lives of rulers, the peace and prosperity of cities. Moreover, the dignity of citizens finds therein its surest guarantee, for they owe it to the high nature of their doctrines to preserve even in obedience that just pride which is the prerogative of the greatness of human nature. They realize that at the judgement seat of God there is no distinction made between the free man and the slave; that all men have one Master, "liberal towards those who invoke Him", and that if subjects are bound to obey and submit themselves to their sovereigns, it is because these represent in some degree the God of Whom it is said that *to serve Him, is to rule*. . . .

Modern theories of political power have already been the cause of great evils, and it is to be feared lest in the future these evils should reach the worst extremes. For indeed, to refuse to refer to God, as to its source, the right to rule men, is in effect to deprive public power of all its dignity and all its vigour. To make it depend upon the will of the people is, first, to commit an error of principle; and, further, to set authority upon a foundation both fragile and inconsistent. Such opinions are a perpetual irritant to popular passions, which will be seen daily growing in boldness, and preparing the public ruin by fraying a way for secret conspiracies or overt sedition.

From Encyclical *Diuturnum* (1881)

THE LAW OF NATURE

It is part of the trend of the day to sever more and more not only morality, but also the foundation of law and jurisprudence, from true belief in God and from His revealed commandments. Here We have in mind particularly the so-called natural law, that is written by the finger of the Creator Himself in the tables of the hearts of men and which can be read on these tables by sound reason not darkened by sin and passion. Every positive law, from whatever lawgiver it may come,

can be examined as to its moral implications, and consequently as to its
moral authority to bind in conscience, in the light of the commandments of the natural law. The laws of man that are in direct contradiction with the natural law bear an initial defect, that no violent means,
no outward display of power, can remedy. By this standard must we
judge the principle: "What helps the people is right." A right meaning
may be given to this sentence if it is understood as expressing that what
is morally illicit can never serve the true interests of the people. But
even ancient paganism recognized that the sentence, to be perfectly
accurate, should be inverted and read: "Never is anything useful, if it is
not at the same time morally good. And not because it is useful is it
morally good, but because it is morally good, it is also useful." Cut
loose from this rule of morality that principle would mean, in international life, a perpetual state of war between the different nations. In
political life within the State, since it confuses considerations of utility
with those of right, it mistakes the basic fact that man as a person
possesses God-given rights, which must be preserved from all attacks
aimed at denying, suppressing, or disregarding them. To pay no heed
to this truth is to overlook the fact, that the true public good is finally
determined and recognized by the nature of man with its harmonious
co-ordination of personal rights and social obligations, as well as by
the purpose of the community which in turn is conditioned by the
same human nature. The community is willed by the Creator as the
means to the full development of the individual and social attainments,
which the individual by a give and take process has to employ to his
own good and that of others. Also those higher and more comprehensive values, that cannot be realized by the individual, but only by the
community, in the final analysis are intended by the Creator for the
sake of the individual, for his natural and supernatural development
and perfection. A deviation from this order loosens the supports on
which the community is placed, and thereby imperils the tranquillity,
security, and even the existence of the community itself.

The believer has an inalienable right to profess his faith and put it
into practice in the manner suited to him. Laws that suppress or make
this profession and practice difficult contradict the law of nature.

Conscientious parents, aware of their duty in the matter of education,
have a primary and original right to determine the education of the
children given to them by God in the spirit of the true faith and in
agreement with its principles and ordinances. Laws or other regulations

concerning schools that disregard the rights of parents guaranteed to them by the natural law, or by threat and violence nullify those rights, contradict the natural law and are utterly and essentially immoral.

From the *Papal Letter to the Church in Germany*:
Mit brennender Sorge (1937)

§2. THE STATE AND THE FAMILY[1]

In choosing a state of life, it is indisputable that all are at full liberty to follow the counsel of Jesus Christ as to observing virginity, or to bind themselves by the marriage tie. No human law can abolish the natural and original right of marriage, nor in any way limit the chief and principal purpose of marriage ordained by God's authority from the beginning: *Increase and multiply*. Hence we have the family; the 'society' of a man's house—a society very small, one must admit, but none the less a true society, and one older than any State. Consequently it has rights and duties peculiar to itself which are quite independent of the State. . . .

Inasmuch as the domestic household is antecedent, as well in idea as in fact, to the gathering of men into a community, the family must necessarily have rights and duties which are prior to those of the community, and founded more immediately in nature. If the citizens of the State—in other words the families—on entering into association and fellowship, were to experience at the hands of the State hindrance instead of help, and were to find their rights attacked instead of being upheld, that association (viz. the State) would rightly be an object of detestation, rather than of desire.

The contention, then, that the civil government should at its option intrude into and exercise intimate control over the family and the household, is a great and pernicious error. True, if a family finds itself in exceeding distress, utterly deprived of the counsel of friends, and without any prospect of extricating itself, it is right that extreme necessity be met with public aid, since each family is a part of the commonwealth. In like manner, if within the precincts of the household there occur grave disturbance of mutual rights, public authority should intervene to force each party to yield to the other its proper due; for this is not to deprive citizens of their rights, but justly and properly to safeguard

---

[1] See also Encyclical *Arcanum* (1880).

and strengthen them. But the rulers of the State must go no further:
here nature bids them stop. Paternal authority can be neither abolished
nor absorbed by the State; for it has the same source as human life
itself. "The child belongs to the father" and is, as it were, the continua-
tion of the father's personality; and, speaking strictly, the child takes
its place in civil society, not of its own right, but in its quality as
member of the family in which it is born. And for the very reason that
"the child belongs to the father", it is, as St Thomas of Aquino says,
"before it attains the use of free will, under the power and the charge of
its parents"....

The State must not absorb the individual or the family; both
should be allowed free and untrammelled action so far as is consistent
with the common good and the interests of others. Rulers should,
nevertheless, anxiously safeguard the community and all its members;
the community, because the conservation thereof is so emphatically the
business of the supreme power, that the safety of the commonwealth is
not only the first law, but it is a governor's whole reason of existence;
and the members, because both philosophy and the Gospel concur in
laying down that the object of the government of the State should be,
not the advantage of the ruler, but the benefit of those over whom he is
placed. As the power to rule comes from God, and is, as it were, a
participation in His, the highest of all sovereignties, it should be
exercised as the power of God is exercised—with a fatherly solicitude
which not only guides the whole, but reaches also to the details.

From Encyclical *Rerum Novarum* (1891)

§3. THE STATE AND ASSOCIATIONS

Lesser societies and the society which constitutes the State differ in
many respects, because their immediate purpose and aim is different.
Civil society exists for the common good, and hence is concerned with
the interests of all in general, albeit with individual interests also in
their due place and degree. It is therefore called a *public* society,
because by its agency, as St Thomas of Aquino says, "Men establish
relations in common with one another in the setting up of a commonwealth". But societies which are formed in the bosom of the State are
styled *private*, and rightly so, since their immediate purpose is the
private advantage of the associates. "Now a private society", says

St Thomas again, "is one which is formed for the purpose of carrying out private objects; as when two or three enter into partnership with the view of trading in common." Private societies, then, although they exist within the State, and are severally part of the State, cannot nevertheless be absolutely, and as such, prohibited by the State. For to enter into a "society" of this kind is the natural right of man; and the State is bound to protect natural rights, not to destroy them; and if it forbids its citizens to form associations, it contradicts the very principle of its own existence; for both they and it exist in virtue of the like principle, namely, the natural tendency of man to dwell in society.

There are occasions, doubtless, when it is fitting that the law should intervene to prevent associations; as when men join together for purposes which are evidently bad, unlawful, or dangerous to the State. In such cases public authority may justly forbid the formation of associations, and may dissolve them if they already exist. But every precaution should be taken not to violate the rights of individuals and not to impose unreasonable regulations under pretence of public benefit. For laws only bind when they are in accordance with right reason, and hence with the eternal law of God.[1]

From Encyclical Rerum Novarum (1891)

When we speak of the reform of institutions, it is principally the State that comes to mind. Not indeed that all salvation is to be hoped from its intervention; but because on account of the evil of "individualism", as We called it, things have come to such a pass that the highly developed social life which once flourished in a variety of associations organically linked with each other, has been damaged and all but ruined, leaving thus virtually only individuals and the State, to the no small detriment of the State itself. Social life has entirely lost its organic form; the State, to-day encumbered with all the burdens once borne by those associations now destroyed, has been submerged and overwhelmed by an infinity of occupations and duties.

It is indeed true, as history clearly proves, that owing to changed circumstances much that was formerly done by small groups can

---

[1] Human law is law only by virtue of its accordance with right reason: and thus far it is manifest that it flows from the eternal law. And in so far as it deviates from right reason it is called an unjust law; in such case it is no law at all, but rather a species of violence. St Thomas, *Summa Theol.* 1 a–2 ae, Q. xciii, art. 3, ad. 2.

nowadays only be done by large associations. None the less, just as it is wrong to withdraw from the individual and commit to a group what private enterprise and industry can accomplish, so too it is an injustice, a grave evil and a disturbance of right order, for a larger and higher association to arrogate to itself functions which can be performed efficiently by smaller and lower societies. This is a fundamental principle of social philosophy, unshaken and unchangeable. Of its very nature the true aim of all social activity should be to help members of the social body, but never to destroy or absorb them.

The State therefore should leave to smaller groups the settlement of business of minor importance, which otherwise would greatly distract it; it will thus carry out with greater freedom, power and success the tasks belonging to it alone, because it alone can effectively accomplish these: directing, watching, stimulating, restraining, as circumstances suggest and necessity demands. Let those in power, therefore, be convinced that the more faithfully this principle of subsidiary function be followed, and a graded hierarchical order exist between various associations, the greater will be both social authority and social efficiency, and the happier and more prosperous the condition of the commonwealth.

Now this is the primary duty of the State and of all good citizens, to abolish disputes between opposing classes, and to create and foster harmony between vocational groups.

The aim of social policy must therefore be the re-establishment of vocational groups. Society to-day still remains in a strained and therefore unstable and uncertain state, because it is founded on classes with divergent aims and hence opposed to each other, and consequently prone to enmity and strife.

Labour, indeed, as has been well said by Our Predecessor in his Encyclical, is not a mere chattel;[1] the human dignity of the working-man must be recognized in it, and consequently it cannot be bought and sold like any piece of merchandize. None the less, as things are now, the wage-system divides men on what is called the labour-market into two sections, resembling armies, and the disputes between these sections transform this labour-market into an arena where the two armies are engaged in fierce combat. To this grave disorder, which is leading society to ruin, a remedy must evidently be applied as speedily as possible. But there cannot be question of any perfect cure unless this

[1] Encyclical *Rerum Novarum.*

opposition be done away with, and well-organized members of the social body be constituted; vocational groups namely, claiming the allegiance of men, not according to the position they occupy in the labour-market, but according to the diverse functions which they exercise in society. For it is natural that just as those who dwell in close proximity constitute townships, so those who practise the same trade or profession, in the economic field or any other, form corporate groups. These groups, with powers of self-government, are considered by many to be, if not essential to civil society, at least natural to it.

Order, as St Thomas well defines, is unity arising from the proper arrangement of a number of objects; hence, true and genuine social order demands that the various members of a society be joined together by some firm bond. Such a bond of union is provided both by the production of goods or the rendering of services in which employers and employees of one and the same vocational group collaborate; and by the common good which all such groups should unite to promote, each in its own sphere, with friendly harmony. Now this union will become powerful and efficacious in proportion to the fidelity with which the individuals and the vocational groups strive to discharge their professional duties and to excel in them.

From this it is easy to conclude that in these corporations the common interests of the whole vocational group must predominate; and among these interests the most important is to promote as much as possible the contribution of each trade or profession to the common good of the State. Regarding cases which may occur in which the particular interests of employers or employees call for special care and protection, the two parties will be able to deliberate separately, or to come to such decisions as the matter may require.

It is hardly necessary to note that what Leo XIII taught concerning the form of political government can in due measure be applied also to professional corporations. Here, too, men may choose whatever form they please, provided that both justice and the common good be taken into account.[1]

Just as the citizens of the same township are wont to form associations with very diverse aims, which each citizen is perfectly free to join or not, similarly, those who are engaged in the same trade or profession will form equally voluntary associations among themselves, for purposes connected in some way with their occupation. Our

[1] Encyclical *Immortale Dei*.

Predecessor of illustrious memory has explained clearly and lucidly the nature of these voluntary associations. We are content, therefore, to emphasize this one point: Not only is man free to institute these unions which are of a private character, but he has "the further right to adopt such rules and regulations as may best conduce to the attainment of the end in view".[1] The same liberty must be asserted for the founding of associations which extend beyond the limits of a single trade or profession. Let those voluntary associations which already flourish and produce salutary fruits make it the goal of their endeavours, in accordance with Christian social doctrine, to prepare the way and to do their best towards the realization of those higher corporations or vocational groups which We have mentioned above.

From Encyclical Quadragesimo Anno (1931)

§ 4. LIBERTY

The unanimous consent and judgement of men, which is the trusty voice of nature, recognizes natural liberty in those only who are endowed with intelligence or reason; and it is by his use of this that man is rightly regarded as responsible for his actions. For, while other animate creatures follow their senses, seeking good and avoiding evil only by instinct, man has reason to guide him in each and every act of his life. Reason sees that whatever things are held to be good upon earth, may exist or may not, and discerning that none of them are of necessity for us, it leaves the will free to choose what it pleases. But man can judge of this *contingency*, as we say, only because he has a soul that is simple, spiritual, and intellectual—a soul, therefore, which is not produced by matter, and does not depend on matter for its existence; but which is created immediately by God, and, for surpassing the condition of things material, has a life and action of its own—so that, knowing the unchangeable and necessary reasons of what is true and good, it sees that no particular kind of good is necessary to us. When, therefore, it is established that man's soul is immortal and endowed with reason and not bound up with things material the foundation of natural liberty is at once most firmly laid.. ..

Such then being the condition of human liberty, it necessarily stands

---

[1] Encyclical *Rerum Novarum*.

in need of light and strength to direct its actions to good and to restrain them from evil. Without this the freedom of our will would be our ruin. First of all there must be *law*; that is, a fixed rule of teaching what is to be done and what is to be left undone. This rule cannot affect the lower animals in any true sense, since they act of necessity, following their natural instinct, and cannot of themselves act in any other way. On the other hand, as was said above, he who is free can either act or not act, can do this or do that, as he pleases, because his judgement precedes his choice. And his judgement not only decides what is right or wrong of its own nature, but also what is practically good and therefore to be chosen, and what is practically evil and therefore to be avoided. In other words the reason prescribes to the will what it should seek after or shun, in order to the eventual attainment of man's last end, for the sake of which all his actions ought to be performed. This ordination of *reason* is called law. In man's free-will, therefore, or in the moral necessity of our voluntary acts being in accordance with reason, lies the very root of the necessity of law. Nothing more foolish can be uttered or conceived than the notion that because man is free by nature, he is therefore exempt from law. Were this the case, it would follow that to become free we must be deprived of reason; whereas the truth is that we are bound to submit to law precisely because we are free by our very nature. For law is the guide of man's actions; it turns him towards good by its rewards, and deters him from evil by its punishments. Foremost in this office comes the *natural law*, which is written and engraved in the mind of every man; and this is nothing but our reason, commanding us to do right and forbidding sin. Nevertheless all prescriptions of human reason can have force of law only inasmuch as they are the voice and the interpreters of some higher power on which our reason and liberty necessarily depend. For, since the force of law consists in the imposing of obligations and the granting of rights, authority is the one and only foundation of all law—the power, that is, of fixing duties and defining rights, as also of assigning the necessary sanctions of rewards and chastisements to each and all of its commands. But all this, clearly, cannot be found in man, if, as his own supreme legislator, he is to be the rule of his own actions. It follows therefore that the law of nature is the same thing as the *eternal law*, implanted in rational creatures, and inclining them *to their right action and end*; and can be nothing else but the eternal reason of God, the Creator and Ruler of all the world. . . .

What has been said of the liberty of individuals is no less applicable
to them when considered as bound together in civil society. For, what
reason and the natural law do for individuals, that *human law*, promulgated for their good, does for the citizens of States. Of the laws
enacted by men, some are concerned with what is good or bad by its
very nature; and they command men to follow after what is right and
to shun what is wrong, adding at the same time a suitable sanction. But
such laws by no means derive their origin from civil society; because,
just as civil society did not create human nature, so neither can it be
said to be the author of the good which befits human nature, or of the
evil which is contrary to it. Laws come before men live together in
society, and have their origin in the natural, and consequently in the
eternal, law. The precepts, therefore, of the natural law, contained
bodily in the laws of men, have not merely the force of human law, but
they possess that higher and more august sanction which belongs to
the law of nature and the eternal law. And within the sphere of this
kind of law, the duty of the civil legislator is, mainly, to keep the
community in obedience by the adoption of a common discipline and
by putting restraint upon refractory and viciously inclined men, so
that, deterred from evil, they may turn to what is good, or at any rate
may avoid causing trouble and disturbance to the State. Now there
are other enactments of the civil authority, which do not follow directly,
but somewhat remotely, from the natural law, and decide many points
which the law of nature treats only in a general and indefinite way. For
instance, though nature commands all to contribute to the public peace
and prosperity, still whatever belongs to the manner, and circumstances,
and conditions under which such service is to be rendered must be
determined by the wisdom of men, and not by nature herself. It is the
constitution of these particular rules of life, suggested by reason and
prudence, and put forth by competent authority, that human law,
properly so called, consists, binding all citizens to work together for
the attainment of the common end proposed to the community, and
forbidding them to depart from this end; and in so far as human law is
in conformity with the dictates of nature, leading to what is good, and
deterring from evil. From this it is manifest that the eternal law of God
is the sole standard and rule of human liberty, not only in each individual man, but also in the community and civil society which men
constitute when united. Therefore, the true liberty of human society
does not consist in every man doing what he pleases, for this would

simply end in turmoil and confusion, and bring on the overthrow of the State; but rather in this, that through the injunction of the civil law all may more easily conform to the prescriptions of the eternal law. Likewise, the liberty of those who are in authority does not consist in the power to lay unreasonable and capricious commands upon their subjects, which would equally be criminal and would lead to the ruin of the commonwealth; but the binding force of human laws is in this, that they are to be regarded as applications of the eternal law, and incapable of sanctioning anything which is not contained in the eternal law, as in the principle of all law. . . .

Therefore, the nature of human liberty, however it be considered, whether in individuals or in society, whether in those who command or in those who obey, supposes the necessity of obedience to some supreme and eternal law, which is no other than the authority of God, commanding good and forbidding evil. And, so far from this most just authority of God over men diminishing, or even destroying their liberty, it protects and perfects it; for the real perfection of all creatures is found in the prosecution and attainment of their respective ends; but the supreme end to which human liberty must aspire is God. . . .

We must now consider briefly *liberty of speech*, and liberty of the Press. It is hardly necessary to say that there can be no such right as this, if it be not used in moderation, and if it pass beyond the bounds and end of all true liberty. For right is a moral power which—as We have before said and must again and again repeat—it is absurd to suppose that nature has accorded indifferently to truth and falsehood, to justice and injustice. Men have a right freely and prudently to propagate throughout the State what things soever are true and honourable, so that as many as possible may possess them; but lying opinions, than which no mental plague is greater, and vices which corrupt the heart and moral life, should be diligently repressed by public authority, lest they insidiously work the ruin of the State. The excesses of an unbridled intellect, which unfailingly end in the oppression of the untutored multitude, are no less rightly controlled by the authority of the law than are the injuries inflicted by violence upon the weak. And this all the more surely, because by far the greater part of the community is either absolutely unable, or able only with great difficulty, to escape from illusions and deceitful subtleties, especially such as flatter the passions. If unbridled licence of speech and of writing be granted to all, nothing will remain sacred and inviolate; even the highest and truest mandates of nature, justly held to be the common and noblest heritage of the human race, will not be spared. Thus, truth gradually being obscured by darkness, pernicious and manifold error, as too often happens, will easily prevail. Thus, too, licence will gain what liberty loses; for liberty will ever be more free and secure, in proportion as licence is kept in fuller restraint. In regard however to all matters of opinion which God leaves to man's free discussion, full liberty of thought and of speech is naturally within the right of every one; for such liberty never leads men to suppress the truth, but often to discover it and to make it known.

From Encyclical *Libertas* (1888)

§5. THE RIGHT OF REVOLUTION

. . . It cannot be said that Catholic Action, in face of the grave problems of Mexico, should occupy a place of secondary importance; and consequently a grievous error would be incurred if this Institution, whose task it is to educate consciences and to form moral qualities, were to be supplanted in any way by an external activity of any kind, even though it be a question of defending necessary religious and civil freedom: for the salvation of Mexico, like that of all human society, lies above all in the eternal and immutable teaching of the Gospels and in the sincere practice of Christian morals.

Nevertheless, once this scale of values and activities is established, it must be admitted that the Christian life requires for its development the support of external and tangible means; that the Church, because it is a society of men, cannot exist or grow if it does not enjoy liberty of action; and that its members have the right to find in civil society the possibility of living in conformity with the dictates of their consciences.

In consequence it is natural that when even the most elementary religious and civil liberties are attacked, Catholic citizens should not passively acquiesce in renouncing such liberties; although circumstances will determine when these just claims should be opportunely made and how energetically they should be furthered.

You have more than once reminded your flock that the Church preserves and encourages peace and order, even at the cost of great sacrifices, and that it condemns as unjust any insurrection against legitimate authority. On the other hand, you have also affirmed that if ever that authority should rise up against justice and truth to·the extent of destroying even the very foundations of Authority, it would be impossible to condemn a movement in which citizens were to unite to defend the Nation and themselves, by lawful and appropriate means, against those who make use of the civil power to drag the Nation to ruin.

Although it is true that the practical solution depends upon concrete circumstances, it is nevertheless Our duty to remind you of some general principles which must always be borne in mind, namely:·

(1) That the active furtherance of these claims is justified as a means, or as a relative end, not as an ultimate and absolute end;

(2) That, as a means, it should be a legitimate action and not intrinsically evil;

(3) That if it is to be a means proportionate to its end recourse should be had to it only in so far as is necessary to obtain the end or to make it possible to attain it either entirely or in part, and in such a way as not to cause greater harm to the community than that which it attempts to remedy;

(4) That the use of such a means, and the exercise of civic and political rights in their entirety, including also all questions of a purely material and technical nature, as well as the question of the defence of these rights by violent resistance, are in no way incumbent upon the Clergy or upon Catholic Action as such; although, on the other hand, it is the task of both to educate Catholics in the just use of their rights and to prepare them for the defence of these rights by all lawful means, as required by the common good;

(5) The Clergy and Catholic Action, being consecrated by their mission of peace and love to the task of uniting all men *in vinculo pacis* (Ephes. IV, 3), must contribute to the prosperity of the nation, chiefly by furthering the union of citizens and of the social classes, and by collaborating in all those social measures that are not opposed to dogma or to the laws of Christian morality. . . .

From the *Apostolic Letter of His Holiness Pope Pius XI to the Mexican Episcopate*, 28 March, 1937

§6. PRIVATE PROPERTY

Every man has by nature the right to possess property as his own. This is one of the chief points of distinction between man and the animal creation, for the brute has no power of self-direction, but is governed by two main instincts, which keep his powers on the alert, impel him to develop them in a fitting manner, and stimulate and determine him to action without any power of choice. One of these instincts is self-preservation, the other the propagation of the species. Both can attain their purpose by means of things which lie within their range; beyond their verge the brute creation cannot go, for they are moved to action by their senses only, and in the special direction which these suggest. But with man it is wholly different. He possesses, on the one hand, the full perfection of the animal being, and hence enjoys, as least as the rest of the animal kind, the fruition of things material. But animal nature, however perfect, is far from representing the human being in its completeness, and is in truth but humanity's humble handmaid, made to serve and to obey. It is the mind, or reason, which is the predominant element in us who are human creatures; it is this which renders a human being human, and distinguishes him essentially from the brute. And on this very account—that man alone among the animal creation is endowed with reason—it must be within his right to possess things not merely for temporary and momentary use, as other living things do, but to have and to hold them in stable possession; he must have not only things that perish in the use, but those also which, though they have been reduced into use, continue for further use in after time.

This becomes still more clearly evident if man's nature be considered a little more deeply. For man, fathoming by his faculty of reason matters without number, linking the future with the present, and being master of his own acts, guides his ways under the eternal law and the power of God, whose Providence governs all things. Wherefore it is in his power to exercise his choice not only as to matters that regard his present welfare, but also about those which he deems may be to his advantage in time yet to come. Hence man not only should possess the fruits of the earth, but also the very soil inasmuch as from the produce of the earth he has to lay by provision for the future. Man's needs do not die out, but for ever recur; although satisfied to-day, they demand fresh supplies for to-morrow. Nature accordingly must have given to man a source that is stable and remaining always with him from which he might look to draw continual supplies. And this stable condition of things he finds solely in the earth and its fruits.

There is no need to bring in the State. Man precedes the State, and possesses, prior to the formation of any State, the right of providing for the sustenance of his body. The fact that God has given the earth for the use and enjoyment of the whole human race can in no way be a bar to the owning of private property. For God has granted the earth to mankind in general, not in the sense that all without distinction can deal with it as they like, but rather that no part of it was assigned to any-one in particular, and that the limits of private possession have been left to be fixed by man's own industry, and by the laws of individual races. Moreover, the earth, even though apportioned among private owners, ceases not thereby to minister to the needs of all, inasmuch as there is no one who does not sustain life from what the land produces. Those who do not possess the soil, contribute their labour; hence it may truly be said that all human subsistence is derived either from labour on one's own land, or from some toil, some calling which is paid for either in the produce of the land itself, or in that which is exchanged for what the land brings forth.

Here, again, we have further proof that private ownership is in accordance with the law of nature. Truly, that which is required for the preservation of life, and for life's well-being, is produced in great abundance from the soil, but not until man has brought it into cultiva-tion and expended upon it his solicitude and skill. Now, when man thus turns the activity of his mind and the strength of his body towards procuring the fruits of nature, by such act he makes his own that portion of nature's field which he cultivates—that portion on which he leaves, as it were, the impress of his individuality; and it cannot but be just that he should possess that portion as his very own, and have a right to hold it without anyone being justified in violating that right. . . .

With reason, then, the common opinion of mankind, little affected by the few dissentients who have contended for the opposite view, has found in the careful study of nature, and in the laws of nature, the foundations of the division of property, and the practice of all ages has consecrated the principle of private ownership, as being pre-eminently in conformity with human nature, and as conducing in the most unmistakable manner to the peace and tranquillity of human existence.

The same principle is confirmed and enforced by the civil laws—laws which, so long as they are just, derive from the law of nature their binding force.

From Encyclical *Rerum Novarum* (1891)

First, let it be made clear beyond all doubt that neither Leo XIII, nor those theologians who have taught under the guidance and direction of the Church, have ever denied or called in question the two-fold aspect of ownership, which is individual or social according as it regards individuals or concerns the common good. Their unanimous assertion has always been that the right to own private property has been given to man by nature, or rather by the Creator Himself, both in order that individuals may be able to provide for their own needs and those of their families, and also that by means of it the goods which the Creator has destined for the whole human race may truly serve this purpose. Now these ends cannot be secured, unless some definite and stable order is maintained.

A double danger must therefore be carefully avoided. On the one hand, if the social and public aspect of ownership be denied or minimized, one falls into "individualism", as it is called, or at least comes near to it; on the other hand, the rejection or diminution of its private and individual character necessarily leads to "collectivism" or something approaching to it. . . .

It follows from the two-fold character of ownership which, as We have said, is both individual and social, that men must take into account in this matter, not only their own advantage, but also the common good. To define in detail these duties, when the need occurs, and when the natural law does not do so, is the function of the civil ruler. Provided that the natural and divine law be observed, the public authority, in view of the true necessities of the common welfare, may specify more accurately what is licit and what is illicit for property-owners in the use of their possessions. Moreover, Leo XIII had wisely taught that "the defining of private possession has been left by God to man's own industry and to the laws of individual peoples". History proves that ownership, like other elements of social life, is not absolutely rigid, and this doctrine We Ourselves have given utterance to on a previous occasion in the following terms: "How varied are the forms which property has assumed. First the primitive form in use amongst rude and savage peoples, which still exists in certain localities even in our own day; then that of the patriarchal age; later various tyrannical types (We use the word 'tyrannical' in its classical meaning); finally, the feudal and monarchic systems down to the varieties of more recent times." It is plain, however, that the State may not discharge this duty in an arbitrary manner. Man's natural right of possessing private property, and transmitting it by inheritance, must remain intact and inviolate, and cannot be taken away by the State; "for man precedes the State" and "the domestic household is antecedent, as well in idea as in fact, to the gathering of men into a community".

From Encyclical *Quadragesimo Anno* (1931)

§7. A JUST WAGE

Let the working man and the employer make free agreements, and in particular let them agree freely as to the wages; nevertheless there underlies a dictate of natural justice more imperious and ancient than any bargain between man and man, namely, that wages ought not to be insufficient to support a frugal and well-behaved wage-earner. If through necessity or fear of a worse evil the workman accept harder conditions because an employer or contractor will afford him no better, he is made the victim of force and injustice. In these and similar conditions, however—such as, for example, the hours of labour in different trades, the sanitary precautions to be observed in factories and workshops, etc.—in order to supersede undue interference on the part of the State, especially as circumstances, times and localities differ so widely, it is advisable that recourse be had to Societies or Boards such as We shall mention presently, or to some other mode of safeguarding the interests of the wage-earners; the State being appealed to, should circumstances require, for its sanction and protection.

From Encyclical *Rerum Novarum* (1891)

Now it is evident that in labour, especially hired labour, as in ownership, there is a social as well as a personal or individual aspect to be considered. For unless a truly social and organic body is established; unless a social and juridical order protects the exercise of labour; unless the various branches of industry, some of which depend upon others, co-operate and complete each other; unless, above all, intelligence, capital and labour combine together for common effort, man's toil cannot produce its adequate fruit. Hence if the social and individual character of labour be overlooked, it can be neither justly valued nor recompensed according to equivalence.

From this double aspect, naturally inherent in human labour, follow important conclusions for the regulation and fixing of wages.

In the first place, the wage paid to the working man must be sufficient for the support of himself and of his family. It is right indeed that the rest of the family contribute according to their power towards the common maintenance, as we see particularly in the families of peasants, but also in those of many artisans and small tradesmen. But it is wrong to abuse the tender years of children, or the weakness of woman. Mothers should carry on their work chiefly at home, or near to it, occupying themselves in caring for the household. Intolerable and at all costs to be abolished is the abuse whereby mothers of families, because of the insufficiency of the father's salary, are forced to engage in painful occupations outside the domestic walls, to the neglect of their own proper cares and duties, particularly the upbringing of their children. Every effort must therefore be made, that fathers of families receive a wage sufficient to meet adequately normal domestic needs. If under present circumstances this is not always feasible, social justice demands that reforms be introduced without delay, which will guarantee such a wage to every adult working-man. In this connexion We praise those who have most prudently and usefully attempted various methods by which an increased wage is paid in view of increased family burdens, and special provision made for special needs.

In settling the amount of wages one must also take into account the business and those in charge of it; for it would be unjust to demand excessive wages, which a business cannot pay without ruin, and without consequent distress amongst the working-people themselves: though if the business make smaller profit on account of want of energy and enterprise, or from neglect of technical and economic progress, this is not a just reason for reducing the workers' wages. If, however, the business does not make enough money to pay the workman a just wage, either because it is overwhelmed with unjust burdens, or because it is compelled to sell its products at an unjustly low price, those who thus injure it are guilty of grievous wrong; for it is they who deprive the workers of a just wage, and force them to accept terms which are unjust.

Let employers, therefore, and employed join in plans and efforts to

overcome all difficulties and obstacles, and let them be aided in this
wholesome endeavour by the wise measures of the public authority.
In the last extreme, counsel must be taken whether the business can
continue, or whether some other provision should be made for the
workers. The guiding spirit in this crucial decision should be one of
mutual understanding and Christian harmony between employers and
workers.

Finally wage-rates must be regulated with a view to the economic
welfare of the whole people. We have already shown how conducive it
is to this common welfare that wage-earners of all kinds be enabled, by
setting aside some portion of their wage after having made provision
for necessary expenses, to attain gradually to the possession of a certain
modest fortune. Another point, however, of scarcely less importance
must not be overlooked, in these our days especially, namely that
opportunities for work be provided for those who are willing and able
to work. This depends in no small measure upon the level of wages,
which multiplies opportunities for work as long as it is fixed at a proper
amount, and reduces them if allowed to depart from this limit. All are
aware that a rate of wages too low or too high causes unemployment.
Now unemployment, particularly if widespread and of long duration,
as We have known it during Our Pontificate, causes misery and tempta-
tion to the workers, ruins the prosperity of nations, and endangers
public order, peace and tranquillity the world over. To lower or raise
wages unduly, with a view to private advantage, and with no consideration for the common good, is therefore contrary to social justice, which
demands that, so far as possible by concerted plans and union of wills,
wages be so regulated as to offer to as many as possible opportunities
of employment, and of securing for themselves suitable means of
livelihood.

A proper proportion between different wages is also a matter of
importance; and with this is intimately connected proper proportions
between the prices charged for the products of the various economic
groups, agricultural, industrial, and so forth. Where this harmonious
proportion is kept, the various branches of production will combine
and unite into one single organism, and as members of a common body
will aid and perfect one another. For then only will the economic and
social order be soundly established and attain its ends, when it offers to
all and each all those goods which the wealth and resources of nature,
technique, and the social organization of economic affairs can give.

These goods should be sufficient both to supply all necessities and reasonable comforts, and to uplift men to that higher standard of life which, provided it be used with prudence, is not only of no hindrance, but is of singular help, to virtue.

From Encyclical *Quadragesimo Anno* (1931)

§8. FROM THE CONSTITUTION OF IRELAND (EIRE), 1937

PREAMBLE:

In the Name of the Most Holy Trinity, from Whom is all authority and to Whom, as our final end, all actions both of men and States must be referred,

We, the people of Eire,

Humbly acknowledging all our obligations to our Divine Lord, Jesus Christ, Who sustained our fathers through centuries of trial,

Gratefully remembering their heroic and unremitting struggle to regain the rightful independence of our Nation,

And seeking to promote the common good, with due observance of Prudence, Justice and Charity, so that the dignity and freedom of the individual may be assured, true social order attained, the unity of our country restored, and concord established with other nations,

Do hereby adopt, enact, and give to ourselves this Constitution.

ARTICLE 6

1. All powers of government, legislative, executive and judicial, derive, under God, from the people, whose right it is to designate the rulers of the State and, in final appeal, to decide all questions of national policy, according to the requirements of the common good.

INTERNATIONAL RELATIONS

ARTICLE 29

1. Ireland affirms its devotion to the ideal of peace and friendly co-operation amongst nations founded on international justice and morality.

2. Ireland affirms its adherence to the principle of the pacific settlement of international disputes by international arbitration or judicial determination.

EDUCATION

ARTICLE 42

1. The State acknowledges that the primary and natural educator of the child is the Family and guarantees to respect the inalienable right and duty of parents to provide, according to their means, for the religious and moral, intellectual, physical and social education of their children.

2. Parents shall be free to provide this education in their homes or in private schools or in schools recognized or established by the State.

3. 1° The State shall not oblige parents in violation of their conscience and lawful preference to send their children to schools established by the State, or to any particular type of school designated by the State.

   2° The State shall, however, as guardian of the common good, require in view of actual conditions that the children receive a certain minimum education, moral, intellectual and social.

4. The State shall provide for free primary education and shall endeavour to supplement and give reasonable aid to private and corporate educational initiative, and, when the public good requires it, provide other educational facilities or institutions with due regard, however, for the rights of parents, especially in the matter of religious and moral formation.

5. In exceptional cases, where the parents for physical or moral reasons fail in their duty towards their children, the State as guardian of the common good, by appropriate means shall endeavour to supply the place of the parents, but always with due regard for the natural and imprescriptible rights of the child.

PRIVATE PROPERTY

ARTICLE 43

1. 1° The State acknowledges that man, in virtue of his rational being, has the natural right, antecedent to positive law, to the private ownership of external goods.

2°   The State, accordingly, guarantees to pass no law attempting to abolish the right of private ownership or the general right to transfer, bequeath, and inherit property.

2.   1°   The State recognizes, however, that the exercise of the rights mentioned in the foregoing provisions of this Article ought, in civil society, to be regulated by the principles of social justice.

2°   The State, accordingly, may as occasion requires delimit by law the exercise of the said rights with a view to reconciling their exercise with the exigencies of the common good.

THE FAMILY

ARTICLE 41

1.   1°   The State recognizes the Family as the natural primary and fundamental unit group of Society, and as a moral institution possessing inalienable and imprescriptible rights, antecedent and superior to all positive law.

2°   The State, therefore, guarantees to protect the Family in its constitution and authority, as the necessary basis of social order and as indispensable to the welfare of the Nation and the State.

2.   1°   In particular, the State recognizes that by her life within the home, woman gives to the State a support without which the common good cannot be achieved.

2°   The State shall, therefore, endeavour to ensure that mothers shall not be obliged by economic necessity to engage in labour to the neglect of their duties in the home.

3.   1°   The State pledges itself to guard with special care the institution of Marriage, on which the Family is founded, and to protect it against attack.

2°   No law shall be enacted providing for the grant of a dissolution of marriage.

3°   No person whose marriage has been dissolved under the civil law of any other State but is a subsisting valid marriage, under the law for the time being in force within the jurisdiction of the Government and Parliament established by this Constitution shall be capable of contracting a valid marriage within that jurisdiction during the lifetime of the other party to the marriage so dissolved.

RELIGION

ARTICLE 44

1.   1°   The State acknowledges that the homage of public worship is due to Almighty God. It shall hold His Name in reverence, and shall respect and honour religion.

2°   The State recognizes the special position of the Holy Catholic Apostolic and Roman Church as the guardian of the Faith professed by the great majority of the citizens.

3°   The State also recognizes the Church of Ireland, the Presbyterian Church in Ireland, the Methodist Church in Ireland, the Religious Society of Friends in Ireland, as well as the Jewish Congregations and the other religious denominations existing in Ireland at the date of the coming into operation of this Constitution.

2.   1°   Freedom of conscience and the free profession and practice of religion are, subject to public order and morality, guaranteed to every citizen.

2°   The State guarantees not to endow any religion.

3°   The State shall not impose any disabilities or make any discrimination on the ground of religious profession, belief or status.

4°   Legislation providing State aid for schools shall not discriminate between schools under the management of different religious denominations, nor be such as to affect prejudicially the right of any child to attend a school receiving public money without attending religious instruction at that school.

5°   Every religious denomination shall have the right to manage its own affairs, own, acquire and administer property, movable and immovable, and maintain institutions for religious or charitable purposes.

6°   The property of any religious denomination or any educational institution shall not be diverted save for necessary works of public utility and on payment of compensation.

DIRECTIVE PRINCIPLES OF
SOCIAL POLICY

ARTICLE 45

The principles of social policy set forth in this Article are intended for
the general guidance of the Oireachtas. The application of those
principles in the making of laws shall be the care of the Oireachtas
exclusively, and shall not be cognizable by any Court under any of
the provisions of this Constitution.

1. The State shall strive to promote the welfare of the whole people
    by securing and protecting as effectively as it may a social order in
    which justice and charity shall inform all the institutions of the
    national life.

2. The State shall, in particular, direct its policy towards securing:

    i. That the citizens (all of whom, men and women equally, have
       the right to an adequate means of livelihood) may through
       their occupations find the means of making reasonable pro-
       vision for their domestic needs.

    ii. That the ownership and control of the material resources of the
        community may be so distributed amongst private individuals
        and the various classes as best to subserve the common good.

    iii. That, especially, the operation of free competition shall not be
         allowed so to develop as to result in the concentration of the
         ownership or control of essential commodities in a few in-
         dividuals to the common detriment.

    iv. That in what pertains to the control of credit the constant and
        predominant aim shall be the welfare of the people as a whole.

    v. That there may be established on the land in economic
       security as many families as in the circumstances shall be
       practicable.

3. 1° The State shall favour and, where necessary, supplement
    private initiative in industry and commerce.

    2° The State shall endeavour to secure that private enterprise shall
    be so conducted as to ensure reasonable efficiency in the production
    and distribution of goods and as to protect the public against unjust
    exploitation.

4.   1°   The State pledges itself to safeguard with especial care the economic interests of the weaker sections of the community, and, where necessary, to contribute to the support of the infirm, the widow, the orphan, and the aged.

2°   The State shall endeavour to ensure that the strength and health of workers, men and women, and the tender age of children shall not be abused and that citizens shall not be forced by economic necessity to enter avocations unsuited to their sex, age or strength.

Dublin, December 1937

BOOK LIST

Rutten. *La Doctrine Sociale de l'Eglise* (1932)
Freppel Cotta. *Economic Planning in Corporative Portugal* (1937)
Principes et Institutions de l'Etat Nouveau Portugais (1935)
J. Maritan. *True Humanism* (1938)

III

COMMUNISM

Through many centuries, Communist ideas found expression mainly in literary descriptions of idealized ways of life in hypothetical commonwealths, or utopias. Plato's *Republic*, depicting a society in which (within the ruling classes, at all events) there was neither private property nor marriage, is the best known example; but Sir Thomas More's *Utopia*, the Italian friar Campanella's *Civitas Solis* ("City of the Sun"), and James Harrington's *Oceana* belong in the list. Communism as a fully developed and dynamic, even though not always entirely coherent, body of doctrine is, however, distinctly modern. To all intents and purposes, it starts with the writings of two mid-nineteenth-century Germans, Karl Marx and Friedrich Engels; and, as Mr Oakeshott points out, the voluminous literature in which it has later been expounded has added relatively little to the form and content imparted by those indefatigable students of industrial society. In 1917, a world which, on the whole, had not taken the doctrine with great seriousness was startled into a keener interest by a revolution which shattered the social order of a major European state, i.e., Russia, and for the first time put Communist theory in a position to be realized in practice on an extended scale; and the materials relating to the doctrine drawn upon by Mr Oakeshott—apart from the writings of Marx and Engels—are found exclusively in the works of the principal author of the new Russian régime, Nicolai Lenin, together with the extraordinary Constitution for the Soviet Union promulgated with high acclaim in 1936.

The progress of the Industrial Revolution in England and Continental Europe in the later eighteenth and earlier nineteenth centuries brought to the fore a multitude of questions concerning the status and interests of manual workers in a capitalistic industrial society; and there arose numerous schools of Socialist opinion—in England, France, Germany, and elsewhere—directed toward solving the economic and social problems of the time on more or less drastic lines. Both Marx and Engels—sprung from well-to-do families, and neither at any time himself a wage-earner—started as Socialists of the more moderate, "evolutionary", type, but gradually advanced to positions where their socialism merged into an extremer form of thought, sometimes characterized as "scientific" socialism, but usually known nowadays as Communism.

Meeting while still young, the two formed a life-long intellectual partnership which early began bearing fruit in challenging articles and tracts; and when, in 1847, a newly established association of radical workingmen, with branches in London, Paris, and other centers, and known as the League of Communists, commissioned Marx to draw up a declaration of principles and a program of action, the *Manifest der Kommunisten*, or "Communist Manifesto" (first printed in London in 1848), emerged from the two men's joint effort. The term "Communist" was deliberately chosen, explains Engels, with a view to emphasizing the contrast between the positive doctrines now set forth and the visionary socialism prevalent at the time; and in the Manifesto (most of which is presented on pp. 82–101 below) is to be found the clearest and most concise statement of the Communist thought of that day and since.

Communism, as expounded and elaborated in the extensive writings of Lenin, and as reduced to practice (at least partially) in the Soviet Union, differs from Marxism at a number of points, yet is grounded firmly on the Marx-Engels Manifesto. Such differences as appear relate not so much to the doctrine itself as to, for example, the Leninist thesis that the revolution ushering in the Communist order is possible in any capitalist country regardless of the stage of its economic development, and to the view that while the working classes are capable of seizing power anywhere, they are capable of maintaining it in a given situation only through some instrumentality of what may be termed paradoxically the proletarian élite, which in Russia means the Communist party. To the charge of inconsistency on the score of retaining, after the revolution of 1917, such a bourgeois institution as a party —and still more, a powerful state, with highly elaborated government—Leninists reply that all this is merely transitional—that in time the state, always as now an organ of class power, will wither away (the phrase comes from Engels), the party disappear, and only pure Communism remain.

References on Communism which American readers will find especially helpful include: F. W. Coker, *Recent Political Thought* (1934), Part I; M. Eastman, *Marx, Lenin, and the Science of Revolution* (1926); M. Hillquit, *From Marx to Lenin* (1921); H. J. Laski, *Communism* (1927); and J. Stalin, *Leninism* (1928).

III

It is natural to represent the social and political doctrine of modern Communism mainly from the writings of Marx and Engels; indeed, it is unavoidable, because most of the later literature, the authoritative literature, of Communism consists in a repetition, often in actual quotation, of what these initiators of the doctrine wrote. It is a doctrine which has received innumerable restatements, but has shown remarkably little power to grow. I have included the greater part of the *Manifesto of the Communist Party*, because that contains the core of the doctrine. I regret that Engels' work, *The Origin of the Family, Private Property and the State*, contains no relevant passage short or long enough for my purpose; but substantial quotations from it appear in the chapters from Lenin's *State and Revolution* which I have included. Marx's criticism of a typical Liberal-Democratic constitution of the last century is contained in the *Critique of the Gotha Programme*, and I have included a short passage from that work which may profitably be compared with some of the provisions of the 1936 Constitution of the U.S.S.R. Of later writers, the contribution of Lenin is the most substantial, but even he is more concerned to reassert and defend than to develop the doctrine. I have included nearly the whole of his pamphlet on *The Teachings of Karl Marx* because, in spite of its cryptic brevity, it is, I think, the best introduction to the doctrine.

It should be remembered that the extracts I have given from some of the official documents of the government of the U.S.S.R. are intended to illustrate, not the working of a regime, but a doctrine.

§ 1. THE NATURE OF SOCIETY

KARL MARX AND FRIEDRICH ENGELS

(i) BOURGEOIS AND PROLETARIANS

The history of all hitherto existing society is the history of class struggles.

Freeman and slave, patrician and plebian, lord and serf, guildmaster and journeyman, in a word, oppressor and oppressed, stood in constant opposition to one another, carried on an uninterrupted now hidden, now open fight, a fight that each time ended, either in a revolutionary reconstitution of society at large, or in the common ruin of the contending classes.

In the earlier epochs of history, we find almost everywhere a complicated arrangement of society into various orders, a manifold gradation of social rank. In ancient Rome we have patricians, knights, plebians, slaves; in the Middle Ages, feudal lords, vassals, guildmasters, journeymen, apprentices, serfs; in almost all of these classes, again, subordinate gradations.

The modern bourgeois society that has sprouted from the ruins of feudal society, has not done away with class antagonisms. It has but established new classes, new conditions of oppression, new forms of struggle in place of the old ones.

Our epoch, the epoch of the bourgeoisie, possesses, however, this distinctive feature: it has simplified the class antagonisms. Society as a whole is more and more splitting up into two great hostile camps, into two great classes directly facing each other—bourgeoisie and proletariat.

From the serfs of the Middle Ages sprang the chartered burghers of the earliest towns. From these burgesses the first elements of the bourgeoisie were developed.

The discovery of America, the rounding of the Cape, opened up fresh ground for the rising bourgeoisie. The East Indian and Chinese markets, the colonization of America, trade with the colonies, the increase in the means of exchange and in commodities generally, gave to commerce, to navigation, to industry, an impulse never before known, and thereby, to the revolutionary element in the tottering feudal society, a rapid development.

The feudal system of industry, in which industrial production was monopolized by closed guilds, now no longer sufficed for the growing wants of the new markets. The manufacturing system took its place. The guildmasters were pushed aside by the manufacturing middle class; division of labour between the different corporate guilds vanished in the face of division of labour in each single workshop.

Meantime the markets kept ever growing, the demand ever rising. Even manufacture no longer sufficed. Thereupon, steam and machinery revolutionized industrial production. The place of manufacture was taken by the giant, modern industry, the place of the industrial middle class, by industrial millionaires, the leaders of whole industrial armies, the modern bourgeois.

Modern industry has established the world market, for which the discovery of America paved the way. This market has given an immense development to commerce, to navigation, to communication by land. This development has, in its turn, reacted on the extension of industry; and in proportion as industry, commerce, navigation, railways extended, in the same proportion the bourgeoisie developed, increased its capital, and pushed into the background every class handed down from the Middle Ages.

We see, therefore, how the modern bourgeoisie is itself the product of a long course of development, of a series of revolutions in the modes of production and exchange.

Each step in the development of the bourgeoisie was accompanied by a corresponding political advance of that class. An oppressed class under the sway of the feudal nobility, an armed and self-governing association in the medieval commune; here independent urban republic (as in Italy and Germany), there taxable "third estate" of the monarchy (as in France); afterwards, in the period of manufacture proper, serving either the semi-feudal or the absolute monarchy as a counterpoise against the nobility, and, in fact, corner-stone of the great monarchies in general, the bourgeoisie has at last, since the establishment of Modern Industry and of the world market, conquered for itself, in the modern representative State, exclusive political sway. The executive of the modern State is but a committee for managing the common affairs of the whole bourgeoisie.

The bourgeoisie, historically, has played a most revolutionary part.

The bourgeoisie, wherever it has got the upper hand, has put an end to all feudal, patriarchal, idyllic relations. It has pitilessly torn asunder the motley feudal ties that bound man to his "natural superiors", and has left no other nexus between man and man than naked self-interest, than callous "cash payment". It has drowned the most heavenly ecstasies of religious fervour, of chivalrous enthusiasm, of philistine sentimentalism, in the icy water of egotistical calculation. It has resolved personal worth into exchange value, and in place of the numberless indefeasible chartered freedoms, has set up that single, unconscionable freedom—Free Trade. In one word, for exploitation, veiled by religious and political illusions, it has substituted naked, shameless, direct, brutal exploitation.

The bourgeoisie has stripped of its halo every occupation hitherto honoured and looked up to with reverent awe. It has converted the physician, the lawyer, the priest, the poet, the man of science, into its paid wage-labourers.

The bourgeoisie has torn away from the family its sentimental veil, and has reduced the family relation to a mere money relation.

The bourgeoisie has disclosed how it came to pass that the brutal display of vigour in the Middle Ages, which reactionaries so much admire, found its fitting complement in the most slothful indolence. It has been the first to show what man's activity can bring about. It has accomplished wonders far surpassing the Egyptian pyramids, Roman aqueducts, and Gothic cathedrals; it has conducted expeditions that put in the shade all the former Exoduses of nations and crusades.

The bourgeoisie cannot exist without constantly revolutionizing the instruments of production, and thereby the relations of production, and with them the whole relations of society. Conservation of the old modes of production in unaltered form, was, on the contrary, the first condition of existence for all earlier industrial classes. Constant revolutionizing of production, uninterrupted disturbance of all social conditions, everlasting uncertainty and agitation distinguish the bourgeois epoch from all earlier ones. All fixed, fast-frozen relations, with their train of ancient and venerable prejudices and opinions, are swept away, all new-formed ones become antiquated before they can ossify. All that is solid melts into air, all that is holy is profaned, and man is at last compelled to face with sober senses his real conditions of life and his relations with his kind.

The need of a constantly expanding market for its products chases the bourgeoisie over the whole surface of the globe. It must nestle everywhere, settle everywhere, establish connexions everywhere.

The bourgeoisie has through its exploitation of the world market given a cosmopolitan character to production and consumption in every country. To the great chagrin of reactionaries, it has drawn from under the feet of industry the national ground on which it stood. All old-established national industries have been destroyed or are daily being destroyed. They are dislodged by new industries, whose introduction becomes a life and death question for all civilized nations, by industries that no longer work up indigenous raw material, but raw material drawn from the remotest zones; industries whose products are consumed, not only at home, but in every quarter of the globe. In place of the old wants, satisfied by the production of the country, we find new wants, requiring for their satisfaction the products of distant lands and climes. In place of the old local and national seclusion and self-sufficiency, we have intercourse in every direction, universal interdependence of nations. And as in material, so also in intellectual productions. The intellectual creations of individual nations become common property. National one-sidedness and narrow-mindedness become more and more impossible, and from the numerous national and local literatures there arises a world literature.

The bourgeoisie, by the rapid improvement of all instruments of production, by the immensely facilitated means of communication, draws all, even the most barbarian, nations into civilization. The cheap prices of its commodities are the heavy artillery with which it batters down all Chinese walls, with which it forces the barbarians' intensely obstinate hatred of foreigners to capitulate. It compels all nations, on pain of extinction, to adopt the bourgeois mode of production; it compels them to introduce what it calls civilization into their midst, i.e. to become bourgeois themselves. In one word, it creates a world after its own image.

The bourgeoisie has subjected the country to the rule of the towns. It has created enormous cities, has greatly increased the urban population as compared to the rural, and has thus rescued a considerable part of the population from the idiocy of rural life. Just as it has made the country dependent on the towns, so it has made barbarian and semi-barbarian countries dependent on the civilized ones, nations of peasants on nations of bourgeois, the East on the West.

The bourgeoisie keeps more and more doing away with the scattered state of the population, of the means of production, and of property. It has agglomerated population, centralized means of production, and has concentrated property in a few hands. The necessary consequence of this was political centralization. Independent, or but loosely connected provinces, with separate interests, laws, governments and systems of taxation, became lumped together into one nation, with one government, one code of laws, one national class interest, one frontier, and one customs tariff.

The bourgeoisie, during its rule of scarce one hundred years, has created more massive and more colossal productive forces, than have all preceding generations together. Subjection of nature's forces to man, machinery, application of chemistry to industry and agriculture, steam-navigation, railways, electric telegraphs, clearing of whole continents for cultivation, canalization of rivers, whole populations conjured out of the ground—what earlier century had even a presentiment that such productive forces slumbered in the lap of social labour?

We see then; the means of production and exchange, on whose foundation the bourgeoisie built itself up, were generated in feudal society. At a certain stage in the development of these means of production and of exchange, the conditions under which feudal society produced and exchanged, the feudal organization of agriculture and manufacturing industry, in one word, the feudal relations of property became no longer compatible with the already developed productive forces; they became so many fetters. They had to be burst asunder; they were burst asunder.

Into their place stepped free competition, accompanied by a social and political constitution adapted to it, and by the economical and political sway of the bourgeois class.

A similar movement is going on before our own eyes. Modern bourgeois society with its relations of production, of exchange and of property, a society that has conjured up such gigantic means of production and exchange, is like the sorcerer who is no longer able to control the powers of the nether world whom he has called up by his spells. For many a decade past the history of industry and commerce is but the history of the revolt of modern productive forces against modern conditions of production, against the property relations that are the conditions for the existence of the bourgeoisie and of its rule. It is enough to mention the commercial crises that by their periodical return put the existence of the entire bourgeois society on its trial, each time more threateningly. In these crises a great part not only of the existing products, but also of the previously created productive forces, are periodically destroyed. In these crises there breaks out an epidemic that, in all earlier epochs, would have seemed an absurdity—the epidemic of over-production. Society suddenly finds itself put back into a state of momentary barbarism; it appears as if famine, a universal war or devastation had cut off the supply of every means of subsistence; industry and commerce seem to be destroyed. And why? Because there is too much civilization, too much means of subsistence, too much industry, too much commerce. The productive forces at the disposal of society no longer tend to further the development of the conditions of bourgeois property; on the contrary, they have become too powerful for these conditions, by which they are fettered, and so soon as they overcome these fetters, they bring disorder into the whole of bourgeois society, endanger the existence of bourgeois property. The conditions of bourgeois society are too narrow to comprise the wealth created by them. And how does the bourgeoisie get over these crises? On the one hand, by enforced destruction of a mass of productive forces; on the other, by the conquest of new markets, and by the more thorough exploitation of the old ones. That is to say, by paving the way for more extensive and more destructive crises, and by diminishing the means whereby crises are prevented.

The weapons with which the bourgeoisie felled feudalism to the ground are now turned against the bourgeoisie itself.

But not only has the bourgeoisie forged the weapons that bring death to itself; it has also called into existence the men who are to wield those weapons—the modern working class—the proletarians.

In proportion as the bourgeoisie, i.e. capital, is developed, in the same proportion is the proletariat, the modern working class, developed—a class of labourers, who live only so long as they find work, and who find work only so long as their labour increases capital. These labourers, who must sell themselves piecemeal, are a commodity, like every other article of commerce, and are consequently exposed to all the vicissitudes of competition, to all the fluctuations of the market.

Owing to the extensive use of machinery and to division of labour, the work of the proletarians has lost all individual character, and, consequently, all charm for the workman. He becomes an appendage of the machine, and it is only the most simple, the most monotonous, and most easily acquired knack, that is required of him. Hence, the cost of production of a workman is restricted, almost entirely, to the means of subsistence that he requires for his maintenance, and for the propagation of his race. But the price of a commodity, and therefore, also of labour, is equal to its cost of production. In proportion, therefore, as the repulsiveness of the work increases, the wage decreases. Nay more, in proportion as the use of machinery and division of labour increases, in the same proportion the burden of toil also increases, whether by prolongation of the working hours, by increase of the work exacted in a given time, or by increased speed of the machinery.

Modern industry has converted the little workshop of the patriarchal master into the great factory of the industrial capitalist. Masses of labourers, crowded into the factory, are organized like soldiers. As privates of the industrial army, they are placed under the command of a positive hierarchy of officers and sergeants. Not only are they slaves of the bourgeois class, and of the bourgeois state; they are daily and hourly enslaved by the machine, by the overseer, and, above all, by the individual bourgeois manufacturer himself. The more openly this despotism proclaims gain to be its end and aim, the more petty, the more hateful and the more embittering it is.

The less the skill and exertion of strength implied in manual labour, in other words, the more modern industry becomes developed, the more is the labour of men superseded by that of women. Differences of age and sex have no longer any distinctive social validity for the working class. All are instruments of labour, more or less expensive to use, according to their age and sex.

No sooner is the exploitation of the labourer by the manufacturer, so far at an end, that he receives his wages in cash, than he is set upon by the other portions of the bourgeoisie, the landlord, the shopkeeper, the pawnbroker, etc.

The lower strata of the middle class—the small tradespeople, shopkeepers, and retired tradesmen generally, the handicraftsmen and the peasants—all these sink gradually into the proletariat, partly because their diminutive capital does not suffice for the scale on which modern industry is carried on, and is swamped in the competition with the large capitalists, partly because their specialized skill is rendered worthless by new methods of production. Thus the proletariat is recruited from all classes of the population.

The proletariat goes through various stages of development. With its birth begins its struggle with the bourgeoisie. At first the contest is carried on by individual labourers, then by the work people of a factory, then by the operatives of one trade, in one locality, against the individual bourgeois who directly exploits them. They direct their attacks not against the bourgeois conditions of production, but against the instruments of production themselves; they destroy imported wares that compete with their labour, they smash to pieces machinery, they set factories ablaze, they seek to restore by force the vanished status of the workman of the Middle Ages.

At this stage the labourers still form an incoherent mass scattered over the whole country, and broken up by their mutual competition. If anywhere they unite to form more compact bodies, this is not yet the consequence of their own active union, but of the union of the bourgeoisie, which class, in order to attain its own political ends, is compelled to set the whole proletariat in motion, and is moreover yet, for a time, able to do so. At this stage, therefore, the proletarians do not fight their enemies, but the enemies of their enemies, the remnants of absolute monarchy, the landowners, the non-industrial bourgeois, the petty bourgeoisie; every victory so obtained is a victory for the bourgeoisie.

But with the development of industry the proletariat not only increases in number; it becomes concentrated in greater masses, its strength grows, and it feels that strength more. The various interests and conditions of life within the ranks of the proletariat are more and more equalized, in proportion as machinery obliterates all distinctions of labour, and nearly everywhere reduces wages to the same low level. The growing competition among the bourgeois, and the resulting commercial crises, make the wages of the workers ever more fluctuating. The unceasing improvement of machinery, ever more rapidly developing, makes their livelihood ever more precarious; the collisions between individual workmen and individual bourgeois take more and more the character of collisions between two classes. Thereupon the workers begin to form combinations (trades' unions) against the bourgeois; they club together in order to keep up the rate of wages; they found permanent associations in order to make provision beforehand for these occasional revolts. Here and there the contest breaks out into riots.

Now and then the workers are victorious, but only for a time. The real fruit of their battle lies, not in the immediate result, but in the ever expanding union of the workers. This union is helped on by the improved means of communication that are created by modern industry, and that place the workers of different localities in contact one with

another. It was just this contact that was needed to centralize the
numerous local struggles, all of the same character, into one national
struggle between classes. But every class struggle is a political struggle.
And that union, to attain which the burghers of the Middle Ages, with
their miserable highways, required centuries, the modern proletarians,
thanks to railways, achieve in a few years.

This organization of the proletarians into a class, and consequently
into a political party, is continually being upset again by the competition
between the workers themselves. But it ever rises up again, stronger,
firmer, mightier. It compels legislative recognition of particular
interests of the workers, by taking advantage of the divisions among
the bourgeoisie itself. Thus the ten-hours' bill in England was carried.

Altogether, collisions between the classes of the old society further
in many ways the course of development of the proletariat. The bourgeoisie finds itself involved in a constant battle. At first with the
aristocracy; later on, with those portions of the bourgeoisie itself,
whose interests have become antagonistic to the progress of industry;
at all times with the bourgeoisie of foreign countries. In all these
battles it sees itself compelled to appeal to the proletariat, to ask for its
help, and thus, to drag it into the political arena. The bourgeoisie itself,
therefore, supplies the proletariat with its own elements of political and
general education, in other words, it furnishes the proletariat with
weapons for fighting the bourgeoisie.

Further, as we have already seen, entire sections of the ruling classes
are, by the advance of industry, precipitated into the proletariat, or are
at least threatened in their conditions of existence. These also supply
the proletariat with fresh elements of enlightenment and progress.

Finally, in time when the class struggle nears the decisive hour, the
process of dissolution going on within the ruling class, in fact within
the whole range of old society, assumes such a violent, glaring character,
that a small section of the ruling class cuts itself adrift, and joins the
revolutionary class, the class that holds the future in its hands. Just as,
therefore, at an earlier period, a section of the nobility went over to the
bourgeoisie, so now a portion of the bourgeoisie goes over to the
proletariat, and in particular, a portion of the bourgeois ideologists,
who have raised themselves to the level of comprehending theoretically
the historical movement as a whole.

Of all the classes that stand face to face with the bourgeoisie to-day,
the proletariat alone is a really revolutionary class. The other classes

decay and finally disappear in the face of modern industry; the proletariat is its special and essential product.

The lower middle class, the small manufacturer, the shopkeeper, the
artizan, the peasant, all these fight against the bourgeoisie, to save from
extinction their existence as fractions of the middle class. They are
therefore not revolutionary, but conservative. Nay more, they are
reactionary, for they try to roll back the wheel of history. If by chance
they are revolutionary, they are so only in view of their impending
transfer into the proletariat; they thus defend not their present, but
their future interests; they desert their own standpoint to place themselves at that of the proletariat.

The "dangerous class", the social scum, that passively rotting mass
thrown off by the lowest layers of old society, may, here and there, be
swept into the movement by a proletarian revolution; its conditions
of life, however, prepare it far more for a bribed tool of reactionary
intrigue.

In the conditions of the proletariat, those of old society at large are
already virtually swamped. The proletarian is without property; his
relation to his wife and children has no longer anything in common
with the bourgeois family relations; modern industrial labour, modern
subjection to capital, the same in England as in France, in America as
in Germany, has stripped him of every trace of national character.
Law, morality, religion, are to him so many bourgeois prejudices,
behind which lurk in ambush just as many bourgeois interests.

All the preceding classes that got the upper hand, sought to fortify
their already acquired status by subjecting society at large to their
conditions of appropriation. The proletarians cannot become masters
of the productive forces of society, except by abolishing their own
previous mode of appropriation, and thereby also every other previous
mode of appropriation. They have nothing of their own to secure and
to fortify; their mission is to destroy all previous securities for, and
insurances of, individual property.

All previous historical movements were movements of minorities,
or in the interests of minorities. The proletarian movement is the
self-conscious, independent movement of the immense majority, in the
interest of the immense majority. The proletariat, the lowest stratum
of our present society, cannot stir, cannot raise itself up, without the
whole superincumbent strata of official society being sprung into
the air.

Though not in substance, yet in form, the struggle of the proletariat with the bourgeoisie is at first a national struggle. The proletariat of each country must, of course, first of all settle matters with its own bourgeoisie.

In depicting the most general phases of the development of the proletariat, we traced the more or less veiled civil war, raging within existing society, up to the point where that war breaks out into open revolution, and where the violent overthrow of the bourgeoisie lays the foundation for the sway of the proletariat.

Hitherto, every form of society has been based, as we have already seen, on the antagonism of oppressing and oppressed classes. But in order to oppress a class, certain conditions must be assured to it under which it can, at least, continue its slavish existence. The serf, in the period of serfdom, raised himself to membership in the commune, just as the petty bourgeois, under the yoke of feudal absolutism, managed to develop into a bourgeois. The modern labourer, on the contrary, instead of rising with the progress of industry, sinks deeper and deeper beneath the conditions of existence of his own class. He becomes a pauper, and pauperism develops more rapidly than population and wealth. And here it becomes evident, that the bourgeoisie is unfit any longer to be the ruling class in society, and to impose its conditions of existence upon society as an over-riding law. It is unfit to rule because it is incompetent to assure an existence to its slave within his slavery, because it cannot help letting him sink into such a state, that it has to feed him, instead of being fed by him. Society can no longer live under this bourgeoisie, in other words, its existence is no longer compatible with society.

The essential condition for the existence and the sway of the bourgeois class, is the formation and augmentation of capital; the condition for capital is wage-labour. Wage-labour rests exclusively on competition between the labourers. The advance of industry, whose involuntary promoter is the bourgeoisie, replaces the isolation of the labourers, due to competition, by their revolutionary competition, due to association. The development of modern industry, therefore, cuts from under its feet the very foundation on which the bourgeoisie produces and appropriates products. What the bourgeoisie therefore produces, above all, are its own grave-diggers. Its fall and the victory of the proletariat are equally inevitable.

(ii) PROLETARIANS AND COMMUNISTS

In what relation do the Communists stand to the proletarians as a whole?

The Communists do not form a separate party opposed to other working class parties.

They have no interests separate and apart from those of the proletariat as a whole.

They do not set up any sectarian principles of their own, by which to shape and mould the proletarian movement.

The Communists are distinguished from the other working class parties by this only: (1) In the national struggles of the proletarians of the different countries, they point out and bring to the front the common interests of the entire proletariat, independently of all nationality. (2) In the various stages of development which the struggle of the working class against the bourgeoisie has to pass through, they always and everywhere represent the interests of the movement as a whole.

The Communists, therefore, are on the one hand, practically, the most advanced and resolute section of the working class parties of every country, that section which pushes forward all others; on the other hand, theoretically, they have over the great mass of the proletariat the advantage of clearly understanding the line of march, the conditions, and the ultimate general results of the proletarian movement.

The immediate aim of the Communists is the same as that of all the other proletarian parties; formation of the proletariat into a class, overthrow of the bourgeois supremacy, conquest of political power by the proletariat.

The theoretical conclusions of the Communists, are in no way based on ideas or principles that have been invented, or discovered, by this or that would-be universal reformer.

They merely express, in general terms, actual relations springing from an existing class struggle, from a historical movement going on under our very eyes. The abolition of existing property relations is not at all a distinctive feature of Communism.

All property relations in the past have continually been subject to historical change consequent upon the change in historical conditions.

The French Revolution, for example, abolished feudal property in favour of bourgeois property.

The distinguishing feature of Communism is not the abolition of property generally, but the abolition of bourgeois property. But modern bourgeois private property is the final and most complete expression of the system of producing and appropriating products that is based on class antagonisms, on the exploitation of the many by the few.

In this sense, the theory of the Communists may be summed up in the single sentence: Abolition of private property.

We Communists have been reproached with the desire of abolishing the right of personally acquiring property as the fruit of a man's own labour, which property is alleged to be the groundwork of all personal freedom, activity and independence.

Hard-won, self-acquired, self-earned property! Do you mean the property of the petty artizan and of the small peasant, a form of property that preceded the bourgeois form? There is no need to abolish that; the development of industry has to a great extent already destroyed it, and is still destroying it daily.

Or do you mean modern bourgeois private property?

But does wage-labour create any property for the labourer? Not a bit. It creates capital, i.e. that kind of property which exploits wage-labour, and which cannot increase except upon condition of begetting a new supply of wage-labour for fresh exploitation. Property, in its present form, is based on the antagonism of capital and wage-labour. Let us examine both sides of this antagonism.

To be a capitalist, is to have not only a purely personal, but a social, *status* in production. Capital is a collective product, and only by the united action of many members, nay, in the last resort, only by the united action of all members of society, can it be set in motion.

Capital is therefore not a personal, it is a social power.

When, therefore, capital is converted into common property, into the property of all members of society, personal property is not thereby transformed into social property. It is only the social character of the property that is changed. It loses its class character.

Let us now take wage-labour.

The average price of wage-labour is the minimum wage, i.e. that quantum of the means of subsistence which is absolutely requisite to keep the labourer in bare existence as a labourer. What, therefore, the wage-labourer appropriates by means of his labour, merely suffices to prolong and reproduce a bare existence. We by no means intend to abolish this personal appropriation of the products of labour, an appropriation that is made for the maintenance and reproduction of human life, and that leaves no surplus with which to command the labour of others. All that we want to do away with is the miserable character of this appropriation under which the labourer lives merely to increase capital, and is allowed to live only in so far as the interest of the ruling class requires it.

In bourgeois society, living labour is but a means to increase accumulated labour. In Communist society, accumulated labour is but a means to widen, to enrich, to promote the existence of the labourer.

In bourgeois society, therefore, the past dominates the present; in Communist society, the present dominates the past. In bourgeois society capital is independent and has individuality, while the living person is dependent and has no individuality.

And the abolition of this state of things is called by the bourgeois, abolition of individuality and freedom! And rightly so. The abolition of bourgeois individuality, bourgeois independence, and bourgeois freedom is undoubtedly aimed at.

By freedom is meant, under the present bourgeois conditions of production, free trade, free selling and buying.

But if selling and buying disappears, free selling and buying disappears also. This talk about free selling and buying, and all the other "brave words" of our bourgeoisie about freedom in general have a meaning, if any, only in contrast with restricted selling and buying, with the fettered traders of the Middle Ages, but have no meaning when opposed to the Communist abolition of buying and selling, of the bourgeois conditions of production, and of the bourgeoisie itself.

You are horrified at our intending to do away with private property. But in your existing society, private property is already done away with for nine-tenths of the population; its existence for the few is solely due to its non-existence in the hands of those nine-tenths. You reproach us, therefore, with intending to do away with a form of property, the necessary condition for whose existence is the non-existence of any property for the immense majority of society.

In one word, you reproach us with intending to do away with your property. Precisely so; that is just what we intend.

From the moment when labour can no longer be converted into capital, money, or rent, into a social power capable of being monopolized, i.e. from the moment when individual property can no longer be transformed into bourgeois property, into capital, from that moment, you say, individuality vanishes.

You must, therefore, confess that by "individual" you mean no other person than the bourgeois, than the middle class owner of property. This person must, indeed, be swept out of the way, and made impossible.

Communism deprives no man of the power to appropriate the products of society; all that it does is to deprive him of the power to subjugate the labour of others by means of such appropriation.

It has been objected, that upon the abolition of private property all work will cease, and universal laziness will overtake us.

According to this, bourgeois society ought long ago to have gone to the dogs through sheer idleness; for those of its members who work, acquire nothing, and those who acquire anything, do not work. The whole of this objection is but another expression of the tautology: there can no longer be any wage-labour when there is no longer any capital.

All objections urged against the Communistic mode of producing and appropriating material products, have, in the same way, been urged against the Communistic modes of producing and appropriating intellectual products. Just as to the bourgeois, the disappearance of class property is the disappearance of production itself, so the disappearance of class culture is to him identical with the disappearance of all culture.

That culture, the loss of which he laments, is, for the enormous majority, a mere training to act as a machine.

But don't wrangle with us so long as you apply, to our intended abolition of bourgeois property, the standard of your bourgeois notions of freedom, culture, law, etc. Your very ideas are but the very outgrowth of the conditions of your bourgeois production and bourgeois property, just as your jurisprudence is but the will of your class made into a law for all, a will, whose essential character and direction are determined by the economical conditions of existence of your class.

The selfish misconception that induces you to transform into eternal laws of nature and of reason, the social forms springing from your present mode of production and form of property—historical relations that rise and disappear in the progress of production—this misconception you share with every ruling class that has preceded you. What you see clearly in the case of ancient property, what you admit in the case of feudal property, you are of course forbidden to admit in the case of your own bourgeois form of property.

Abolition of the family! Even the most radical flare up at this infamous proposal of the Communists.

On what foundation is the present family, the bourgeois family, based? On capital, on private gain. In its completely developed form this family exists only among the bourgeoisie. But this state of things finds its complement in the practical absence of the family among the proletarians, and in public prostitution.

The bourgeois family will vanish as a matter of course when its complement vanishes, and both will vanish with the vanishing of capital.

Do you charge us with wanting to stop the exploitation of children by their parents? To this crime we plead guilty.

But, you will say, we destroy the most hallowed of relations, when we replace home education by social.

And your education! Is not that also social, and determined by the social conditions under which you educate, by the intervention, direct or indirect, of society, by means of schools, etc.? The Communists have not invented the intervention of society in education; they do but seek to alter the character of that intervention, and to rescue education from the influence of the ruling class.

The bourgeois claptrap about the family and education, about the hallowed correlation of parent and child, becomes all the more disgusting, the more, by the action of modern industry, all family ties among the proletarians are torn asunder, and their children transformed into simple articles of commerce and instruments of labour.

But you Communists would introduce community of women, screams the whole bourgeoisie in chorus.

The bourgeois sees in his wife a mere instrument of production. He hears that the instruments of production are to be exploited in common, and, naturally, can come to no other conclusion than that the lot of being common to all will likewise fall to the women.

He has not even a suspicion that the real point aimed at is to do away with the status of women as mere instruments of production.

For the rest, nothing is more ridiculous than the virtuous indignation of our bourgeois at the community of women which, they pretend, is to be openly and officially established by the Communists. The Communists have no need to introduce community of women; it has existed almost from time immemorial.

Our bourgeois, not content with having the wives and daughters of their proletarians at their disposal, not to speak of common prostitutes, take the greatest pleasure in seducing each other's wives.

Bourgeois marriage is in reality a system of wives in common and thus, at the most, what the Communists might possibly be reproached with is that they desire to introduce, in substitution for a hypocritically concealed, an openly legalized community of women. For the rest, it is self-evident, that the abolition of the present system of production must bring with it the abolition of the community of women springing from that system, i.e. of prostitution both public and private.

The Communists are further reproached with desiring to abolish countries and nationality.

The working men have no country. We cannot take from them what they have not got. Since the proletariat must first acquire political supremacy, must rise to be the leading class of the nation, must constitute itself *the* nation, it is, so far, itself national, though not in the bourgeois sense of the word.

National differences and antagonisms between peoples are daily more and more vanishing, owing to the development of the bourgeoisie to freedom of commerce, to the world market, to uniformity in the mode of production and in the conditions of life corresponding thereto.

The supremacy of the proletariat will cause them to vanish still faster. United action of the leading civilized countries at least, is one of the first conditions for the emancipation of the proletariat.

In proportion as the exploitation of one individual by another is put an end to, the exploitation of one nation by another will also be put an end to. In proportion as the antagonism between classes within the nation vanishes, the hostility of one nation to another will come to an end.

The charges against Communism made from a religious, a philosophical and, generally, from an ideological standpoint, are not deserving of serious examination.

Does it require deep intuition to comprehend that man's ideas, views, and conceptions, in one word, man's consciousness, changes with every change in the conditions of his material existence, in his social relations and in his social life?

What else does the history of ideas prove, than that intellectual production changes its character in proportion as material production is changed? The ruling ideas of each age have ever been the ideas of its ruling class.

When people speak of ideas that revolutionize society, they do but express the fact, that within the old society, the elements of a new one have been created, and that the dissolution of the old ideas keeps even pace with the dissolution of the old conditions of existence.

When the ancient world was in its last throes, the ancient religions were overcome by Christianity. When Christian ideas succumbed in the eighteenth century to rationalist ideas, feudal society fought its death-battle with the then revolutionary bourgeoisie. The ideas of religious liberty and freedom of conscience, merely gave expression to the sway of free competition within the domain of knowledge.

"Undoubtedly," it will be said, "religious, moral, philosophical and juridical ideas have been modified in the course of historical development. But religion, morality, philosophy, political science, and law, constantly survived this change."

"There are, besides, eternal truths, such as Freedom, Justice, etc., that are common to all states of society. But Communism abolishes eternal truths, it abolishes all religion, and all morality, instead of constituting them on a new basis; it therefore acts in contradiction to all past historical experience."

What does this accusation reduce itself to? The history of all past society has consisted in the development of class antagonisms, antagonisms that assumed different forms at different epochs.

But whatever form they may have taken, one fact is common to all past ages, viz. the exploitation of one part of society by the other. No wonder, then, that the social consciousness of past ages, despite all the multiplicity and variety it displays, moves within certain common forms, or general ideas, which cannot completely vanish except with the total disappearance of class antagonisms.

The Communist revolution is the most radical rupture with traditional property relations; no wonder that its development involves the most radical rupture with traditional ideas.

But let us have done with the bourgeois objections to Communism.

We have seen above, that the first step in the revolution by the working class, is to raise the proletariat to the position of ruling class, to win the battle of democracy.

The proletariat will use its political supremacy, to wrest, by degrees, all capital from the bourgeoisie, to centralize all instruments of production in the hands of the state, i.e. of the proletariat organized as the ruling class; and to increase the total of productive forces as rapidly as possible.

Of course, in the beginning, this cannot be effected except by means of despotic inroads on the rights of property, and on the conditions of bourgeois production; by means of measures, therefore, which appear economically insufficient and untenable, but which, in the course of the movement, outstrip themselves, necessitate further inroads upon the old social order, and are unavoidable as a means of entirely revolutionizing the mode of production.

These measures will of course be different in different countries.

Nevertheless, in the most advanced countries, the following will be pretty generally applicable: .

1. Abolition of property in land and application of all rents of land to public purposes.

2. A heavy progressive or graduated income tax.

3. Abolition of all right of inheritance.

4. Confiscation of the property of all emigrants and rebels.

5. Centralization of credit in the hands of the state, by means of a national bank with state capital and an exclusive monopoly.

6. Centralization of the means of communication and transport in the hands of the state.

7. Extension of factories and instruments of production owned by the state; the bringing into cultivation of waste lands, and the improvement of the soil generally in accordance with a common plan.

8. Equal obligation of all to work. Establishment of industrial armies, especially for agriculture.

9. Combination of agriculture with manufacturing industries; gradual abolition of the distinction between town and country, by a more equable distribution of the population over the country.

10. Free education for all children in public schools. Abolition of children's factory labour in its present form. Combination of education with industrial production, etc.

When, in the course of development, class distinctions have disappeared, and all production has been concentrated in the hands of a vast association of the whole nation, the public power will lose its political character. Political power, properly so called, is merely the organized power of one class for oppressing another. If the proletariat during its contest with the bourgeoisie is compelled, by the force of circumstances, to organize itself as a class; if, by means of a revolution, it makes itself the ruling class, and, as such, sweeps away by force the old conditions of production, then it will, along with these conditions, have swept away the conditions for the existence of class antagonisms and of classes generally, and will thereby have abolished its own supremacy as a class.

In place of the old bourgeois society, with its classes and class antagonisms, we shall have an association, in which the free development of each is the condition for the free development of all.

From *Manifesto of the Communist Party* (1848)

§2. THE TEACHINGS OF KARL MARX

LENIN

Marxism is the system of the views and teachings of Marx. Marx was the genius who continued and completed the three chief ideological currents of the nineteenth century, represented respectively by the three most advanced countries of humanity: classical German philosophy, classical English political economy, and French Socialism combined with French revolutionary doctrines. The remarkable consistency and unity of conception of Marx's views, acknowledged even by his opponents, which in their totality constitute modern materialism and modern scientific Socialism as the theory and programme of the labour movement in all the civilized countries of the world, make it necessary that we present a brief outline of his world conception in general before proceeding to the chief contents of Marxism, namely, the economic doctrine of Marx.

PHILOSOPHIC MATERIALISM

Beginning with the years 1844-5, when his views were definitely formed, Marx was a materialist, and especially a follower of Feuerbach; even in later times, he saw Feuerbach's weak side only in this, that his materialism was not sufficiently consistent and comprehensive. For Marx, Feuerbach's world-historic and "epoch-making" significance consisted in his having decisively broken away from the idealism of Hegel, and in his proclamation of materialism, which even in the eighteenth century, especially in France, had become "a struggle not only against the existing political institutions, and against...religion and theology, but also...against every form of metaphysics" (as "intoxicated speculation" in contradistinction to "sober philosophy").

For Hegel—wrote Marx, in the preface to the second edition of the first volume of *Capital*—the thought process (which he actually transforms into an independent subject, giving to it the name of "idea") is the demiurge [creator] of the real.... In my view, on the other hand, the ideal is nothing other than the material when it has been transposed and translated inside the human head.

In full conformity with Marx's materialist philosophy, and expounding it, Engels wrote in *Anti-Dühring* (which Marx read in the manuscript):

The unity of the world does not consist in its existence. . . . The real unity of the world consists in its materiality, and this is proved . . . by the long and laborious development of philosophy and natural science. . . . Motion is the form of existence of matter. Never and nowhere has there been or can there be matter without motion. . . . Matter without motion is just as unthinkable as motion without matter. . . . If we enquire . . . what thought and consciousness are, whence they come, we find that they are products of the human brain, and that man himself is a product of nature, developing in and along with his environment. Obviously, therefore, the products of the human brain, being in the last analysis likewise products of nature, do not contradict the rest of nature, but correspond to it.

Again: "Hegel was an idealist; that is to say, for him the thoughts in his head were not more or less abstract reflexions of real things and processes; but, on the contrary, things and their evolution were, for Hegel, only reflexions in reality of the Idea that existed somewhere even prior to the world."

In his *Ludwig Feuerbach*—in which Engels expounds his own and Marx's views on Feuerbach's philosophy, and which Engels sent to the press after re-reading an old manuscript, written by Marx and himself in 1844–5, on Hegel, Feuerbach, and the materialist conception of history—Engels writes:

The great basic question of all, and especially of recent, philosophy, is the question of the relationship between thought and existence, between spirit and nature. . . . Which is prior to the other: spirit or nature? Philosophers are divided into two great camps, according to the way in which they have answered this question. Those who declare that spirit existed before nature, and who, in the last analysis, therefore, assume in one way or another that the world was created . . . have formed the idealist camp. The others, who regard nature as primary, belong to the various schools of materialism.

Any other use (in a philosophic sense) of the terms idealism and materialism is only confusing. Marx decidedly rejected not only idealism, always connected in one way or another with religion, but also the views of Hume and Kant, that are especially widespread in our day, as well as agnosticism, criticism, positivism in various forms; he considered such philosophy as a "reactionary" concession to idealism, at best as a "shamefaced manner of admitting materialism through the back door while denying it before the world". It is especially important that we should note Marx's opinion concerning the relation between freedom and necessity: "Freedom is the recognition of necessity. Necessity is blind only in so far as it is not understood" (Engels, *Anti-Dühring*). This means acknowledgement of the objective reign of law in nature and of the dialectical transformation of necessity into freedom (at the same time, an acknowledgement of the transformation of the unknown but knowable "thing-in-itself" into the "thing-for-us", of the "essence of things" into "phenomena"). Marx and Engels pointed out the following major shortcomings of the "old" materialism, including Feuerbach's (and, *a fortiori*, the "vulgar" materialism of Büchner, Vogt and Moleschott): (1) it was "predominantly mechanical", not taking into account the latest developments of chemistry and biology (in our day it would be necessary to add the electric theory of matter); (2) it was non-historical, non-dialectical (was metaphysical, in the sense of being anti-dialectical), and did not apply the standpoint of evolution consistently and all-sidedly; (3) it regarded "human nature" abstractly, and not as a "synthesis" of (definite, concrete-historical) "social relationships"—and thus only "interpreted" the world, whereas it was a question of "changing" it, that is, it did not grasp the significance of "practical revolutionary activity".

DIALECTICS

Marx and Engels regarded Hegelian dialectics, the theory of evolution most comprehensive, rich in content and profound, as the greatest achievement of classical German philosophy. All other formulations of the principle of development, of evolution, they considered to be one-sided, poor in content, distorting and mutilating the actual course of development of nature and society (a course often consummated in leaps and bounds, catastrophes, revolutions).

Marx and I were almost the only persons who rescued conscious dialectics ...[from the swamp of idealism, including Hegelianism] by transforming it into the materialist conception of nature.... Nature is the test of dialectics, and we must say that science has supplied a vast and daily increasing mass of material for this test, thereby proving that, in the last analysis, nature proceeds dialectically and not metaphysically [this was written before the discovery of radium, electrons, the transmutation of elements, etc.].

Again, Engels writes:

The great basic idea that the world is not to be viewed as a complex of fully fashioned objects, but as a complex of processes, in which apparently stable objects, no less than the images of them inside our heads (our concepts), are undergoing incessant changes, arising here and disappearing there, and which with all apparent accident and in spite of all momentary retrogression, ultimately constitutes a progressive development—this great basic idea has, particularly since the time of Hegel, so deeply penetrated the general consciousness that hardly any one will now venture to dispute it in its general form. But it is one thing to accept it in words, quite another thing to put it in practice on every occasion and in every field of investigation.

In the eyes of dialectic philosophy, nothing is established for all time, nothing is absolute or sacred. On everything and in everything it sees the stamp of inevitable decline; nothing can resist it save the unceasing process of formation and destruction, the unending ascent from the lower to the higher—a process of which that philosophy itself is only a simple reflexion within the thinking brain.

Thus dialectics, according to Marx, is "the science of the general laws of motion both of the external world and of human thinking".

This revolutionary side of Hegel's philosophy was adopted and developed by Marx. Dialectical materialism "does not need any philosophy towering above the other sciences". Of former philosophies there remain "the science of thinking and its laws—formal logic and dialectics". Dialectics, as the term is used by Marx in conformity with Hegel, includes what is now called the theory of cognition, or epistemology, or gnoseology, a science that must contemplate its subject-matter in the same way—historically, studying and generalizing the origin and development of cognition, the transition from non-consciousness to consciousness. In our times, the idea of development, of evolution, has almost fully penetrated social consciousness, but it has done so in other ways, not through Hegel's philosophy. Still, the same idea, as formulated by Marx and Engels on the basis of Hegel's philosophy, is much more comprehensive, much more abundant in content than the current theory of evolution. A development that repeats, as it were, the stages already passed, but repeats them in a different way, on a higher plane ("negation of negation"); a development, so to speak, in spirals, not in a straight line; a development in leaps and bounds, catastrophes, revolutions; "intervals of gradualness"; transformation of quantity into quality; inner impulses for development, imparted by the contradiction, the conflict of different forces and tendencies reacting on a given body or inside a given phenomenon or within a given society; interdependence, and the closest, indissoluble connexion between *all* sides of every phenomenon (history disclosing ever new sides), a connexion that provides the one world-process of motion proceeding according to law—such are some of the features of dialectics as a doctrine of evolution more full of meaning than the current one.

MATERIALIST CONCEPTION OF HISTORY

Realizing the inconsistency, the incompleteness, and the onesidedness of the old materialism, Marx became convinced that it was necessary "to harmonize the science of society with the materialist basis, and to reconstruct it in accordance with this basis". If, speaking generally, materialism explains consciousness as the outcome of existence, and not conversely, then, applied to the social life of mankind, materialism must explain *social* consciousness as the outcome of *social* existence. "Technology", writes Marx in the first volume of *Capital*, "reveals man's dealings with nature, discloses the direct productive activities of his life, thus throwing light upon social relations and the resultant mental conceptions". In the preface to *A Contribution to the Critique of Political Economy* Marx gives an integral formulation of the fundamental principles of materialism as applied to human society and its history, in the following words:

In the social production of the means of life, human beings enter into definite and necessary relations which are independent of their will—production relations which correspond to a definite stage of the development of their productive forces. The totality of these production relations constitutes the economic structure of society, the real basis upon which a legal and political superstructure arises and to which definite forms of social consciousness correspond. The mode of production of the material means of life determines, in general, the social, political, and intellectual processes of life. It is not the consciousness of human beings that determines their existence, but, conversely, it is their social existence that determines their consciousness. At a certain stage of their development, the material productive forces of society come into conflict with existing production relationships, or, what is but a legal expression for the same thing, with the property relationships within which they have hitherto moved. From forms of development of the productive forces, these relationships turn into their fetters. A period of social revolution then begins. With the change in the economic foundation, the whole gigantic superstructure is more or less rapidly transformed. In considering such transformations we must always distinguish between the material changes in the economic conditions of production, changes which can be determined with the precision of natural science, and the legal, political, religious, æsthetic, or philosophic, in short, ideological forms, in which human beings become conscious of this conflict and fight it out to an issue.

Just as little as we judge an individual by what he thinks of himself, just so little can we appraise such a revolutionary epoch in accordance with its own

consciousness of itself. On the contrary, we have to explain this consciousness as the outcome of the contradictions of material life, of the conflict
existing between social productive forces and production relationships. . . .
In broad outline we can designate the Asiatic, the classical, the feudal, and
the modern bourgeois forms of production as progressive epochs in the
economic formation of society.

The discovery of the materialist conception of history, or, more
correctly, the consistent extension of materialism to the domain of
social phenomena, obviated the two chief defects in earlier historical
theories. For, in the first place, those theories, at best, examined only
the ideological motives of the historical activity of human beings
without investigating the origin of these ideological motives, or
grasping the objective conformity to law in the development of the
system of social relationships, or discerning the roots of these social
relationships in the degree of development of material production. In
the second place, the earlier historical theories ignored the activities of
the *masses*, whereas historical materialism first made it possible to
study with scientific accuracy the social conditions of the life of the
masses and the changes in these conditions. At best, pre-Marxist
"sociology" and historiography gave an accumulation of raw facts
collected at random, and a description of separate sides of the historic
process. Examining the *totality* of all the opposing tendencies, reducing
them to precisely definable conditions in the mode of life and the
method of production of the various *classes* of society, discarding
subjectivism and free will in the choice of various "leading" ideas or in
their interpretation, showing how all the ideas and all the various
tendencies, without exception, have their roots in the condition of the
material forces of production, Marxism pointed the way to a comprehensive, an all-embracing study of the rise, development, and decay of
socio-economic structures. People make their own history; but what
determines their motives, that is, the motives of people in the mass;
what gives rise to the clash of conflicting ideas and endeavours; what is
the sum total of all these clashes among the whole mass of human
societies; what are the objective conditions for the production of the
material means of life that form the basis of all the historical activity
of man; what is the law of the development of these conditions—to all
these matters Marx directed attention, pointing out the way to a scientific
study of history as a unified and true-to-law process despite its being
extremely variegated and contradictory.

CLASS STRUGGLE

That in any given society the strivings of some of the members conflict with the strivings of others; that social life is full of contradictions; that history discloses to us a struggle among peoples and societies, and also within each nation and each society, manifesting in addition an alternation between periods of revolution and reaction, peace and war, *how the*
stagnation and rapid progress or decline—these facts are generally *also pm*
known. Marxism provides a clue which enables us to discover the reign of law in this seeming labyrinth and chaos: the theory of the class struggle. Nothing but the study of the totality of the strivings of all the members of a given society, or group of societies, can lead to the scientific definition of the result of these strivings. Now, the conflict of strivings arises from differences in the situation and modes of life of the *classes* into which society is divided.

The history of all human society, past and present [wrote Marx in 1848, in the *Communist Manifesto*; except the history of the primitive community, Engels added], has been the history of class struggles. Freeman and slave, patrician and plebeian, lord and serf, guild-master and journeyman—in a word, oppressor and oppressed—stood in sharp opposition each to the other. They carried on perpetual warfare, sometimes masked, sometimes open and acknowledged; a warfare that invariably ended either in a revolutionary change in the whole structure of society or else in the common ruin of contending classes. . . . Modern bourgeois society, rising out of the ruins of feudal society, did not make an end of class antagonisms. It merely set up new classes in place of the old; new conditions of oppression; new embodiments of struggle. Our own age, the bourgeois age, is distinguished by this —that it has simplified class antagonisms. More and more, society is splitting up into two great hostile camps, into two great and directly contraposed classes: bourgeoisie and proletariat.

Since the time of the great French Revolution, the class struggle as the actual motive force of events has been most clearly manifest in all European history. During the Restoration period in France, there were already a number of historians (Thierry, Guizot, Mignet, Thiers) who, generalizing events, could not but recognize in the class struggle the key to the understanding of all the history of France. In the modern age—the epoch of the complete victory of the bourgeoisie, of representative institutions, of extended (if not universal) suffrage, of cheap daily newspapers widely circulated among the masses, etc., of powerful and ever-expanding organizations of workers and employers, etc.—the class struggle (though sometimes in a highly one-sided, "peaceful", "constitutional" form) has shown itself still more obviously to be the mainspring of events.

The following passage from Marx's *Communist Manifesto* will show us what Marx demanded of social sciences as regards an objective analysis of the situation of every class in modern society as well as analysis of the conditions of development of every class.

Among all the classes that confront the bourgeoisie to-day, the proletariat alone is really revolutionary. Other classes decay and perish with the rise of large-scale industry, but the proletariat is the most characteristic product of that industry. The lower middle class—small manufacturers, small traders, handicraftsmen, peasant proprietors—one and all fight the bourgeoisie in the hope of safeguarding their existence as sections of the middle class. They are, therefore, not revolutionary, but conservative. Nay, more, they are reactionary, for they are trying to make the wheels of history turn backwards. If they ever become revolutionary, it is only because they are afraid of slipping down into the ranks of the proletariat; they are not defending their present interests, but their future interests; they are forsaking their own standpoint, in order to adopt that of the proletariat.

In a number of historical works, Marx gave brilliant and profound examples of materialist historiography, an analysis of the position of *each* separate class, and sometimes of that of various groups or strata within a class, showing plainly why and how "every class struggle is a political struggle". The above-quoted passage is an illustration of what a complex network of social relations and *transitional stages* between one class and another, between the past and the future, Marx analyses in order to arrive at the resultant of the whole historical development.

Marx's economic doctrine is the most profound, the most many-sided, and the most detailed confirmation and application of his teaching.

Marx's Economic Doctrine

"It is the ultimate aim of this work to reveal the economic law of motion of modern society" (that is to say, capitalist, bourgeois society), writes Marx in the preface to the first volume of *Capital*. The study of the production relationships in a given, historically determinate society, in their genesis, their development, and their decay—such is the content of Marx's economic teaching. In capitalist society the dominant feature is the production of *commodities*, and Marx's analysis therefore begins with an analysis of commodity.

Value

A commodity is, firstly, something that satisfies a human need; and, secondly, it is something that is exchanged for something else. The utility of a thing gives it *use-value*. Exchange-value (or simply, value) presents itself first of all as the proportion, the ratio, in which a certain number of use-values of one kind are exchanged for a certain number of use-values of another kind. Daily experience shows us that by millions upon millions of such exchanges, all and sundry use-values, in themselves very different and not comparable one with another, are equated to one another. Now, what is common in these various things which are constantly weighed one against another in a definite system of social relationships? That which is common to them is that they are *products of labour*. In exchanging products, people equate to one another most diverse kinds of labour. The production of commodities is a system of social relationships in which different producers produce various products (the social division of labour), and in which all these products are equated to one another in exchange. Consequently, the element common to all commodities is not concrete labour in a definite branch of production, not labour of one particular kind, but *abstract* human labour—human labour in general. All the labour power of a given society, represented in the sum total of values of all commodities, is one and the same human labour power. Millions upon millions of acts of exchange prove this. Consequently, each particular commodity represents only a certain part of *socially necessary* labour time. The magnitude of the value is determined by the amount of socially necessary labour, or by the labour time that is socially requisite for the production of the given commodity, of the given use-value. "...Exchanging labour products of different kinds one for another, they equate the values of the exchanged products; and in doing so they equate the different kinds of labour expended in production, treating them as homogeneous human labour. They do not know that they are doing this, but they do it." As one of the earlier economists said, value is a relationship between two persons, only he should have added that it is a relationship hidden beneath a material wrapping. We can only understand what value is when we consider it from the point of view of a system of social production relationships in one particular historical type of society; and, moreover, of relationships which present themselves in a mass form, the phenomenon of exchange repeating itself millions upon millions of times. "As values, all commodities are only definite quantities of congealed labour time." Having made a detailed analysis of the twofold character of the labour incorporated in commodities, Marx goes on to analyse the *form of value and of money*. His main task, then, is to study the *origin* of the money form of value, to study the *historical process* of the development of exchange, beginning with isolated and casual acts of exchange ("simple, isolated, or casual value form", in which a given quantity of one commodity is exchanged for a given quantity of another), passing on to the universal form of value, in which a number of different commodities are exchanged for one and the same particular commodity, and ending with the money form of value, when gold becomes this particular commodity, the universal equivalent. Being the highest product of the development of exchange and of commodity production, money masks the social character of individual labour, and hides the social tie between the various producers who come together in the market. Marx analyses in great detail the various functions of money; and it is essential to note that here (as generally in the opening chapters of *Capital*) what appears to be an abstract and at times purely deductive mode of exposition in reality reproduces a gigantic collection of facts concerning the history of the development of exchange and commodity production.

Money...presupposes a definite level of commodity exchange. The various forms of money (simple commodity equivalent or means of circulation, or means of payment, treasure, or international money) indicate, according to the different extent to which this or that function is put into application, and according to the comparative predominance of one or other of them, very different grades of the social process of production.

Surplus Value

At a particular stage in the development of commodity production, money becomes transformed into capital. The formula of commodity circulation was C.M.C. (commodity—money—commodity); the sale of one commodity for the purpose of buying another. But the general formula of capital, on the contrary, is M.C.M. (money—commodity—money); purchase for the purpose of selling—at a profit. The designation "surplus value" is given by Marx to the increase over the original value of money that is put into circulation. The fact of this "growth" of money in capitalist society is well known. Indeed, it is this "growth" which transforms money into *capital*, as a special, historically defined, social relationship of production. Surplus value cannot arise out of the circulation of commodities, for this represents nothing more than the exchange of equivalents; it cannot arise out of an advance in prices, for the mutual losses and gains of buyers and sellers would equalize one another; and we are concerned here, not with what happens to individuals, but with a mass or average or social phenomenon. In order that he may be able to receive surplus value, "Moneybags must...find in the market a commodity whose use-value has the peculiar quality of being a source of value"—a commodity, the actual process of whose use is at the same time the process of the creation of value. Such a commodity exists. It is human labour power. Its use is labour, and labour creates value. The owner of money buys labour power at its value, which is determined, like the value of every other commodity, by the socially necessary labour time requisite for its production (that is to say, the cost of maintaining the worker and his family). Having bought labour power, the owner of money is entitled to use it, that is to set it to work for the whole day—twelve hours, let us suppose. Meanwhile, in the course of six hours ("necessary" labour time) the labourer produces sufficient to pay back the cost of his own maintenance; and in the course of the next six hours ("surplus" labour time), he produces a "surplus" product for which the capitalist does not pay him—surplus product or surplus value. In capital, therefore, from the viewpoint of the process of production, we have to distinguish between two parts: first, constant capital, expended for the means of production (machinery, tools, raw materials, etc.), the value of this being (all at once or part by part) transferred, unchanged, to the finished product; and, secondly, variable capital, expended for labour power. The value of this latter capital is not constant, but grows in the labour process, creating surplus value. To express the degree of exploitation of labour power by capital, we must therefore compare the surplus value, not with the whole capital, but only with the variable capital. Thus, in the example just given, the rate of surplus value, as Marx calls this relationship, will be 6 : 6, i.e., 100 per cent.

There are two historical prerequisites to the genesis of capital: first, accumulation of a considerable sum of money in the hands of individuals living under conditions in which there is a comparatively high development of commodity production. Second, the existence of workers who are "free" in a double sense of the term: free from any constraint or restriction as regards the sale of their labour power; free

from any bondage to the soil or to the means of production in general
—i.e. of propertyless workers, of "proletarians" who cannot maintain
their existence except by the sale of their labour power.

There are two fundamental ways in which surplus value can be
increased: by an increase in the working day ("absolute surplus
value"); and by a reduction in the necessary working day ("relative
surplus value"). Analysing the former method, Marx gives an impressive picture of the struggle of the working class for shorter hours and
of governmental interference, first (from the fourteenth century to the
seventeenth) in order to lengthen the working day, and subsequently
(factory legislation of the nineteenth century) to shorten it. Since the
appearance of *Capital*, the history of the working-class movement in
all lands provides a wealth of new facts to amplify this picture.

Analysing the production of relative surplus value, Marx investigates
the three fundamental historical stages of the process whereby capitalism has increased the productivity of labour: (1) simple co-operation;
(2) division of labour, and manufacture; (3) machinery and large-scale
industry. How profoundly Marx has here revealed the basic and typical
features of capitalist development is shown by the fact that investigations
of the so-called "kustar" industry of Russia furnish abundant material
for the illustration of the first two of these stages. The revolutionizing
effect of large-scale machine industry, described by Marx in 1867, has
become evident in a number of "new" countries, such as Russia, Japan,
etc., in the course of the last fifty years.

But to continue. Of extreme importance and originality is Marx's
analysis of the *accumulation of capital*, that is to say, the transformation
of a portion of surplus value into capital and the applying of this
portion to additional production, instead of using it to supply the
personal needs or to gratify the whims of the capitalist. Marx pointed
out the mistake made by earlier classical political economy (from Adam
Smith on), which assumed that all the surplus value which was transformed into capital became variable capital. In actual fact, it is divided
into *means of production* plus variable capital. The more rapid growth
of constant capital as compared with variable capital in the sum total
of capital is of immense importance in the process of development of
capitalism and in that of the transformation of capitalism into Socialism.

The accumulation of capital, accelerating the replacement of workers
by machinery, creating wealth at the one pole and poverty at the other,
gives birth to the so-called "reserve army of labour", to a "relative

overabundance" of workers or to "capitalist over-population". This assumes the most diversified forms, and gives capital the possibility of expanding production at an exceptionally rapid rate. This possibility, in conjunction with enhanced facilities for credit and with the accumulation of capital in the means of production, furnishes, among other things, the key to the understanding of the *crises* of overproduction that occur periodically in capitalist countries—first about every ten years, on an average, but subsequently in a more continuous form and with a less definite periodicity. From accumulation of capital upon a capitalist foundation we must distinguish the so-called "primitive accumulation": the forcible severance of the worker from the means of production, the driving of the peasants off the land, the stealing of the communal lands, the system of colonies and national debts, of protective tariffs, and the like. "Primitive accumulation" creates, at one pole, the "free" proletarian: at the other, the owner of money, the capitalist.

The "*historical tendency of capitalist accumulation*" is described by Marx in the following well-known terms:

The expropriation of the immediate producers is effected with ruthless vandalism, and under the stimulus of the most infamous, the basest, the meanest, and the most odious of passions. Self-earned private property [of the peasant and the handicraftsman], the private property that may be looked upon as grounded on a coalescence of the isolated, individual, and independent worker with his working conditions, is supplemented by capitalist private property, which is maintained by the exploitation of others' labour, but of labour which in a formal sense is free. . . . What has now to be expropriated is no longer the labourer working on his own account, but the capitalist who exploits many labourers. This expropriation is brought about by the operation of the immanent laws of capitalist production, by the centralization of capital. One capitalist lays a number of his fellow capitalists low. Hand in hand with this centralization, concomitantly with the expropriation of many capitalists by a few, the co-operative form of the labour process develops to an ever-increasing degree; therewith we find a growing tendency towards the purposive application of science to the improvement of technique; the land is more methodically cultivated; the instruments of labour tend to assume forms which are only utilizable by combined effort; the means of production are economized through being turned to account only by joint, by social labour; all the peoples of the world are enmeshed in the net of the world market, and therefore the capitalist regime tends more and more to assume an international character. While there is thus a progressive diminution in the number of the capitalist magnates (who usurp and monopolize all the advantages of this transformative process), there occurs a corresponding increase in the mass of poverty, oppression, enslavement, degeneration, and exploitation; but at the same time there is a steady intensification of the wrath of the working class—a class which grows ever more numerous, and is disciplined, unified, and organized by the very mechanism of the capitalist method of production. Capitalist monopoly becomes a fetter upon the method of production which has flourished with it and under it. The centralization of the means of production and the socialization of labour reach a point where they prove incompatible with their capitalist husk. This bursts asunder. The knell of capitalist private property sounds. The expropriators are expropriated.

Of great importance and quite new is Marx's analysis, in the second volume of *Capital*, of the reproduction of social capital, taken as a whole. Here, too, Marx is dealing, not with an individual phenomenon, but with a mass phenomenon; not with a fractional part of the economy of society, but with economy as a whole. Having corrected the above-mentioned mistake of the classical economists, Marx divides the whole of social production into two great sections: production of the means of production, and production of articles for consumption. Using figures for an example, he makes a detailed examination of the circulation of all social capital taken as a whole—both when it is reproduced in its previous proportions and when accumulation takes place. The third volume of *Capital* solves the problem of how the average rate of profit is formed on the basis of the law of value. It is an immense advance in economic science that Marx conducts his analysis from the point of view of mass economic phenomena, of the aggregate of social economy, and not from the point of view of individual cases or upon the purely superficial aspects of competition—a limitation of view so often met with in vulgar political economy and in the contemporary "theory of marginal utility". First, Marx analyses the origin of surplus value, and then he goes on to consider its division into profit, interest, and ground-rent. Profit is the ratio between the surplus value and all the capital invested in an undertaking. Capital with a "high organic composition" (i.e. with a preponderance of constant capital over variable capital to an extent above the social average) yields a below-average rate of profit; capital with a "low organic composition" yields an above-average rate of profit. Competition among the capitalists, who are free to transfer their capital from one branch of production to another, reduces the rate of profit in both cases to the average. The sum total of the values of all the commodities in a given society coincides with the sum total of the prices of all the commodities; but in separate undertakings, and in separate branches of production, as a result of competition, commodities are sold, not in accordance with their values, but in accordance with the *prices of production*, which are equal to the expended capital plus the average profit.

In this way the well-known and indisputable fact of the divergence between prices and values and of the equalization of profits is fully explained by Marx in conformity with the law of value; for the sum total of the values of all the commodities coincides with the sum total of all the prices. But the adjustment of value (a social matter) to price (an individual matter) does not proceed by a simple and direct way. It is an exceedingly complex affair. Naturally, therefore, in a society made up of separate producers of commodities, linked solely through the market, conformity to law can only be an average, a general manifestation, a mass phenomenon, with individual and mutually compensating deviations to one side and the other.

An increase in the productivity of labour means a more rapid growth of constant capital as compared with variable capital. Inasmuch as surplus value is a function of variable capital alone, it is obvious that the rate of profit (the ratio of surplus value to the whole capital, and not to its variable part alone) has a tendency to fall. Marx makes a detailed analysis of this tendency and of the circumstances that incline to favour it or to counteract it. Without pausing to give an account of the extra-ordinarily interesting parts of the third volume of *Capital* that are devoted to the consideration of usurer's capital, commercial capital, and money capital, I shall turn to the most important subject of that volume, the theory of *ground-rent*. Due to the fact that the land area is limited, and that in capitalist countries it is all occupied by private owners, the production price of agricultural products is determined by the cost of production, not on soil of average quality, but on the worst soil, and by the cost of bringing goods to the market, not under average conditions, but under the worst conditions. The difference between this price and the price of production on better soil (or under better conditions) constitutes *differential* rent. Analysing this in detail, and showing how it arises out of variations in the fertility of the individual plots of land and in the extent to which capital is applied to the land, Marx fully exposes the error of Ricardo, who considered that differential rent is only obtained when there is a continual transition from better to worse lands. Advances in agricultural technique, the growth of towns, and so on, may, on the contrary, act inversely, may transfer land from one category into the other; and the famous "law of diminishing returns", charging nature with the insufficiencies, limitations, and contradictions of capitalism, is a great mistake. Moreover, the equalization of profit in all branches of industry and national economy in general, presupposes complete freedom of competition, the free mobility of capital from one branch to another. But the private ownership of land, creating monopoly, hinders this free mobility. Thanks to this monopoly, the products of agriculture, where a low organic composition of capital prevails, and, consequently, individually, a higher rate of profit can be secured, are not exposed to a perfectly free process of equalization of the rate of profit. The landowner, being a monopolist, can keep the price of his produce above the average, and this monopoly price is the source of *absolute rent*. Differential rent cannot be done away with so long as capitalism exists; but absolute rent *can* be abolished even under capitalism—for instance, by nationalization of the land, by making all the land state property. Nationalization of the land would put an end to the monopoly of private landowners, with the result that free competition would be more consistently and fully applied in the domain of agriculture. That is why, as Marx states, in the course of history the radical bourgeois have again and again come out with this progressive bourgeois demand of land nationalization, which, however, frightens away the majority of the bourgeoisie, for it touches upon another monopoly that is highly important and "touchy" in our days—the monopoly of the means of production in general. For the history of ground-rent it is also important to note Marx's analysis which shows how rent paid in labour service (when the peasant creates a surplus product by labouring on the lord's land) is transformed into rent paid in produce or rent in kind (the peasant creating a surplus product on his own land and handing this over to the lord of the soil under stress of "non-economic constraint"); then into monetary rent (which is the monetary equivalent of rent in kind, the *obrok* of old Russia, money having replaced produce thanks to the development of commodity production), and finally into capitalist rent, when the place of the peasant has been taken by the agricultural entrepreneur cultivating the soil with the help of wage-labour. In connexion with this analysis of the "genesis of capitalist ground-rent" must be noted Marx's *profound* ideas concerning the *evolution of capitalism in agriculture* (this is of especial importance in its bearing on backward countries, such as Russia).

The transformation of rent in kind into money rent is not only necessarily accompanied, but even anticipated by the formation of a class of propertyless day labourers, who hire themselves out for wages. During the period of their rise, when this new class appears but sporadically, the custom necessarily develops among the better situated tributary farmers of exploiting agricultural labourers for their own account, just as the wealthier serfs in feudal times used to employ serfs for their own benefit. In this way they gradually acquire the ability to accumulate a certain amount of wealth and to transform themselves even into future capitalists. The old self-employing possessors of the land thus gave rise among themselves to a nursery for capitalist tenants, whose development is conditioned upon the general development of capitalist production outside of the rural districts. . . .

The expropriation of part of the country folk, and the hunting of them off the land, does not merely "set free" the workers for the uses of industrial capital, together with their means of subsistence and the materials of their labour; in addition it creates the home market.

The impoverishment and the ruin of the agricultural population lead, in their turn, to the formation of a reserve army of labour for capital. In every capitalist country, "part of the rural population is continually on the move, in course of transference to join the urban proletariat, the manufacturing proletariat. . . . (In this connexion, the term 'manufacture' is used to include all non-agricultural industry.) This source of a relative surplus population is, therefore, continually flowing. . . . The agricultural labourer, therefore, has his wages kept down to the minimum, and always has one foot in the swamp of pauperism." The peasant's private ownership of the land he tills constitutes the basis of small-scale production and causes the latter to flourish and attain its classical form. But such petty production is only compatible with a narrow and primitive type of production, with a narrow and primitive framework of society. Under capitalism, the exploitation of the peasants "differs from the exploitation of the industrial proletariat only in point of form. The exploiter is the same: capital. The individual capitalists exploit the individual peasants through mortgages and usury, and the capitalist class exploits the peasant class through state taxation." "Peasant agriculture, the smallholding system, is merely an expedient whereby the capitalist is enabled to extract profit, interest, and rent from the land, while leaving the peasant proprietor to pay himself his own wages as best he may." As a rule, the peasant hands over to the capitalist society, i.e. to the capitalist class, part of the wages of his own labour, sinking "down to the level of the Irish tenant—all this on the pretext of being the owner of private property". Why is it that "the price of cereals is lower in countries with a predominance of small farmers than in countries with a capitalist method of production"? The answer is that the peasant presents part of his surplus product as a free gift to society (i.e. to the capitalist class). "This lower price [of bread and other agricultural products] is also a result of the poverty of the producers and by no means of the productivity of their labour." Peasant proprietorship, the smallholding system, which is the normal form of petty production, degenerates, withers, perishes under capitalism.

Small peasants' property excludes by its very nature the development of the social powers of production of labour, the social forms of labour, the social concentration of capital, cattle raising on a large scale, and a progressive application of science. Usury and a system of taxation must impoverish it everywhere. The expenditure of capital in the price of the land withdraws this capital from cultivation. An infinite dissipation of means of production and an isolation of the producers themselves go with it. [Co-operatives, i.e. associations of small peasants, while playing an unusually progressive bourgeois role, only weaken this tendency without eliminating it; one must not forget besides, that these co-operatives do much for the well-to-do peasants and very little, almost nothing, for the mass of the poor peasants, also that the associations themselves become exploiters of wage labour.] Also an enormous waste of human energy. A progressive deterioration of the conditions of production and a raising of the price of means of production is a necessary law of small peasants' property.

In agriculture as in industry, capitalism improves the production process only at the price of the "martyrdom of the producers".

The dispersion of the rural workers over large areas breaks down their powers of resistance at the very time when concentration is increasing the powers of the urban operatives in this respect. In modern agriculture, as in urban industry, the increased productivity and the greater mobility of labour are purchased at the cost of devastating labour power and making it a prey to disease. Moreover, every advance in capitalist agriculture is an advance in the art, not only of robbing the worker, but also of robbing the soil. . . . Capitalist production, therefore, is only able to develop the technique and the combination of the social process of production by simultaneously undermining the foundations of all wealth—the land and the workers.

SOCIALISM

From the foregoing it is manifest that Marx deduces the inevitability of the transformation of capitalist society into Socialist society wholly and exclusively from the economic law of the movement of contemporary society. The chief material foundation of the inevitability of the coming of Socialism is the socialization of labour in its myriad forms, advancing ever more rapidly, and conspicuously so, throughout the half-century that has elapsed since the death of Marx—being especially plain in the growth of large-scale production, of capitalist cartels, syndicates, and trusts; but also in the gigantic increase in the dimensions and the power of finance capital. The intellectual and moral driving force of this transformation is the proletariat, the physical carrier trained by capitalism itself. The contest of the proletariat with the bourgeoisie, assuming various forms which grow continually richer in content, inevitably becomes a political struggle aiming at the conquest of political power by the proletariat ("the dictatorship of the proletariat"). The socialization of production cannot fail to lead to the transfer of the means of production into the possession of society, to the "expropriation of the expropriators". An immense increase in the productivity of labour; a reduction in working hours; replacement of the remnants, the ruins of petty, primitive, individual production by collective and perfected labour—such will be the direct consequences of this transformation. Capitalism breaks all ties between agriculture and industry; but at the same time, in the course of its highest development, it prepares new elements for the establishment of a connexion between the two, uniting industry and agriculture upon the basis of the conscious use of science and the combination of collective labour, the redistribution of population (putting an end at one and the same time to rural seclusion and unsociability and savagery, and to the unnatural concentration of enormous masses of population in huge cities). A new kind of family life, changes in the position of women and in the upbringing of the younger generation, are being prepared by the highest forms of modern capitalism; the labour of women and children, the break-up of the patriarchal family by capitalism, necessarily assume in contemporary society the most terrible, disastrous, and repulsive forms. Nevertheless,

. . .large-scale industry, by assigning to women and to young persons and children ot both sexes a decisive role in the socially organized process of production, and a role which has to be fulfilled outside the home, is building the new economic foundation for a higher form of the family and of the relations between the sexes. I need hardly say that it is just as stupid to regard the Christo-Teutonic form of the family as absolute, as it is to take the same view of the classical Roman form or of the classical Greek form, or of the Oriental form—which, by the by, constitute an historically interconnected developmental series. It is plain, moreover, that the composition of the combined labour personnel out of individuals of both sexes and various ages —although in its spontaneously developed and brutal capitalist form (wherein the worker exists for the process of production instead of the process of production existing for the worker) it is a pestilential source of corruption and slavery—under suitable conditions cannot fail to be transformed into a source of human progress.

In the factory system are to be found "the germs of the education of the future....This will be an education which, in the case of every child over a certain age, will combine productive labour with instruction and physical culture, not only as a means for increasing social production, but as the only way of producing fully-developed human beings." Upon the same historical foundation, not with the sole idea of throwing light on the past, but with the idea of boldly foreseeing the future and boldly working to bring about its realization, the Socialism of Marx propounds the problems of nationality and the state. The nation is a necessary product, an inevitable form, in the bourgeois epoch of social development. The working class cannot grow strong, cannot mature, cannot consolidate its forces, except by "establishing itself as the nation", except by being "national" ("though by no means in the bourgeois sense of the term"). But the development of capitalism tends more and more to break down the partitions that separate the nations one from another, does away with national isolation, substitutes class antagonisms for national antagonisms. In the more developed capitalist countries, therefore, it is perfectly true that "the workers have no fatherland", and that "united action" of the workers, in the civilized countries at least, "is one of the first conditions requisite for the emancipation of the workers". The state, which is organized oppression, came into being inevitably at a certain stage in the development of society, when this society had split into irreconcilable classes, and when it could not exist without an "authority" supposed to be standing above society and to some extent separated from it. Arising out of class contradictions, the state becomes

...the state of the most powerful economic class that by force of its economic supremacy becomes also the ruling political class, and thus acquires new means of subduing and exploiting the oppressed masses. The ancient state was therefore the state of the slave-owners for the purpose of holding the slaves in check. The feudal state was the organ of the nobility for the oppression of the serfs and dependent farmers. The modern representative state is the tool of the capitalist exploiters of wage labour. [Engels, *The Origin of the*

Family, Private Property, and the State, a work in which the writer expounds his own views and Marx's.]

This condition of affairs persists even in the democratic republic, the freest and most progressive kind of bourgeois state; there is merely a change of form (the government becoming linked up with the stock exchange, and the officialdom and the press being corrupted by direct or indirect means). Socialism, putting an end to classes, will thereby put an end to the state.

The first act, writes Engels in *Anti-Dühring*, whereby the state really becomes the representative of society as a whole, namely, the expropriation of the means of production for the benefit of society as a whole, will likewise be its last independent act as a state. The interference of the state authority in social relationships will become superfluous, and will be discontinued in one domain after another. The government over persons will be transformed into the administration of things and the management of the process of production. The state will not be "abolished"; it will "die out".

The society that is to recognize production on the basis of a free and equal association of the producers, will transfer the machinery of state where it will then belong: into the museum of antiquities, by the side of the spinning-wheel and the bronze axe. [Engels, *The Origin of the Family, Private Property, and the State.*]

If, finally, we wish to understand the attitude of Marxian Socialism towards the small peasantry, which will continue to exist in the period of the expropriation of the expropriators, we must turn to a declaration by Engels expressing Marx's views. In an article on "The Peasant Problem in France and Germany", which appeared in the *Neue Zeit*, he says:

When we are in possession of the powers of the state, we shall not even dream of forcibly expropriating the poorer peasants, the smallholders (with or without compensation), as we shall have to do in relation to the large land-owners. Our task as regards the smallholders will first of all consist in trans-forming their individual production and individual ownership into co-operative production and co-operative ownership, not forcibly, but by way of example, and by offering social aid for this purpose. We shall then have the means of showing the peasant all the advantages of this change—advantages which even now should be obvious to him.

From *The Teachings of Karl Marx* (1920)

§3. CLASS SOCIETY AND THE STATE

LENIN

1. THE STATE AS THE PRODUCT OF THE IRRECONCILABILITY OF CLASS ANTAGONISMS

What is now happening to Marx's doctrine has, in the course of history, often happened to the doctrines of other revolutionary thinkers and leaders of oppressed classes struggling for emancipation. During the lifetime of great revolutionaries, the oppressing classes relentlessly persecute them, treat their teachings with malicious hostility and fierce hatred, and subject them to an unscrupulous campaign of lies and slanders. After their deaths, attempts are made to convert them into harmless icons, to canonize them, so to speak, and to surround their *names* with a certain halo for the "consolation" of the oppressed classes and with the object of duping them, while at the same time emasculating the revolutionary doctrine of its content, vulgarizing it and blunting its revolutionary edge. At the present time, the bourgeoisie and the opportunists in the labour movement concur in this "revision" of Marxism. They omit, obliterate and distort the revolutionary side of its doctrine, its revolutionary soul. They push to the foreground and extol what is or seems acceptable to the bourgeoisie. All the social-chauvinists are now "Marxists" (don't laugh!). And more and more frequently, German bourgeois professors, erstwhile specialists in the extermination of Marxism, are speaking of the "national-German" Marx, who, they aver, trained the labour unions which are so splendidly organized for the purpose of conducting a predatory war!

In such circumstances, in view of the incredibly widespread nature of the distortions of Marxism, our first task is to *restore* the true doctrine of Marx on the state. For this purpose it will be necessary to quote at length from the works of Marx and Engels. Of course, long quotations will make the text cumbersome and will not help to make it popular reading, but we cannot possibly avoid them. All, or at any rate, all the most essential passages in the works of Marx and Engels on the subject of the state must necessarily be given as fully as possible, in order that the reader may form an independent opinion on the totality of views of the founders of scientific socialism, and on the development of those views, and in order that their distortion by the now prevailing "Kautskyism" may be documentarily proved and clearly demonstrated.

Let us begin with the most popular of Engels' work, *The Origin of the Family, Private Property, and the State*, the sixth edition of which was published in Stuttgart as far back as 1894. We must translate the quotations from the German originals, as the Russian translations, although very numerous, are for the most part either incomplete or very unsatisfactory.

Summing up his historical analysis, Engels says:

The state is therefore by no means a power imposed on society from the outside; just as little is it "the reality of the moral idea", "the image and reality of reason", as Hegel asserts. Rather, it is a product of society at a certain stage of development; it is the admission that this society has become entangled in an insoluble contradiction with itself, that it is cleft into irreconcilable antagonisms, which it is powerless to dispel. But in order that these antagonisms, classes with conflicting economic interests, might not consume themselves and society in sterile struggle, a power apparently standing above society became necessary for the purpose of moderating the conflict and keeping it within the bounds of "order"; and this power, arising out of society, but placing itself above it, and increasingly alienating itself from it, is the state.

This fully expresses the basic idea of Marxism on the question of the historical role and meaning of the state. The state is the product and the manifestation of the *irreconcilability* of class antagonisms. The state arises when, where and to the extent that class antagonisms *cannot* be objectively reconciled. And, conversely, the existence of the state proves that the class antagonisms *are* irreconcilable.

It is precisely on this most important and fundamental point that distortions of Marxism, proceeding along two main lines, begin.

On the one hand, the bourgeois ideologists, and particularly the petty-bourgeois ideologists, compelled by the pressure of indisputable historical facts to admit that the state exists only where there are class antagonisms and the class struggle, "correct" Marx in a way that makes it appear that the state is an organ for the *conciliation* of classes. According to Marx, the state could neither arise nor continue to exist if it were possible to conciliate classes. According to the petty-bourgeois and philistine professors and publicists—frequently on the strength of well-meaning references to Marx!—the state conciliates classes.

According to Marx, the state is an organ of class *rule*, an organ for the *oppression* of one class by another (it creates "order"), which legalizes and perpetuates this oppression by moderating the collisions between the classes. In the opinion of the petty-bourgeois politicians, order means the conciliation of classes, and not the oppression of one class by another; to moderate collisions means conciliating and not depriving the oppressed classes of definite means and methods of fighting to overthrow the oppressors.

For instance, when, in the Revolution of 1917, the question of the real meaning and role of the state arose in all its magnitude as a practical question demanding immediate action on a wide mass scale, all the Socialist-Revolutionaries and Mensheviks immediately and completely sank to the petty-bourgeois theory that the "state" "conciliates" classes. There were innumerable resolutions and articles by politicians of both these parties thoroughly saturated with this purely petty-bourgeois and philistine "conciliation" theory. Petty-bourgeois democracy is never able to understand that the state is the organ of the rule of a definite class which *cannot* be reconciled with its antipode (the class opposite to it). Their attitude towards the state is one of the most striking proofs that our Socialist-Revolutionaries and Mensheviks are not socialists at all (which we Bolsheviks have always maintained), but petty-bourgeois democrats with near-Socialist phraseology.

On the other hand, the "Kautskyan" distortion of Marxism is far more subtle. "Theoretically", it is not denied that the state is the organ of class rule, or that class antagonisms are irreconcilable. But what is lost sight of or glossed over is this: if the state is the product of irreconcilable class antagonisms, if it is a power standing *above society* and *"increasingly alienating itself from it"*, it is clear that the liberation of the oppressed class is impossible, not only without a violent revolution, *but also without the destruction* of the apparatus of state power which was created by the ruling class and which is the embodiment of this "alienation". As we shall see later, Marx very definitely drew this theoretically self-evident conclusion from a concrete historical analysis of the tasks of the revolution. And—as we shall show fully in our subsequent remarks—it is precisely this conclusion which Kautsky has "forgotten" and distorted.

2. SPECIAL BODIES OF ARMED MEN, PRISONS, ETC.

Engels continues:

As against the ancient *gentile* organization, the primary distinguishing feature of the state is the division of the subjects of the state *according to territory*.

Such a division seems "natural" to us, but it cost a prolonged struggle against the old form of tribal or gentile society.

...The second is the establishment of a *public power*, which is no longer directly identical with the population organizing itself as an armed power. This special public power is necessary, because a self-acting armed organization of the population has become impossible since the cleavage into classes. ...This public power exists in every state; it consists not merely of armed men, but of material appendages, prisons and coercive institutions of all kinds, of which gentile society knew nothing.. ..

Engels further elucidates the concept of the "power" which is termed the state—a power which arises from society, but which places itself above it and becomes more and more alienated from it. What does this power mainly consist of? It consists of special bodies of armed men which have prisons, etc., at their disposal.

We are justified in speaking of special bodies of armed men, because the public power which is an attribute of every state is not "directly identical" with the armed population, with its "self-acting armed organization".

Like all the great revolutionary thinkers, Engels tried to draw the attention of the class-conscious workers to the very fact which prevailing philistinism regards as least worthy of attention, as the most common and sanctified, not only by long standing, but one might say by petrified prejudices. A standing army and police are the chief instruments of state power. But can it be otherwise?

From the point of view of the vast majority of Europeans of the end of the nineteenth century whom Engels was addressing, and who had not lived through or closely observed a single great revolution, it could not be otherwise. They completely failed to understand what a "self-acting armed organization of the population" was. To the question, whence arose the need for special bodies of armed men, standing above society and becoming alienated from it (police and standing army), the West European and Russian philistines are inclined to answer with a few phrases borrowed from Spencer or Mikhailovsky, by referring to the complexity of social life, the differentiation of functions, and so forth.

Such a reference seems "scientific"; it effectively dulls the senses of the average man and obscures the most important and basic fact, namely, the cleavage of society into irreconcilably antagonistic classes. Had this cleavage not existed, the "self-acting armed organization of the population" might have differed from the primitive organization of a tribe of monkeys grasping sticks, or of primitive man, or of men united in a tribal form of society, by its complexity, its high technique, and so forth; but it would still have been possible.

It is not possible now, because civilized society is divided into antagonistic and, indeed, irreconcilably antagonistic classes, the "self-acting" arming of which would lead to an armed struggle between them. A state arises, a special force is created in the form of special bodies of armed men, and every revolution, by destroying the state apparatus, demonstrates to us how the ruling class strives to restore the special bodies of armed men which serve *it*, and how the oppressed class strives to create a new organization of this kind, capable of serving not the exploiters but the exploited.

In the above argument, Engels raises theoretically the very question which every great revolution raises practically, palpably and on a mass scale of action, namely, the question of the relation between special bodies of armed men and the "self-acting armed organization of the population". We shall see how this is concretely illustrated by the experience of the European and Russian revolutions.

But let us return to Engels' exposition.

He points out that sometimes, in certain parts of North America, for example, this public power is weak (he has in mind a rare exception in capitalist society, and parts of North America in its pre-imperialist days where the free colonist predominated), but that in general it grows stronger:

It [the public power] grows stronger, however, in proportion as the class antagonisms within the state become more acute, and with the growth in size and population of the adjacent states. We have only to look at our present-day Europe, where class struggle and rivalry in conquest have screwed up the public power to such a pitch that it threatens to devour the whole of society and even the state itself.

This was written no later than the beginning of the nineties of the last century, Engels' last preface being dated 16 June 1891. The turn towards imperialism—meaning by that the complete domination of the trusts, the omnipotence of the big banks, a colonial policy on a grand scale, and so forth—was only just beginning in France, and was even weaker in North America and in Germany. Since then "rivalry in conquest" has made gigantic strides—especially as, by the beginning of the second decade of the twentieth century, the whole world had been finally divided up among these "rivals in conquest", i.e. among the great predatory powers. Since then, military and naval armaments have grown to monstrous proportions, and the predatory war of 1914–7 for the domination of the world by England or Germany, for the division of the spoils, has brought the "devouring" of all the forces of society by the rapacious state power to the verge of complete catastrophe.

As early as 1891 Engels was able to point to "rivalry in conquest" as one of the most important distinguishing features of the foreign policy of the Great Powers, but in 1914–7, when this rivalry, many times intensified, has given birth to an imperialist war, the rascally social-chauvinists cover up their defence of the predatory interests of "their" bourgeoisie by phrases about "defence of the fatherland", "defence of the republic and the revolution", etc.!

3. The State as an Instrument for the Exploitation of the Oppressed Class

For the maintenance of a special public power standing above society, taxes and state loans are needed:

...Possessing the public power and the right to exact taxes, the officials now exist as organs of society standing *above* society. The free, voluntary respect which was accorded to the organs of the gentile organization does not satisfy them, even if they could have it.

Special laws are enacted proclaiming the sanctity and immunity of the officials. "The shabbiest police servant" has more "authority" than all the representatives of the tribe put together, but even the head of the military power of a civilized state may well envy a tribal chief the "unfeigned and undisputed respect" the latter enjoys.

Here the question of the privileged position of the officials as organs of state power is stated. The main point indicated is: what puts them *above* society? We shall see how this theoretical problem was solved in practice by the Paris Commune in 1871 and how it was slurred over in a reactionary manner by Kautsky in 1912.

As the state arose out of the need to hold class antagonisms in check, but as it, at the same time, arose in the midst of the conflict of these classes, it is, as a rule, the state of the most powerful, economically dominant class, which through the medium of the state became also the dominant class politically, and thus acquired new means of holding down and exploiting the oppressed class. . . .

It was not only the ancient and feudal states that were organs for the exploitation of the slaves and serfs but

. . . the contemporary representative state is an instrument of exploitation of wage-labour by capital. By way of exception, however, periods occur when the warring classes are so nearly balanced that the state power, ostensibly appearing as a mediator, acquires, for the moment, a certain independence in relation to both. . . .

Such, for instance, were the absolute monarchies of the seventeenth and eighteenth centuries, the Bonapartism of the First and Second Empires in France, and the Bismarck regime in Germany. Such, we add, is the present Kerensky government in republican Russia, since it began to persecute the revolutionary proletariat at a moment when, thanks to the leadership of the petty-bourgeois democrats, the Soviets had *already* become impotent while the bourgeoisie was *not yet* strong enough openly to disperse them.

In a democratic republic, Engels continues, "wealth wields its power indirectly, but all the more effectively", first, by means of the "direct corruption of the officials" (America); second, by means of "the alliance between the government and the Stock Exchange" (France and America).

At the present time, imperialism and the domination of the banks have "developed" both these methods of defending and asserting the omnipotence of wealth in democratic republics of all descriptions to an unusually fine art. For instance, in the very first months of the Russian democratic republic, one might say during the honeymoon of the union of the "Socialist" S. R.'s and the Mensheviks with the bourgeoisie, Mr Palchinsky, in the coalition government, obstructed every measure intended for the purpose of restraining the capitalists and their marauding practices, their plundering of the public treasury by means of war contracts. When Mr Palchinsky resigned (and, of course, was replaced by an exactly similar Palchinsky), the capitalists "rewarded" him with a "soft" job and a salary of 120,000 roubles per annum. What would you call this—direct or indirect corruption? An alliance between the government and the syndicates, or "only" friendly relations? What role do the Chernovs, Tseretellis, Avksentyevs and Skobelevs play? Are they the "direct" or only the indirect allies of the millionaire treasury looters?

The omnipotence of "wealth" is thus more *secure* in a democratic republic, since it does not depend on the faulty political shell of capitalism. A democratic republic is the best possible political shell for capitalism, and, therefore, once capital has gained control of this very best shell (through the Palchinskys, Chernovs, Tseretellis and Co.), it establishes its powers so securely, so firmly, that *no* change, either of persons, of institutions, or of parties in the bourgeois-democratic republic, can shake it.

We must also note that Engels very definitely calls universal suffrage an instrument of bourgeois rule. Universal suffrage, he says, obviously summing up the long experience of German Social-Democracy, is

. . .an index of the maturity of the working class. It cannot and never will be anything more in the modern state.

The petty-bourgeois democrats, such as our Socialist-Revolutionaries and Mensheviks, and also their twin brothers, the social-chauvinists and opportunists of Western Europe, all expect "more" from universal suffrage. They themselves share and instil into the minds of the people the wrong idea that universal suffrage "in the *modern* state" is really capable of expressing the will of the majority of the toilers and of ensuring its realization.

Here we can only note this wrong idea, only point out that Engels' perfectly clear, precise and concrete statement is distorted at every step in the propaganda and agitation conducted by the "official" (i.e. opportunist) Socialist Parties. A detailed elucidation of the utter falsity of this idea, which Engels brushes aside, is given in our further account of the views of Marx and Engels on the "*modern*" state.

Engels gives a general summary of his views in the most popular of his works in the following words:

The state, therefore, has not existed from all eternity. There have been societies which managed without it, which had no conception of the state and state power. At a certain stage of economic development, which was necessarily bound up with the cleavage of society into classes, the state became a necessity owing to this cleavage. We are now rapidly approaching a stage in the development of production at which the existence of these classes has not only ceased to be a necessity, but is becoming a positive hindrance to production. They will fall as inevitably as they arose at an earlier stage. Along with them, the state will inevitably fall. The society that organizes production anew on the basis of the free and equal association of the producers will put the whole state machine where it will then belong: in the museum of antiquities, side by side with the spinning-wheel and the bronze axe.

We do not often come across this passage in the propaganda and agitation literature of present-day Social-Democracy. But even when we do come across it, it is generally quoted in the same manner as one bows before an icon, i.e. it is done merely to show official respect for Engels, and no attempt is made to gauge the breadth and depth of the revolution that this relegating of "the whole state machine...to the museum of antiquities" presupposes. In most cases we do not even find an understanding of what Engels calls the state machine.

4. The "Withering Away" of the State and Violent Revolution

Engels' words regarding the "withering away" of the state are so widely known, they are so often quoted, and they reveal the significance of the customary painting of Marxism to look like opportunism so clearly that we must deal with them in detail. We shall quote the whole passage from which they are taken.

The proletarian seizes the state power and transforms the means of production in the first instance into state property. But in doing this, it puts an end to itself as the proletariat, it puts an end to all class differences and class antagonisms, it puts an end also to the state as the state. Former society, moving in class antagonisms, had need of the state, that is, an organization of the exploiting class, at each period for the maintenance of its external conditions of production; that is, therefore, for the forcible holding down of the exploited class in the conditions of oppression (slavery, villeinage or serfdom, wage-labour) determined by the existing mode of production. The state was the official representative of society as a whole, its embodiment in a visible corporation; but it was this only in so far as it was the state of that class which itself, in its epoch, represented society as a whole: in ancient times, the state of the slave-owning citizens; in the Middle Ages, of the feudal nobility; in our epoch, of the bourgeoisie. When ultimately it becomes really representative of society as a whole, it makes itself superfluous. As soon as there is no longer any class of society to be held in subjection; as soon as, along with class domination and the struggle for individual existence based on the former anarchy of production, the collisions and excesses arising from these have also been abolished, there is nothing more to be repressed, which would make a special repressive force, a state, necessary. The first act in which the state really comes forward as the representative of society as a whole—the taking possession of the means of production in the name of society—is at the same time its last independent act as a state. The interference of the state power in social relations becomes superfluous in one sphere after another, and then ceases of itself. The government of persons is replaced by the administration of things and the direction of the process of production. The state is not "abolished", *it withers away*. It is from this standpoint that we must appraise the phrase "free people's state"—both its justification at times for agitational purposes, and its ultimate scientific inadequacy—and also the demand of the so-called anarchists that the state should be abolished overnight. [Engels, *Anti-Dühring*.]

It may be said without fear of error that of this argument of Engels', which is so singularly rich in ideas, only one point has become an integral part of socialist thought among modern Socialist Parties, namely, that according to Marx the state "withers away"—as distinct from the anarchist doctrine of the "abolition of the state". To emasculate Marxism in such a manner is to reduce it to opportunism for such an "interpretation" only leaves the hazy conception of a slow, even, gradual change, of absence of leaps and storms, of absence of revolution. The current, widespread, mass, if one may say so, conception of the "withering away" of the state undoubtedly means the slurring over, if not the repudiation, of revolution.

Such an "interpretation" is the crudest distortion of Marxism, advantageous only to the bourgeoisie; in point of theory, it is based on a disregard for the most important circumstances and considerations pointed out, for example, in the "summary" of Engels' argument we have just quoted in full.

In the first place, Engels at the very outset of his argument says that, in assuming state power, the proletariat by that "puts an end to the state...as the state". It is not "good form" to ponder over what this means. Generally, it is either ignored altogether, or it is considered to be a piece of "Hegelian weakness" on Engels' part. As a matter of fact, however, these words briefly express the experience of one of the great proletarian revolutions, the Paris Commune of 1871. As a matter of fact, Engels speaks here of the "abolition" of the *bourgeois* state by the proletarian revolution, while the words about its withering away refer to the remnants of the *proletarian* state *after* the socialist revolution. According to Engels the bourgeois state does not "wither away", but is "*put an end to*" by the proletariat in the course of the revolution. What withers away after the revolution is the proletarian state or semi-state.

Secondly, the state is a "special repressive force". Engels gives this splendid and extremely profound definition here with complete lucidity. And from it follows that the "special repressive force" for the suppression of the proletariat by the bourgeoisie, for the suppression of the millions of toilers by a handful of the rich, must be superseded by a "special repressive force" for the suppression of the bourgeoisie by the proletariat (the dictatorship of the proletariat). This is precisely what is meant by putting an end to "the state as the state". This is precisely the "act" of taking possession of the means of production in the name of society. And it is obvious that such a substitution of one (proletarian) "special repressive force" for another (bourgeois) "special repressive force" cannot possibly take place in the form of "withering away".

Thirdly, in regard to the state "withering away", and the even more expressive and colourful "ceasing of itself", Engels refers quite clearly and definitely to the period *after* the state has "taken possession of the means of production in the name of society", that is, *after* the socialist revolution. We all know that the political form of the "state" at that time is the most complete democracy. But it never enters the head of any of the opportunists who shamelessly distort Marxism that Engels here speaks of *democracy* "withering away", or "ceasing of itself". This seems very strange at first sight; but it is "unintelligible" only to those who have not pondered over the fact that democracy is *also* a state and that, consequently, democracy will also disappear when the state disappears. Revolution alone can "put an end" to the bourgeois state. The state in general, i.e. the most complete democracy, can only "wither away".

Fourthly, after formulating his famous proposition that "the state withers away", Engels at once explains concretely that this proposition is directed equally against the opportunists and the anarchists. In doing this, however, Engels puts in the forefront the conclusion deduced from the proposition, the "state withers away", which is directed against the opportunists.

One can wager that out of every 10,000 persons who have read or heard about the "withering away" of the state, 9990 do not know, or do not remember, that Engels did not direct the conclusions he deduced from this proposition against the anarchists *alone*. Of the remaining ten, probably nine do not know the meaning of "free people's state" or why an attack on this watchword contains an attack on the opportunists. This is how history is written! This is how a great revolutionary doctrine is imperceptibly falsified and adapted to prevailing philistinism! The conclusion drawn against the anarchists has been repeated thousands of times, vulgarized, dinned into people's heads in the crudest fashion and has acquired the strength of a prejudice; whereas the conclusion drawn against the opportunists has been hushed up and "forgotten"!

The "free people's state" was a programme demand and a popular slogan of the German Social-Democrats in the 'seventies. The only political content of this slogan is a pompous philistine description of the concept democracy. In so far as it hinted in a lawful manner at a democratic republic, Engels was prepared to "justify" its use "for a time" from an agitational point of view. But it was an opportunist slogan, for it not only expressed an embellishment of bourgeois democracy, but also lack of understanding of the socialist criticism of the state in general. We are in favour of a democratic republic as the best form of state for the proletariat under capitalism; but we have no right to forget that wage-slavery is the lot of the people even in the most democratic bourgeois republic. Furthermore, every state is a "special repressive force" for the suppression of the oppressed class. Consequently, *no* state is a "free" or a "people's state". Marx and Engels explained this repeatedly to their party comrades in the 'seventies.

Fifthly, this very same work of Engels', of which everyone remembers the argument about the "withering away" of the state, also contains a disquisition on the significance of violent revolution. Engels' historical analysis of its role becomes a veritable panegyric on violent revolution. This "no one remembers"; it is not good form in modern Socialist Parties to talk or even think about the importance of this idea, and it plays no part whatever in their daily propaganda and agitation among the masses. And yet, it is inseparably bound up with the "withering away" of the state into one harmonious whole.

Here is Engels' argument:

That force, however, plays yet another role [other than that of a diabolical power] in history, a revolutionary role; that, in the words of Marx, it is the midwife of every old society which is pregnant with the new; that it is the instrument by the aid of which the social movement forces its way through and shatters the dead, fossilized, political forms—of this there is not a word in Herr Dühring. It is only with sighs and groans that he admits the possibility that force will perhaps be necessary for the overthrow of the economic system of exploitation—unfortunately, because all use of force, forsooth, demoralizes the person who uses it. And this in spite of the immense moral and spiritual impetus which has resulted from every victorious revolution! And this in Germany, where a violent collision—which indeed may be forced on the people—would at least have the advantage of wiping out the servility which has permeated the national consciousness as a result of the humiliation of the Thirty Years' War. And this parson's mode of thought—lifeless, insipid and impotent—claims to impose itself on the most revolutionary party which history has known!

How can this panegyric on violent revolution, which Engels insistently brought to the attention of the German Social-Democrats between 1878 and 1894, i.e. right up to the time of his death, be combined with the theory of the "withering away" of the state to form a single doctrine?

Usually the two views are combined by means of eclecticism, by an unprincipled, or sophistic, arbitrary selection (or a selection to please the powers that be) of one or another argument, and in ninety-nine cases out of a hundred (if not more often), it is the idea of the "withering away" that is specially emphasized. Eclecticism is substituted for dialectics—this is the most usual, the most widespread phenomenon to be met with in present-day official Social-Democratic literature on Marxism. This sort of substitution is not new, of course, it is observed even in the history of classic Greek philosophy. In painting Marxism to look like opportunism, the substitution of eclecticism for dialectics is the best method of deceiving the masses; it gives an illusory satisfaction; it seems to take into account all sides of the process, all tendencies of development, all the conflicting influences, and so forth, whereas in reality it presents no consistent and revolutionary conception of the process of social development at all.

We have already said above, and shall show more fully later, that the doctrine of Marx and Engels concerning the inevitability of a violent revolution refers to the bourgeois state. The latter *cannot* be superseded by the proletarian state (the dictatorship of the proletariat) in the process of "withering away"; as a general rule, this can happen only by means of a violent revolution. The panegyric Engels sang in its honour, and which fully corresponds to Marx's repeated declarations (recall the concluding passages of *The Poverty of Philosophy* and *The Communist Manifesto*, with their proud and open declaration of the inevitability of a violent revolution; recall Marx's *Critique of the Gotha*

Programme of 1875, in which, almost thirty years later, he mercilessly castigates the opportunist character of that programme)—this panegyric is by no means a mere "impulse", a mere declamation or a polemical sally. The necessity of systematically imbuing the masses with *this* and precisely this view of violent revolution lies at the root of the *whole* of Marx's and Engels' doctrine. The betrayal of their doctrine by the now predominant social-chauvinist and Kautskyan trends is brought out in striking relief by the neglect of *such* propaganda and agitation by both these trends.

The substitution of the proletarian state for the bourgeois state is impossible without a violent revolution. The abolition of the proletarian state, i.e. of the state in general, is impossible except through the process of "withering away".

State and Revolution. Chapter 1 (1917)

§4. THE ECONOMIC BASIS OF THE WITHERING AWAY OF THE STATE

LENIN

Marx explains this question most thoroughly in his *Critique of the Gotha Programme.* The polemical part of this remarkable work, consisting of a criticism of Lassalleanism, has, so to speak, overshadowed its positive part, namely, the analysis of the connexion between the development of communism and the withering away of the state.

1. Marx's Presentation of the Question

From a superficial comparison of Marx's letter to Bracke (5 May 1875) with Engels' letter to Bebel (28 March 1875), it might appear that Marx was much more "pro-state" than Engels, and that the difference of opinion between the two writers on the question of the state was very considerable.

Engels suggested to Bebel that all the chatter about the state be dropped; that the word "state" be eliminated from the programme and the word "community" substituted for it. Engels even declared that the Commune was really no longer a state in the proper sense of the word, while Marx spoke of the "future state in communist society", i.e. apparently he recognized the need for a state even under communism.

But such a view would be fundamentally wrong. A closer examination shows that Marx's and Engels' views on the state and its withering away were completely identical, and that Marx's expression quoted above refers merely to this *withering away* of the state.

Clearly, there can be no question of defining the exact moment of the *future* withering away—the more so since it must obviously be a rather lengthy process. The apparent difference between Marx and Engels is due to the different subjects they dealt with, the different aims they were pursuing. Engels set out to show Bebel plainly, sharply and in broad outline the absurdity of the prevailing prejudices concerning the state, shared to no small degree by Lassalle. Marx, on the other hand, only touched upon *this* question in passing, being interested mainly in another subject, viz. the *development* of communist society.

The whole theory of Marx is an application of the theory of development—in its most consistent, complete, thought-out and replete form —to modern capitalism. It was natural for Marx to raise the question of applying this theory both to the *forthcoming* collapse of capitalism and to the *future* development of *future* communism.

On the basis of what *data* can the question of the future development of future communism be raised?

On the basis of the fact that *it has its origin* in capitalism, that it develops historically from capitalism, that it is the result of the action of a social force to which capitalism *has given birth*. There is no trace of an attempt on Marx's part to conjure up a Utopia, to make idle guesses about what cannot be known. Marx treats the question of communism in the same way as a naturalist would treat the question of the development of, say, a new biological species, if he knew that such and such was its origin, and such and such the direction in which it was changing.

Marx, first of all, brushes aside the confusion the Gotha Programme brings into the question of the relation between state and society. He writes:

"Present-day society" is capitalist society, which exists in all civilized countries, more or less free from medieval admixture, more or less modified by the special historical development of each country and more or less developed. On the other hand the "present-day state" varies with every state boundary. It is different in the Prusso-German Empire from what it is in Switzerland, it is different in England from what it is in the United States. "The present-day state" is therefore a fiction.

Nevertheless the different states of the different civilized countries, in spite of their varied diversity of form, all have this in common that they are based on modern bourgeois society, only either more or less capitalistically developed. They have therefore also certain essential features in common. In this sense it is possible to speak of the "present-day state", in contrast to the future, in which its present root, bourgeois society, will have died away.

The question then arises: what transformation will the state undergo in communist society? In other words, what social functions will survive there analogous to the present functions of the state? This question can only be answered scientifically and one does not get a flea-hop nearer to the problem however many thousand times the word "people" is combined with the word "state".

Having thus ridiculed all talk about a "people's state", Marx formulates the question and warns us, as it were, that to arrive at a scientific answer one must rely only on firmly established scientific data.

The first fact that has been established with complete exactitude by the whole theory of development, by science as a whole—a fact which the Utopians forgot, and which is forgotten by present-day opportunists who are afraid of the socialist revolution—is that, historically, there must undoubtedly be a special stage or epoch of *transition* from capitalism to communism.

2. THE TRANSITION FROM CAPITALISM TO COMMUNISM

Marx continues:

Between capitalist and communist society lies the period of the revolutionary transformation of the one into the other. There corresponds to this also a political transition period in which the state can be nothing but *the revolutionary dictatorship of the proletariat.*

Marx bases this conclusion on an analysis of the role played by the proletariat in modern capitalist society, on the data concerning the development of this society, and on the irreconcilability of the antagonistic interests of the proletariat and the bourgeoisie.

Earlier the question was put in this way: in order to achieve its emancipation, the proletariat must overthrow the bourgeoisie, conquer political power and establish its own revolutionary dictatorship.

Now the question is put somewhat differently: the transition from capitalist society—which is developing towards communism—to a communist society is impossible without a "political transition period", and the state in this period can only be the revolutionary dictatorship of the proletariat.

What, then, is the relation of this dictatorship to democracy?

We have seen that *The Communist Manifesto* simply places the two ideas side by side: "to raise the proletariat to the position of the ruling class" and "to win the battle of democracy". On the basis of all that has been said above, it is possible to determine more precisely how democracy changes in the transition from capitalism to communism.

In capitalist society, under the conditions most favourable to its development, we have more or less complete democracy in the democratic republic. But this democracy is always restricted by the narrow framework of capitalist exploitation, and consequently always remains, in reality, a democracy for the minority, only for the possessing classes, only for the rich. Freedom in capitalist society always remains about the same as it was in the ancient Greek republics: freedom for the slave-owners. Owing to the conditions of capitalist exploitation the modern wage-slaves are also so crushed by want and poverty that "they cannot be bothered with democracy", "they cannot be bothered with politics"; in the ordinary peaceful course of events the majority of the population is debarred from participating in social and political life.

The correctness of this statement is perhaps most clearly proved by Germany, precisely because in that country constitutional legality lasted and remained stable for a remarkably long time—for nearly half a century (1871–1914)—and because during this period Social-Democracy was able to achieve far more in Germany than in other countries in the way of "utilizing legality", and was able to organize a larger proportion of the working class into a political party than anywhere else in the world.

What is this largest proportion of politically conscious and active wage-slaves that has so far been observed in capitalist society? One million members of the Social-Democratic Party—out of fifteen million wage-workers! Three million organized in trade unions—out of fifteen million!

Democracy for an insignificant minority, democracy for the rich— that is the democracy of capitalist society. If we look more closely into the mechanism of capitalist democracy, everywhere, in the "petty"— so-called petty—details of the suffrage (residential qualification, exclusion of women, etc.), and in the technique of the representative institutions, in the actual obstacles to the right of assembly (public buildings are not for "beggars"!), in the purely capitalist organization of the daily press, etc., etc.—on all sides we see restriction after restriction upon democracy. These restrictions, exceptions, exclusions, obstacles for the poor, seem slight, especially in the eyes of one who has never known want himself and has never been in close contact with the oppressed classes in their mass life (and nine-tenths, if not ninety-nine hundredths, of the bourgeois publicists and politicians are of this category); but in their sum total these restrictions exclude and squeeze out the poor from politics, from taking an active part in democracy.

Marx grasped this *essence* of capitalist democracy splendidly, when, in analysing the experience of the Commune, he said that the oppressed were allowed, once every few years, to decide which particular representatives of the oppressing class should misrepresent them in parliament!

But from this capitalist democracy—inevitably narrow, tacitly repelling the poor, and therefore hypocritical and false to the core—development does not proceed simply, smoothly and directly to "greater and greater democracy", as the liberal professors and petty-bourgeois opportunists would have us believe. No, development—towards communism—proceeds through the dictatorship of the proletariat; it cannot do otherwise, for the *resistance* of the capitalist exploiters cannot be *broken* by anyone else or in any other way.

But the dictatorship of the proletariat, i.e. the organization of the vanguard of the oppressed as the ruling class for the purpose of crushing the oppressors, cannot result merely in an expansion of democracy. *Simultaneously* with an immense expansion of democracy which *for the first time* becomes democracy for the poor, democracy for the people, and not democracy for the rich, the dictatorship of the proletariat imposes a series of restrictions on the freedom of the oppressors, the exploiters, the capitalists. We must crush them in order to free humanity from wage-slavery; their resistance must be broken by force; it is clear that where there is suppression there is also violence, there is no freedom, no democracy.

Engels expressed this splendidly in his letter to Bebel when he said, as the reader will remember, that

so long as the proletariat still *uses* the state it does not use it in the interests of freedom but in order to hold down its adversaries, and as soon as it becomes possible to speak of freedom the state as such ceases to exist.

Democracy for the vast majority of the people, and suppression by force, i.e. exclusion from democracy, of the exploiters and oppressors of the people—this is the change democracy undergoes during the *transition* from capitalism to communism.

Only in communist society, when the resistance of the capitalists has been completely broken, when the capitalists have disappeared, when there are no classes (i.e. when there is no difference between the members of society as regards their relation to the social means of production), *only then* does "the state...cease to exist", and it "*becomes possible to speak of freedom*". Only then will really complete democracy, democracy without any exceptions, be possible and be realized. And only then will democracy itself begin to *wither away* owing to the simple fact that, freed from capitalist slavery, from the untold horrors, savagery, absurdities and infamies of capitalist exploitation, people will gradually *become accustomed* to observing the elementary rules of social life that have been known for centuries and repeated for thousands of years in all copy-book maxims; they will become accustomed to observing them without force, without compulsion, without subordination, without the *special apparatus* for compulsion which is called the state.

The expression "the state *withers away*" is very well chosen, for it indicates both the gradual and the spontaneous nature of the process. Only habit can, and undoubtedly will, have such an effect; for we see around us millions of times how readily people become accustomed to observing the necessary rules of social life if there is no exploitation, if there is nothing that causes indignation, that calls forth protest and revolt and has to be *suppressed*.

Thus, in capitalist society we have a democracy that is curtailed, wretched, false; a democracy only for the rich, for the minority. The dictatorship of the proletariat, the period of transition to communism, will, for the first time, create democracy for the people, for the majority, in addition to the necessary suppression of the minority—the exploiters. Communism alone is capable of giving really complete democracy, and the more complete it is the more quickly will it become unnecessary and wither away of itself.

In other words: under capitalism we have a state in the proper sense of the word, that is, a special machine for the suppression of one class by another, and of the majority by the minority at that. Naturally, the successful discharge of such a task as the systematic suppression of the exploited majority by the exploiting minority calls for the greatest ferocity and savagery in the work of suppression, it calls for seas of blood through which mankind has to wade in slavery, serfdom and wage-labour.

Furthermore, during the *transition* from capitalism to communism, suppression is *still* necessary; but it is the suppression of the exploiting minority by the exploited majority. A special apparatus, a special machine for suppression, the "state", is *still* necessary, but this is now a transitory state; it is no longer a state in the proper sense; for the suppression of the minority of exploiters by the majority of the wage-slaves *of yesterday* is comparatively so easy, simple and natural a task that it will entail far less bloodshed than the suppression of the risings of slaves, serfs or wage-labourers, and it will cost mankind far less. This is compatible with the diffusion of democracy among such an overwhelming majority of the population that the need for a *special machine* of suppression will begin to disappear. The exploiters are, naturally, unable to suppress the people without a very complex machine for performing this task; but *the people* can suppress the exploiters with a very simple "machine", almost without a "machine", without a special apparatus, by the simple *organization of the armed masses* (such as the Soviets of Workers' and Soldiers' Deputies, we may remark, running ahead a little).

Finally, only communism makes the state absolutely unnecessary, for there is *no one* to be suppressed—"no one" in the sense of a *class*, in the sense of a systematic struggle against a definite section of the population. We are not Utopians, and we do not in the least deny the possibility and inevitability of excesses on the part of *individual persons*, or the need to suppress *such excesses*. But, in the first place, no special machine, no special apparatus of repression is needed for this: this will be done by the armed people itself, as simply and as readily as any crowd of civilized people, even in modern society, parts two people who are fighting, or interferes to prevent a woman from being assaulted. And, secondly, we know that the fundamental social cause of excesses, which consist in violating the rules of social life, is the exploitation of the masses, their want and their poverty. With the removal of this chief cause, excesses will inevitably begin to "*wither away*". We do not know how quickly and in what order, but we know that they will wither away. With their withering away, the state will also *wither away*.

Without dropping into Utopias, Marx defined more fully what can be defined *now* regarding this future, namely the difference between the lower and higher phases (degrees, stages) of communist society.

3. THE FIRST PHASE OF COMMUNIST SOCIETY

In the *Critique of the Gotha Programme*, Marx goes into some detail to disprove Lassalle's idea that under socialism the worker will receive the "undiminished" or "whole proceeds of his labour". Marx shows that from the whole of the social labour of society it is necessary to deduct a reserve fund, a fund for the expansion of production, for the replacement of "worn-out" machinery, and so on; then, also, from the means of consumption must be deducted a fund for the expenses of management, for schools, hospitals, homes for the aged, and so on.

Instead of Lassalle's hazy, obscure, general phrase—"the whole proceeds of his labour to the worker"—Marx makes a sober estimate of exactly how socialist society will have to manage its affairs. Marx proceeds to make a *concrete* analysis of the conditions of life of a society in which there is no capitalism, and says:

What we have to deal with here [in analysing the programme of the Party] is a communist society not as it has *developed* on its own foundations, but on the contrary as it *emerges from capitalist society*; which is thus in every respect economically, morally and intellectually still stamped with the birthmarks of the old society from whose womb it emerges.

And it is this communist society—a society which has just come into the world out of the womb of capitalism and which, in every respect, bears the birth-marks of the old society—that Marx terms the "first", or lower, phase of communist society.

The means of production are no longer the private property of individuals. The means of production belong to the whole of society. Every member of society, performing a certain part of socially-necessary labour, receives a certificate from society to the effect that he has done such and such an amount of work. According to this certificate, he receives from the public warehouses, where articles of consumption are stored, a corresponding quantity of products. Deducting that proportion of labour which goes to the public fund, every worker, therefore, receives from society as much as he has given it.

"Equal right" seems to reign supreme.

But when Lassalle, having such a social order in view (generally called socialism, but termed by Marx the first phase of communism), speaks of this as "equitable distribution", and says that this is "the equal right" of "all members of society" to "equal proceeds of labour", he is mistaken, and Marx exposes his error.

"Equal right", says Marx, we indeed have here; but it is *still* a "bourgeois right", which, like every right, *presupposes inequality*. Every right is an application of the *same* measure to *different* people who, in fact, are not the same and are not equal to one another; that is why "equal right" is really a violation of equality and an injustice. As a matter of fact, every man having performed as much social labour as another receives an equal share of the social product (less the above-mentioned deductions).

But people are not alike: one is strong, another is weak; one is married, another is not; one has more children, another has less, and so on. And the conclusion Marx draws is:

...with an equal output and hence an equal share in the social consumption fund, one will in fact receive more than another, one will be richer than another and so on. To avoid all these defects, right, instead of being equal, would have to be unequal.

Hence, the first phase of communism cannot produce justice and equality; differences, and unjust differences, in wealth will still exist, but the *exploitation* of man by man will have become impossible, because it will be impossible to seize the *means of production*, the factories, machines, land, etc., as private property. In smashing Lassalle's petty-bourgeois, confused phrases about "equality" and "justice" *in general*, Marx shows the *course of development* of communist society, which, at first, is compelled to abolish *only* the "injustice" of the means of production having been seized by private individuals and which *cannot* at once abolish the other injustice of the distribution of articles of consumption "according to the amount of work performed" (and not according to needs).

The vulgar economists, including the bourgeois professors and also "our" Tugan-Baranovsky, constantly reproach the Socialists with forgetting the inequality of people and with "dreaming" of abolishing this inequality. Such a reproach, as we see, only proves the extreme ignorance of Messieurs the bourgeois ideologists.

Marx not only scrupulously takes into account the inevitable inequality of men; he also takes into account the fact that the mere conversion of the means of production into the common property of the whole of society (generally called "socialism") *does not remove* the defects of distribution and the inequality of "bourgeois right" which *continue to prevail* as long as the products are divided "according to the amount of work performed". Continuing, Marx says:

> But these defects are inevitable in the first phase of communist society as it is when it has just emerged after prolonged birth-pangs from capitalist society. Right can never be higher than the economic structure of society and the cultural development thereby determined.

And so, in the first phase of communist society (generally called socialism) "bourgeois right" is *not* abolished in its entirety, but only in part, only in proportion to the economic transformation so far attained, i.e. only in respect of the means of production. "Bourgeois right" recognizes them as the private property of separate individuals. Socialism converts them into *common* property. *To that extent*, and to that extent alone, "bourgeois right" disappears.

However, it continues to exist so far as its other part is concerned; it remains in the capacity of regulator (determining factor) in the distribution of products and allotment of labour among the members of society. The socialist principle: "He who does not work, neither shall he eat", is *already* realized; the other socialist principle: "An equal amount of labour for an equal quantity of products", is also *already* realized. But this is not yet communism, and it does not abolish "bourgeois right", which gives to unequal individuals, in return for an unequal (actually unequal) amount of work, an equal quantity of products.

This is a "defect", says Marx, but it is unavoidable in the first phase of communism; for if we are not to fall into Utopianism, we cannot imagine that, having overthrown capitalism, people will at once learn to work for society *without any standard of right*; indeed, the abolition of capitalism *does not immediately* create the economic prerequisites for *such* a change.

And there is as yet no other standard than that of "bourgeois right". To this extent, therefore, there is still need for a state, which, while safeguarding the public ownership of the means of production, would safeguard the equality of labour and equality in the distribution of products.

The state withers away in so far as there are no longer any capitalists, any classes, and consequently, no *class* can be *suppressed*.

But the state has not yet completely withered away, since there still remains the protection of "bourgeois right" which sanctifies actual inequality. For the complete withering away of the state, complete communism is necessary.

4. THE HIGHER PHASE OF COMMUNIST SOCIETY

Marx continues:

In a higher phase of communist society after the enslaving subordination of individuals under division of labour and therewith the antithesis between mental and physical labour has vanished; after labour has become not merely a means to live but has become itself the primary necessity of life; after the productive forces have also increased with the all-round development of the individual, and all the springs of co-operative wealth flow more abundantly —only then can the narrow horizon of bourgeois right be fully left behind and society inscribe on its banner: from each according to his ability, to each according to his needs!

Only now can we appreciate to the full the correctness of Engels' remarks in which he mercilessly ridiculed the absurdity of combining the words "freedom" and "state". While the state exists there is no freedom. When freedom exists, there will be no state.

The economic basis for the complete withering away of the state is the high stage of development of communism in which the antithesis between mental and physical labour disappears, that is to say, when one of the principal sources of modern *social* inequality—a source, moreover, which cannot be removed immediately by the mere conversion of the means of production into public property, by the mere expropriation of the capitalists—disappears.

This expropriation will *facilitate* the enormous development of the productive forces. And seeing how capitalism is already *retarding* this development to an incredible degree, seeing how much progress could be achieved even on the basis of the present level of modern technique, we have a right to say with the fullest confidence that the expropriation of the capitalists will inevitably result in an enormous development of the productive forces of human society. But how rapidly this development will proceed, how soon it will reach the point of breaking away from the division of labour, of removing the antithesis between mental and physical labour, of transforming work into the "primary necessity of life"—we do not and *cannot* know.

That is why we have a right to speak only of the inevitable withering away of the state; we must emphasize the protracted nature of this process and its dependence upon the rapidity of development of the *higher phase* of communism; and we leave the question of length of time, or the concrete forms of the withering away, quite open, because *no material is available* to enable us to answer these questions.

The state will be able to wither away completely when society can apply the rule: "From each according to his ability, to each according to his needs", i.e. when people have become so accustomed to observing the fundamental rules of social life and when their labour is so productive that they will voluntarily work *according to their ability*. "The narrow horizon of bourgeois right", which compels one to calculate with the shrewdness of a Shylock whether he has not worked half an hour more than another, whether he is not getting less pay than another —this narrow horizon will then be left behind. There will then be no need for society to make an exact calculation of the quantity of products to be distributed to each of its members; each will take freely "according to his needs".

From the bourgeois point of view, it is easy to declare such a social order to be "a pure Utopia", and to sneer at the Socialists for promising everyone the right to receive from society, without any control of the labour of the individual citizen, any quantity of truffles, automobiles, pianos, etc. Even now, most bourgeois "savants" make shift with such sneers, thereby displaying at once their ignorance and their selfish defence of capitalism.

Ignorance—for it has never entered the head of any Socialist to "promise" that the higher phase of communism will arrive; and the great Socialists, in *foreseeing* its arrival, presupposed both a productivity of labour unlike the present and a person *unlike the present* man-in-the-street who, like the seminary students in Pomyalovsky's story, is capable of damaging the stores of social wealth "just for fun", and of demanding the impossible.

Until the "higher" phase of communism arrives, the Socialists demand the *strictest* control, by society *and by the state*, of the amount of labour and the amount of consumption; but this control must *start* with the expropriation of the capitalists, with the establishment of workers' control over the capitalists, and must be carried out, not by a state of bureaucrats, but by a state of *armed workers*.

The selfish defence of capitalism by the bourgeois ideologists (and their hangers-on, like Messrs Tseretelli, Chernov and Co.) lies in their *substituting* controversies and discussions about the distant future for the essential imperative questions of *present-day* policy, viz. the expropriation of the capitalists, the conversion of *all* citizens into workers and employees of *one* huge "syndicate"—the whole state—and the complete subordination of the whole of the work of this syndicate to the really democratic state of the *Soviets of Workers' and Soldiers' Deputies.*

In reality, when a learned professor, and following him some philistine, and following the latter Messrs Tseretelli and Chernov, talk of the unreasonable Utopias, of the demagogic promises of the Bolsheviks, of the impossibility of "introducing" socialism, it is the higher stage or phase of communism which they have in mind, and which no one has ever promised, or has even thought of "introducing", because, generally speaking, it cannot be "introduced".

And this brings us to the question of the scientific difference between socialism and communism which Engels touched on in his above-quoted argument about the incorrectness of the name "Social-Democrat". The political difference between the first, or lower, and the higher phase of communism will in time, no doubt, be tremendous; but it would be ridiculous to take cognizance of this difference now, under capitalism; only some isolated anarchist, perhaps, could invest it with primary importance (if there are still any people among the anarchists who have learned nothing from the "Plekhanovist" conversion of the Kropotkins, the Graveses, the Cornelisens and other "leading lights" of anarchism into social-chauvinists or "anarcho-*Jusquaubout*-ists", as Gé, one of the few anarchists who has still preserved a sense of honour and a conscience, has expressed it).

But the scientific difference between socialism and communism is clear. What is generally called socialism was termed by Marx the "first" or lower phase of communist society. In so far as the means of production become *common* property, the word "communism" is also applicable here, providing we do not forget that it is *not* complete communism. The great significance of Marx's explanations lies in that here, too, he consistently applies materialist dialectics, the theory of development, and regards communism as something which develops *out of* capitalism. Instead of scholastically invented, "concocted" definitions and fruitless disputes about words (What is socialism? What is communism?), Marx gives an analysis of what may be called stages in the economic ripeness of communism.

In its first phase, or first stage, communism *cannot* as yet be economically ripe and entirely free from all the traditions and all traces of capitalism. Hence the interesting phenomenon that communism in its first phase retains "the narrow horizon of *bourgeois* right". Of course, bourgeois right in regard to distribution of articles of *consumption* inevitably presupposes the existence of the *bourgeois state*, for right is nothing without an apparatus capable of *enforcing* the observance of the standards of right.

Consequently, for a certain time not only bourgeois right, but even the bourgeois state remains under communism, without the bourgeoisie!

This may sound like a paradox or simply a dialectical puzzle which Marxism is often accused of inventing by people who would not take the slightest trouble to study its extraordinarily profound content.

As a matter of fact, however, the remnants of the old surviving in the new confront us in life at every step, in nature as well as in society. Marx did not smuggle a scrap of "bourgeois" right into communism of his own accord; he indicated what is economically and politically inevitable in the society which is emerging *from the womb* of capitalism.

Democracy is of great importance for the working class in its struggle for freedom against the capitalists. But democracy is by no means a boundary that must not be overstepped; it is only one of the stages in the process of development from feudalism to capitalism, and from capitalism to communism.

Democracy means equality. The great significance of the proletariat's struggle for equality and the significance of equality as a slogan will be clear if we correctly interpret it as meaning the abolition of *classes*. But democracy means only *formal* equality. As soon as equality is obtained for all members of society *in relation to* the ownership of the means of production, that is, equality of labour and equality of wages, humanity will inevitably be confronted with the question of going beyond formal equality to real equality, i.e. to applying the rule, "from each according to his ability, to each according to his needs". By what stages, by what practical measures humanity will proceed to this higher aim—we do not and cannot know. But it is important to realize how infinitely mendacious is the ordinary bourgeois conception of socialism as something lifeless, petrified, fixed once for all, whereas in reality *only* under socialism will a rapid, genuine, really mass movement, embracing first the majority and then the whole of the population, commence in all spheres of social and individual life.

Democracy is a form of state, one of its varieties. Consequently, like every state, it, on the one hand, represents the organized, systematic application of force against persons; but, on the other hand, it signifies the formal recognition of the equality of all citizens, the equal right of all to determine the structure and administration of the state. This, in turn, is connected with the fact that, at a certain stage in the development of democracy, it first rallies the proletariat as a revolutionary class against capitalism, and gives it the opportunity to crush, to smash to atoms, to wipe off the face of the earth the bourgeois, even the republican bourgeois, state machine, the standing army, the police and bureaucracy; to substitute for all this a *more* democratic, but still a state machine in the shape of the armed masses of workers who become transformed into a universal people's militia.

Here "quantity is transformed into quality"; *such* a degree of democracy is connected with overstepping the boundaries of bourgeois society, with the beginning of its socialist reconstruction. If, indeed, *all* take part in the administration of the state, capitalism cannot retain its hold. The development of capitalism, in turn, itself creates the *pre-requisites* that *enable* indeed "all" to take part in the administration of the state. Some of these prerequisites are: universal literacy, already achieved in most of the advanced capitalist countries, then the "training and disciplining" of millions of workers by the huge, complex and socialized apparatus of the post-office, the railways, the big factories, large-scale commerce, banking, etc., etc.

With such *economic* prerequisites it is quite possible, immediately, overnight, after the overthrow of the capitalists and bureaucrats, to supersede them in the *control* of production and distribution, in the work of *keeping account* of labour and its products by the armed workers, by the whole of the armed population. (The question of control and accounting must not be confused with the question of the scientifically educated staff of engineers, agronomists and so on. These gentlemen are working to-day and obey the capitalists; they will work even better to-morrow and obey the armed workers.)

Accounting and control—these are the *principal* things that are necessary for the "setting-up" and correct functioning of the *firs phase* of communist society. *All* citizens are transformed into the salaried employees of the state, which consists of the armed workers. *All* citizens become employees and workers of a *single* national state "syndicate". All that is required is that they should work equally—do their proper share of work—and get paid equally. The accounting and control necessary for this have been so utterly *simplified* by capitalism that they have become the extraordinarily simple operations of checking, recording and issuing receipts, which anyone who can read and write and who knows the first four rules of arithmetic can perform.

When the *majority* of the people themselves begin everywhere to keep such accounts and maintain such control over the capitalists (now converted into employees) and over the intellectual gentry, who preserve their capitalist habits, this control will really become universal, general, national; and there will be no way of getting away from it, there will be "nowhere to go".

The whole of society will have become a single office and a single factory with equality of work and equality of pay.

But this "factory" discipline, which the proletariat will extend to the whole of society after the defeat of the capitalists and the overthrow of the exploiters, is by no means our ideal, or our ultimate goal. It is but a necessary *step* for the purpose of thoroughly purging society of all the hideousness and foulness of capitalist exploitation, *and for the purpose of advancing further.*

From the moment all members of society, or even only the over-whelming majority, have learned to administer the state *themselves*, have taken this business into their own hands, have "set up" control over the insignificant minority of capitalists, over the gentry, who wish to preserve their capitalist habits, and over the workers who have been completely demoralized by capitalism—from this moment the need for government begins to disappear. The more complete democracy becomes, the nearer the moment approaches when it becomes unnecessary. The more democratic the "state" of the armed workers—which is "no longer a state in the proper sense of the word"—becomes, the more rapidly does *the state* begin to wither away.

For when *all* have learned the art of administration, and will indeed independently administer social production, will independently keep accounts, control the idlers, the gentlefolk, the swindlers and similar "guardians of capitalist traditions", the escape from this national accounting and control will inevitably become so increasingly difficult, such a rare exception, and will probably be accompanied by such swift and severe punishment (for the armed workers are practical men and not sentimental intellectuals, and they will scarcely allow anyone to trifle with them), that very soon the *necessity* of observing the simple, fundamental rules of human intercourse will become a *habit*.

The door will then be wide open for the transition from the first phase of communist society to its higher phase, and with it to the complete withering away of the state.

State and Revolution. Chapter v (1917)

§5. EQUALITY IN THE COMMUNIST SOCIETY

KARL MARX

Within the co-operative commonwealth based on the social ownership of the means of production, the producers do not exchange their products; just as little does the labour embodied in the products appear here as the *value* of these products, as a material quality possessed by them, since now, in contrast to capitalist society, the individual labour no longer exists as an indirectly but as a directly constituent part of the total labour. The phrase "proceeds of labour" is objectionable nowadays any way on account of its ambiguity and has thus lost any meaning it ever had.

What we have to deal with here is a communist society, not as if it had *developed on a basis of its own,* but on the contrary as *it emerges from capitalist society,* which is thus in every respect economically, morally and intellectually still stamped with the birthmarks of the old society from whose womb it is emerging. In this way the individual producer receives back again from society, with deductions, exactly what he gives. What he has given to society is his individual amount of labour. For example, the social working-day consists of the sum of the individuals' hours of work. The individual working-time of the individual producer is that part of the social working-day contributed by him, his part thereof. He receives from society a voucher that he has contributed such and such a quantity of work (after deduction from his work for the common fund) and draws through this voucher on the social storehouse as much of the means of consumption as the same quantity of work costs. The same amount of work which he has given to society in one form, he receives back in another.

Here obviously the same principle prevails as that which regulates the exchange of commodities so far as this exchange is of equal values. Content and form are changed because under the changed conditions no one can contribute anything except his labour and, on the other hand, nothing can pass into the possession of individuals except individual objects of consumption. But, so far as the distribution of the latter among individual producers is concerned, the same principle prevails as in the exchange of commodity-equivalents, i.e. equal quantities of labour in one form are exchanged for equal quantities of labour in another form.

The equal right is here still based on the same principle as bourgeois right, although principle and practice are no longer at daggers drawn, while the exchange of equivalents in commodity exchange only exists *for the average* and not for the individual case.

In spite of this advance, this *equal right* is still continually handicapped by bourgeois limitations. The right of the producers is *proportional* to the amount of labour they contribute; the equality consists in the fact that everything is measured by an *equal measure*, labour.

But one man will excel another physically or intellectually and so contributes in the same time more labour, or can labour for a longer time; and labour, to serve as a measure, must be defined by its duration or intensity, otherwise it ceases to be a standard measure. This *equal* right is an unequal right for unequal work. It recognizes no class differences because every worker ranks as a worker like his fellows, but it tacitly recognizes unequal individual endowment, and thus capacities for production, as natural privileges. It is therefore a right of unequality in its content, as in general is every right. Right can by its very nature only consist in the application of an equal standard; but unequal individuals (and they would not be different individuals if they were not unequal) are only measurable by an equal standard in so far as they can be brought under an equal observation, be regarded from one *definite* aspect only, e.g. in the case under review, they must be considered *only as workers* and nothing more be seen in them, everything else being ignored. Further, one worker is married, another single, one has more children than another and so on. Given an equal capacity for labour and thence an equal share in the funds for social consumption, the one will in practice receive more than the other, the one will be richer than the other and so forth. To avoid all these inconveniences, rights must be unequal instead of being equal.

But these deficiencies are unavoidable in the first phase of communist society when it is just emerging after prolonged birth-pangs from capitalist society. Right can never be higher than the economic structure and the cultural development of society conditioned by it.

In a higher phase of communist society, after the tyrannical sub-ordination of individuals according to the distribution of labour and thereby also the distinction between manual and intellectual work, have disappeared, after labour has become not merely a means to live but is in itself the first necessity of living, after the powers of production have also increased and all the springs of co-operative wealth are gushing more freely together with the all-round development of the individual, then and only then can the narrow horizon of bourgeois rights be left far behind and society inscribe on its banner: "From each according to his capacity, to each according to his need."

From *Critique of the Gotha Programme* (1875)

§6. DECLARATION OF THE RIGHTS OF THE LABOURING AND EXPLOITED PEOPLES[1]

LENIN

1. Russia is declared a republic of soviets of workers, soldiers and peasants' deputies. All central and local authority is invested in these soviets.

2. The Russian Soviet Republic is established on the basis of a free union of free nations, as a federation of national soviet republics.

3. Within the fundamental aim of suppressing all exploitation of man by man, of abolishing for ever the division of society into classes, of ruthlessly suppressing all exploiters, of bringing about the socialist organization of society and the triumph of socialism in all countries, the Third All-Russian Congress of Soviets of workers, soldiers and peasants' deputies further decrees:

(*a*) In order to establish the socialization of land, private ownership of land is abolished; all land is declared national property and is handed over to the labouring masses, without compensation, on the basis of an equitable division giving the right of use only.

(*b*) All forests, underground mineral wealth, and waters of national importance, all live-stock and appurtenances together with all model farms and agricultural enterprises are proclaimed national property.

(*c*) As the first step towards the complete transfer of factories, works, shops, mines, railways and other means of production and of

[1] This translation is taken from W. S. Batsell, *Soviet Rule in Russia*, by permission of the Macmillan Company, publishers.

transport to the ownership of the workers' and peasants' Soviet Republic, and in order to ensure the supremacy of the labouring masses over the exploiters, the Congress ratifies the soviet law on the workers' control of industry, and that on the Supreme Economic Council.

Preamble to the Fundamental Law of 10 *July* 1918

§7. THE CONSTITUTION OF THE U.S.S.R., 1936

THE STRUCTURE OF SOCIETY

Article 1. The Union of Soviet Socialist Republics is a socialist state of workers and peasants.

Article 2. The political foundation of the U.S.S.R. consists of soviets of working people's deputies, which grew up and became strong as a result of the overthrow of the power of landlords and capitalists and the winning of the dictatorship of the proletariat.

Article 3. All power in the U.S.S.R. belongs to the working people of town and country as represented by soviets of working people's deputies.

Article 4. The economic foundation of the U.S.S.R. consists of the socialist economic system and the socialist ownership of the tools and means of production, firmly established as a result of the liquidation of the capitalist economic system, the abolition of private ownership of the tools and means of production, and the abolition of the exploitation of man by man.

Article 5. Socialist property in the U.S.S.R. has either the form of State property (the wealth of the whole people) or the form of co-operative-collective property (property of separate collective farms, property of co-operative associations).

Article 6. The land, its deposits, waters, forests, mills, factories, mines, railways, water and air transport, banks, means of communication, large state-organized farm enterprises (state farms, machine-tractor stations, etc.) and also the basic housing facilities in cities and industrial localities are state property, that is, the wealth of the whole people.

Article 7. Public enterprises in collective farms and co-operative organizations, with their livestock and equipment, products raised or manufactured by the collective farms or co-operative organizations, as well as their public structures, constitute the public, socialist property of the collective farms and co-operative organizations.

Aside from the basic income from socialized collective farm husbandry, every collective farm household shall have for personal use a plot of land attached to the house and, as personal property, the subsidiary husbandry of the plot, the house, the productive livestock, poultry, and small farm tools—according to the statutes of the farming artel.

Article 8. The land occupied by collective farms is secured to them without payment and without time limit, that is, for ever.

Article 9. Alongside the socialist system of economy, which is the dominant form of economy in the U.S.S.R., the law allows small-scale private enterprise of individual peasants and handicraftsmen based on their personal labour, provided there is no exploitation of the labour of others.

Article 10. The right of personal property of citizens in their income from work and in their savings, in their dwellinghouse and auxiliary husbandry, in household articles and utensils and articles for personal use and comfort, as well as the right of inheritance of personal property of citizens, is protected by law.

Article 11. The economic life of the U.S.S.R. is determined and directed by a state plan of national economy in the interests of increasing the public wealth, of steadily raising the material and cultural standard of the working people, and of strengthening the independence of the U.S.S.R. and its capacity for defence.

Article 12. Work in the U.S.S.R. is a duty and a matter of honour for every able-bodied citizen, on the principle: "He who does not work shall not eat."

In the U.S.S.R. the principle of socialism is realized: "From each according to his ability, to each according to his work."

JUSTICE AND THE COURTS

Article 102. Justice in the U.S.S.R. shall be administered by the Supreme Court of the U.S.S.R., the Supreme Courts of the constituent republics, territorial and provincial courts, courts of autonomous republics and autonomous provinces, special courts of the U.S.S.R. created by resolution of the Supreme Soviet of the U.S.S.R., and the people's courts.

Article 103. Cases in all courts shall be tried with the participation of people's associate judges except in cases specially provided for by law.

Article 109. The people's courts shall be elected for a term of three years by the citizens of the district, by secret vote, on the basis of universal, direct and equal suffrage.

Article 111. In all courts of the U.S.S.R. cases shall be heard in public unless otherwise provided by law, and the accused shall be guaranteed the right of defence.

Article 112. The judges are independent and shall be subordinate only to the law.

BASIC RIGHTS AND DUTIES OF CITIZENS

Article 118. Citizens of the U.S.S.R. have the right to work, that is, the right to guaranteed employment and payment for their work in accordance with its quantity and quality.

The right to work is ensured by the socialist organization of the national economy, the steady growth of the productive forces of Soviet society, the elimination of the possibility of economic crises, and the abolition of unemployment.

Article 119. Citizens of the U.S.S.R. have the right to rest.

The right to rest is ensured by the reduction of the working day to seven hours for the overwhelming majority of the workers, the institution of annual holidays with pay for workers and other employees, and the provision of a wide network of sanatoria, rest houses and clubs serving the needs of the working people.

Article 120. Citizens of the U.S.S.R. have the right to material security in old age and also in the case of sickness or loss of capacity to work.

This right is ensured by the wide development of social insurance of workers and other employees at state expense, free medical service for the working people, and the provision of a wide network of health resorts at the disposal of the working people.

Article 121. Citizens of the U.S.S.R. have the right to education.

This right is ensured by universal compulsory elementary education, by education free of charge including higher education, by a system of state stipends for the overwhelming majority of students in higher schools, by instruction in schools in the native language, and by the organization in factories, state farms, machine-tractor stations and collective farms of free industrial, technical and agricultural education for the working people.

Article 122. Women in the U.S.S.R. are accorded equal rights with men in all spheres of economic, state, cultural, social and political life.

The realization of these rights of women is ensured by affording equally with men the right to work, payment for work, rest, social insurance and education, and by state protection of the interests of mother and child, pregnancy leave with pay, and the provision of a wide network of maternity homes, nurseries and kindergartens.

Article 123. Equal rights for citizens of the U.S.S.R., irrespective of their nationality or race, in all spheres of economic, state, cultural, social and political life, shall be an irrevocable law.

Any direct or indirect limitation of these rights, or conversely, any establishment of direct or indirect privileges for citizens on account of their race and nationality, as well as any propagation of racial or national exclusiveness or hatred and contempt, shall be punished by law.

Article 124. In order to ensure to citizens freedom of conscience, the church in the U.S.S.R. shall be separated from the state, and the school from the church. Freedom of religious worship and freedom of anti-religious propaganda shall be recognized for all citizens.

Article 125. In accordance with the interests of the working people, and in order to strengthen the socialist system, the citizens of the U.S.S.R. are guaranteed by law:

(*a*) Freedom of speech.

(*b*) Freedom of the press.

(*c*) Freedom of assembly and meetings.

(*d*) Freedom of street processions and demonstrations.

These rights of citizens are ensured by placing at the disposal of the working people and their organizations printing shops, supplies of paper, public buildings, the streets, means of communication and other material requisites for the exercise of these rights.

Article 126. In accordance with the interests of the working people, and for the purpose of developing the organized self-expression and political activity of the masses of the people, citizens of the U.S.S.R. are ensured the right to unite in public organizations—trade unions, co-operative associations, youth organizations, sport and defence organizations, cultural, technical and scientific societies; and the most active and politically conscious citizens from the ranks of the working class and other strata of the working people unite in the All-Union Communist Party (of Bolsheviks), which is the vanguard of the working people in their struggle to strengthen and develop the socialist system and which represents the leading nucleus of all organizations of the working people, both social and state.

Article 127. Citizens of the U.S.S.R. are guaranteed inviolability of the person. No one may be subject to arrest except by an order of the court or with the sanction of a state attorney.

Article 128. The inviolability of the houses of citizens and secrecy of correspondence are protected by law.

Article 129. The U.S.S.R. grants the right of asylum to foreign citizens persecuted for defending the interests of the working people or for scientific activity or for their struggle for national liberation.

Article 130. It is the duty of every citizen of the U.S.S.R. to observe the constitution of the Union of Soviet Socialist Republics, to carry out the laws, to maintain labour discipline, honestly to perform his public duties and to respect the rules of the socialist community.

Article 131. It is the duty of every citizen to safeguard and strengthen public socialist property as the sacred and inviolable foundation of the Soviet system, as the source of the wealth and the might of the fatherland, as the source of the prosperous and cultural life of all the working people.

Persons making attacks on public socialist property shall be regarded as enemies of the people.

Article 132. Universal military duty shall be the law.

Military service in the Workers' and Peasants' Red Army represents an honourable duty of the citizens of the U.S.S.R.

Article 133. The defence of the fatherland is the sacred duty of every citizen of the U.S.S.R. Treason to the homeland: violation of the oath, desertion to the enemy, impairing the military might of the state, espionage: shall be punished with the full severity of the law as the gravest crime.

THE ELECTORAL SYSTEM

Article 134. Election of deputies to all the soviets of working people's deputies . . . shall be effected by vote on the basis of universal, equal and direct suffrage, by secret ballot.

Article 135. The elections of deputies shall be universal: all the citizens of the U.S.S.R. who have reached the age of 18, irrespective of race and nationality, religion, educational gratifications, residence, social origin, property status or past activity, shall have the right to take part in the elections of deputies and to be elected, with the exception of insane persons and persons condemned by court with deprivation of electoral rights.

Article 136. The election of deputies shall be equal: every citizen shall have one vote; all citizens shall take part in the elections on an equal basis.

Article 137. Women shall have the right to elect and to be elected on equal terms with men.

Article 140. The voting at elections of deputies shall be secret.

Article 141. Candidates for elections shall be nominated by electoral districts.

The right to nominate candidates shall be ensured to public organizations and societies of working people; Communist Party organizations; trade unions; organizations of youth; cultural societies.

Article 142. Every deputy shall be obliged to report to the electors on his work and on the work of the soviets of working people's deputies and may at any time be recalled by a decision of a majority of the electors in the manner prescribed by law.

Moscow, 5 *December* 1936

BOOK LIST

J. Strachey. *Theory and Practice of Socialism* (1936)

L. von Mises. *Socialism* (1936)

S. and B. Webb. *Soviet Communism* (2nd edition, 1937)

A. Strong. *The New Soviet Constitution* (1937)

M. M. Bober. *Karl Marx's Interpretation of History* (1927)

IV

FASCISM

With deep erudition and great dialectical skill, Marx formulated and Lenin developed and matured the doctrinal content of contemporary Communism. For Italian Fascism, no one ever performed a like service. To be sure, writers like Alfredo Rocco, Giovanni Gentile, and Luigi Federzoni contributed to the movement more or less ample expositions of its ideological background and content. There is, however, among these commentators no full agreement, and they leave many basic questions unanswered. To be sure, too, Mussolini himself, in 1932, contributed to Volume XIV of the *Enciclopedia Italiana* a famous article entitled "The Doctrine of Fascism", which Mr Oakeshott reproduces in full in the ensuing section of this book; and, because of its authority, this document must be taken, so far as it goes, as an official statement on the subject. The article, however, is brief; prepared, moreover, by a man of no great intellectual power, it moves rather fitfully and emotionally over the surface of things, without often penetrating deeply into social phenomena after the manner of the monumental works to which one resorts for Communist and various other bodies of modern thought.

It has often been said, indeed, that Fascism has no doctrinal basis, being, instead, wholly pragmatic and empirical. Mussolini himself lent color to the charge by asserting on one occasion: "Fascism is based on reality, bolshevism is based on theory. . . . We want to be definite and real. We want to come out of the cloud of discussion and theory. My program . . . is action, not talk." At a different time, however, he conceded that even Fascism "has a doctrine, or, if you will, a particular philosophy with regard to all the questions which beset the human mind today"; and while one is privileged to doubt whether the boastful leader quite comprehended the sweep of his claim, he at least was right in asserting that his movement has had somewhat of a creed, even though arrived at largely by rationalization of experience rather than through the intellectual creativeness of a Marx or a Lenin.

As will be observed, the encyclopedia article falls into two parts —one labelled "Fundamental Ideas", the other, "Political and Social Doctrines", with the first part only a condensed abstract statement of the second. The second, indeed, may profitably be read before the first. Viewed as a whole, the document undertakes to do three things: (1) to discredit and repudiate individualistic liberalism, democracy, socialism, communism, and every idea and creed not squaring with the concept of the all-embracing, ever-enduring, and self-sufficient totalitarian state; (2) to give Fascism a positive definition in terms of its rootage in history, its concepts of human values, its own peculiar, but avowedly superior, form of "liberty", and (3) to elucidate the notion of the Fascist state as "the highest and most powerful form of personality", embracing within the orbit of its regulative and creative authority the life and action of every person in every relationship and direction.

As supplementing the *Enciclopedia* article, Mr Oakeshott includes in his collection the Charter of Labor of 1927—a sufficiently pertinent document in that the essence of it largely appears also in the article. Although, to be sure, not a legislative act in origin or in form, the Charter has now, in piecemeal fashion, been extensively translated into law; and those of its principles not yet so incorporated have been recognized by the country's highest court as morally binding in the interpretation of laws already existent. One will look into this document especially to find Fascism's position on private initiative in industry, the right of the state to intervene in economic production, the individual's obligation to perform useful work, the right of workers to organize syndicates or unions, the rights of occupational organizations of employers, the methods prescribed for settling industrial disputes, and the rôle assigned industry and labor in the slowly evolving corporative system. The antecedent law of 1926 (p. 186) forbidding strikes and lockouts is, of course, pertinent. Both documents are to be studied especially as illustrative of the extension of Fascist theory into a particularly controversial field of social and political action.

Section 5, on the press, gives some indication of the technique of subjecting newspapers and their editors to governmental regulation, but only by implication suggests the rigors of censorship which have reduced the press, in all totalitarian states, to an enslaved agency of the régime.

To Mr Oakeshott's reference list may be added: F. W. Coker, *Recent Political Thought* (1934), Chap. XVII; C. Gini, "The Scientific Basis of Fascism", *Polit. Sci. Quar.*, Mar., 1927; G. Gentile, "The Philosophic Basis of Fascism", *Foreign Affairs*, Jan., 1928; and B. Mussolini, *My Autobiography* (1928).

IV

Before 1932 there existed no official exposition of the doctrine of Fascism, but in that year an article entitled *The Doctrine of Fascism* appeared in the *Enciclopedia Italiana*. It is the work of Mussolini himself (though the first part of it, at least, shows the influence of the philosopher of Fascism, Gentile), and since 1932 it has frequently been reprinted. I give it in full because it remains the sole reliable statement of the doctrine.

For the rest I have had to depend upon passages from the laws of the present regime in Italy, the most important of which, for my purpose, is the *Charter of Labour* (1927). Dictatorship is, in Italy, a theory as well as a fact, but it has been difficult to find any satisfactory exposition of the theory. It appears to be conceived primarily in military terms; but nothing exists for Italy comparable to the elaborate doctrine of Leadership which has been developed in Germany. Consequently I have had to be content for my statement of this element of Fascist doctrine with the passing references which the official exposition of Fascist doctrine and the provisions of the Constitution of the Grand Fascist Council contain. The two versions of the *Fascist Decalogue* I have printed come from the years 1934 and 1938. They are not the only versions which have received currency from time to time in Italy; and though the differences between the two are striking, and may be important in practical politics, it is the similarities which make them important as statements of doctrine. I have included them for the insight they give into the spirit of this regime rather than for the relevance of any of the different clauses to the doctrine of Fascism.

§1. THE DOCTRINE OF FASCISM

BENITO MUSSOLINI

(i) FUNDAMENTAL IDEAS

1. Like every sound political conception, Fascism is both practice and thought; action in which a doctrine is immanent, and a doctrine which, arising out of a given system of historical forces, remains embedded in them and works there from within. Hence it has a form correlative to the contingencies of place and time, but it has also a content of thought which raises it to a formula of truth in the higher level of the history of thought. In the world one does not act spiritually as a human will dominating other wills without a conception of the transient and particular reality under which it is necessary to act, and of the permanent and universal reality in which the first has its being and its life. In order to know men it is necessary to know man; and in order to know man it is necessary to know reality and its laws. There is no concept of the State which is not fundamentally a concept of life: philosophy or intuition, a system of ideas which develops logically or is gathered up into a vision or into a faith, but which is always, at least virtually, an organic conception of the world.

2. Thus Fascism could not be understood in many of its practical manifestations as a party organization, as a system of education, as a discipline, if it were not always looked at in the light of its whole way of conceiving life, a spiritualized way. The world seen through Fascism is not this material world which appears on the surface, in which man is an individual separated from all others and standing by himself, and in which he is governed by a natural law that makes him instinctively live a life of selfish and momentary pleasure. The man of Fascism is an individual who is nation and fatherland, which is a moral law, binding together individuals and the generations into a tradition and a mission, suppressing the instinct for a life enclosed within the brief round of pleasure in order to restore within duty a higher life free from the limits of time and space: a life in which the individual, through the denial of himself, through the sacrifice of his own private interests, through death itself, realizes that completely spiritual existence in which his value as a man lies.

3. Therefore it is a spiritualized conception, itself the result of the general reaction of modern times against the flabby materialistic

positivism of the nineteenth century. Anti-positivistic, but positive: not sceptical, nor agnostic, nor pessimistic, nor passively optimistic, as are, in general, the doctrines (all negative) that put the centre of life outside man, who with his free will can and must create his own world. Fascism desires an active man, one engaged in activity with all his energies: it desires a man virilely conscious of the difficulties that exist in action and ready to face them. It conceives of life as a struggle, considering that it behoves man to conquer for himself that life truly worthy of him, creating first of all in himself the instrument (physical, moral, intellectual) in order to construct it. Thus for the single individual, thus for the nation, thus for humanity. Hence the high value of culture in all its forms (art, religion, science), and the enormous importance of education. Hence also the essential value of work, with which man conquers nature and creates the human world (economic, political, moral, intellectual).

4. This positive conception of life is clearly an ethical conception. It covers the whole of reality, not merely the human activity which controls it. No action can be divorced from moral judgement; there is nothing in the world which can be deprived of the value which belongs to everything in its relation to moral ends. Life, therefore, as conceived by the Fascist, is serious, austere, religious: the whole of it is poised in a world supported by the moral and responsible forces of the spirit. The Fascist disdains the "comfortable" life.

5. Fascism is a religious conception in which man is seen in his immanent relationship with a superior law and with an objective Will that transcends the particular individual and raises him to conscious membership of a spiritual society. Whoever has seen in the religious politics of the Fascist regime nothing but mere opportunism has not understood that Fascism besides being a system of government is also, and above all, a system of thought.

6. Fascism is an historical conception, in which man is what he is only in so far as he works with the spiritual process in which he finds himself, in the family or social group, in the nation and in the history in which all nations collaborate. From this follows the great value of tradition, in memories, in language, in customs, in the standards of social life. Outside history man is nothing. Consequently Fascism is opposed to all the individualistic abstractions of a materialistic nature like those of the eighteenth century; and it is opposed to all Jacobin utopias and innovations. It does not consider that "happiness" is

possible upon earth, as it appeared to be in the desire of the economic literature of the eighteenth century, and hence it rejects all teleological theories according to which mankind would reach a definitive stabilized condition at a certain period in history. This implies putting oneself outside history and life, which is a continual change and coming to be. Politically, Fascism wishes to be a realistic doctrine; practically, it aspires to solve only the problems which arise historically of themselves and that of themselves find or suggest their own solution. To act among men, as to act in the natural world, it is necessary to enter into the process of reality and to master the already operating forces.

7. Against individualism, the Fascist conception is for the State; and it is for the individual in so far as he coincides with the State, which is the conscience and universal will of man in his historical existence. It is opposed to classical Liberalism, which arose from the necessity of reacting against absolutism, and which brought its historical purpose to an end when the State was transformed into the conscience and will of the people. Liberalism denied the State in the interests of the particular individual; Fascism reaffirms the State as the true reality of the individual. And if liberty is to be the attribute of the real man, and not of that abstract puppet envisaged by individualistic Liberalism, Fascism is for liberty. And for the only liberty which can be a real thing, the liberty of the State and of the individual within the State. Therefore, for the Fascist, everything is in the State, and nothing human or spiritual exists, much less has value, outside the State. In this sense Fascism is totalitarian, and the Fascist State, the synthesis and unity of all values, interprets, develops and gives strength to the whole life of the people.

8. Outside the State there can be neither individuals nor groups (political parties, associations, syndicates, classes). Therefore Fascism is opposed to Socialism, which confines the movement of history within the class struggle and ignores the unity of classes established in one economic and moral reality in the State; and analogously it is opposed to class syndicalism. Fascism recognizes the real exigencies for which the socialist and syndicalist movement arose, but while recognizing them wishes to bring them under the control of the State and give them a purpose within the corporative system of interests reconciled within the unity of the State.

9. Individuals form classes according to the similarity of their interests, they form syndicates according to differentiated economic

activities within these interests; but they form first, and above all, the State, which is not to be thought of numerically as the sum-total of individuals forming the majority of a nation. And consequently Fascism is opposed to Democracy, which equates the nation to the majority, lowering it to the level of that majority; nevertheless it is the purest form of democracy if the nation is conceived, as it should be, qualitatively and not quantitatively, as the most powerful idea (most powerful because most moral, most coherent, most true) which acts within the nation as the conscience and the will of a few, even of One, which ideal tends to become active within the conscience and the will of all—that is to say, of all those who rightly constitute a nation by reason of nature, history or race, and have set out upon the same line of development and spiritual formation as one conscience and one sole will. Not a race,[1] nor a geographically determined region, but as a community historically perpetuating itself, a multitude unified by a single idea, which is the will to existence and to power: consciousness of itself, personality.

10. This higher personality is truly the nation in so far as it is the State. It is not the nation that generates the State, as according to the old naturalistic concept which served as the basis of the political theories of the national States of the nineteenth century. Rather the nation is created by the State, which gives to the people, conscious of its own moral unity, a will and therefore an effective existence. The right of a nation to independence derives not from a literary and ideal consciousness of its own being, still less from a more or less unconscious and inert acceptance of a *de facto* situation, but from an active consciousness, from a political will in action and ready to demonstrate its own rights: that is to say, from a state already coming into being. The State, in fact, as the universal ethical will, is the creator of right.

11. The nation as the State is an ethical reality which exists and lives in so far as it develops. To arrest its development is to kill it. Therefore the State is not only the authority which governs and gives the form of laws and the value of spiritual life to the wills of individuals, but it is also a power that makes its will felt abroad, making it known and respected, in other words, demonstrating the fact of its universality in all the necessary directions of its development. It is consequently organization and expansion, at least virtually. Thus it can be likened to

[1] "Race; it is an emotion, not a reality; ninety-five per cent of it is emotion." Mussolini.

the human will which knows no limits to its development and realizes itself in testing its own limitlessness.

12. The Fascist State, the highest and most powerful form of personality, is a force, but a spiritual force, which takes over all the forms of the moral and intellectual life of man. It cannot therefore confine itself simply to the functions of order and supervision as Liberalism desired. It is not simply a mechanism which limits the sphere of the supposed liberties of the individual. It is the form, the inner standard and the discipline of the whole person; it saturates the will as well as the intelligence. Its principle, the central inspiration of the human personality living in the civil community, pierces into the depths and makes its home in the heart of the man of action as well as of the thinker, of the artist as well as of the scientist: it is the soul of the soul.

13. Fascism, in short, is not only the giver of laws and the founder of institutions, but the educator and promoter of spiritual life. It wants to remake, not the forms of human life, but its content, man, character, faith. And to this end it requires discipline and authority that can enter into the spirits of men and there govern unopposed. Its sign, therefore, is the Lictors' rods, the symbol of unity, of strength and justice.

(ii) POLITICAL AND SOCIAL DOCTRINE

1. When in the now distant March of 1919 I summoned to Milan, through the columns of the *Popolo d' Italia*, my surviving supporters who had followed me since the constitution of the Fasces of Revolutionary Action, founded in January 1915, there was no specific doctrinal plan in my mind. I had known and lived through only one doctrine, that of the Socialism of 1903-4 up to the winter of 1914, almost ten years. My experience in this had been that of a follower and of a leader, but not that of a theoretician. My doctrine, even in that period, had been a doctrine of action. An unequivocal Socialism, universally accepted, did not exist after 1905, when the Revisionist Movement began in Germany under Bernstein and there was formed in opposition to that, in the see-saw of tendencies, an extreme revolutionary movement, which in Italy never emerged from the condition of mere words, whilst in Russian Socialism it was the prelude to Bolshevism. Reform, Revolution, Centralization—even the echoes of the terminology are now spent; whilst in the great river of Fascism are to be found the

streams which had their source in Sorel, Peguy, in the Lagardelle of the *Mouvement Socialiste* and the groups of Italian Syndicalists, who between 1904 and 1914 brought a note of novelty into Italian Socialism, which by that time had been devitalized and drugged by fornication with Giolitti, in *Pagine Libere* of Olivetti, *La Lupa* of Orano and *Divenire Sociale* of Enrico Leone.

In 1919, at the end of the War, Socialism as a doctrine was already dead: it existed only as hatred, it had still only one possibility, especially in Italy, that of revenge against those who had wished for the War and who should be made to expiate it. The *Popolo d' Italia* expressed it in its sub-title—"The Newspaper of Combatants and Producers". The word "producers" was already the expression of a tendency. Fascism was not given out to the wet nurse of a doctrine elaborated beforehand round a table: it was born of the need for action; it was not a party, but in its first two years it was a movement against all parties, The name which I gave to the organization defined its characteristics. Nevertheless, whoever rereads, in the now crumpled pages of the time, the account of the constituent assembly of the *Fasci italiani di Combattimento* will not find a doctrine, but a series of suggestions, of anticipations, of admonitions, which when freed from the inevitable vein of contingency, were destined later, after a few years, to develop into a series of doctrinal attitudes which made of Fascism a self-sufficient political doctrine able to face all others, both past and present. "If the bourgeoisie", I said at that time, 'thinks to find in us a lightning-conductor, it is mistaken. We must go forward in opposition to Labour. . . . We want to accustom the working classes to being under a leader, to convince them also that it is not easy to direct an industry or a commercial undertaking successfully. . . . We shall fight against technical and spiritual retrogression. . . . The successors of the present regime still being undecided, we must not be unwilling to fight for it. We must hasten; when the present regime is superseded, we must be the ones to take its place. The right of succession belongs to us because we pushed the country into the War and we lead it to victory. The present method of political representation cannot be sufficient for us, we wish for a direct representation of individual interests. . . . It might be said against this programme that it is a return to the corporations. It doesn't matter! . . . I should like, nevertheless, the Assembly to accept the claims of national syndicalism from the point of view of economics. . . . "

Is it not surprising that from the first day in the Piazza San Sepolcro there should resound the word "Corporation" which was destined in the course of the revolution to signify one of the legislative and social creations at the base of the regime?

2. The years preceding the March on Rome were years during which the necessity of action did not tolerate enquiries or complete elaborations of doctrine. Battles were being fought in the cities and villages. There were discussions, but—and this is more sacred and important—there were deaths. People knew how to die. The doctrine—beautiful, well-formed, divided into chapters and paragraphs and surrounded by a commentary—might be missing; but there was present something more decisive to supplant it—Faith. Nevertheless, he who recalls the past with the aid of books, articles, votes in Parliament, the major and the minor speeches, he who knows how to investigate and weigh evidence, will find that the foundations of the doctrine were laid while the battle was raging. It was precisely in these years that Fascist thought armed itself, refined itself, moving towards one organization of its own. The problems of the individual and the State; the problems of authority and liberty; political and social problems and those more specifically national; the struggle against liberal, democratic, socialist, Masonic, demagogic doctrines was carried on at the same time as the "punitive expeditions". But since the "system" was lacking, adversaries ingenuously denied that Fascism had any power to make a doctrine of its own, while the doctrine rose up, even though tumultuously, at first under the aspect of a violent and dogmatic negation, as happens to all ideas that break new ground, then under the positive aspect of a constructive policy which, during the years 1926, 1927, 1928, was realized in the laws and institutions of the regime.

Fascism is to-day clearly defined not only as a regime but as a doctrine. And I mean by this that Fascism to-day, self-critical as well as critical of other movements, has an unequivocal point of view of its own, a criterion, and hence an aim, in face of all the material and intellectual problems which oppress the people of the world.

3. Above all, Fascism, in so far as it considers and observes the future and the development of humanity quite apart from the political considerations of the moment, believes neither in the possibility nor in the utility of perpetual peace. It thus repudiates the doctrine of Pacifism —born of a renunciation of the struggle and an act of cowardice in the face of sacrifice. War alone brings up to their highest tension all human

energies and puts the stamp of nobility upon the peoples who have the
courage to meet it. All other trials are substitutes, which never really
put a man in front of himself in the alternative of life and death. A
doctrine, therefore, which begins with a prejudice in favour of peace is
foreign to Fascism; as are foreign to the spirit of Fascism, even though
acceptable by reason of the utility which they might have in given
political situations, all internationalistic and socialistic systems which,
as history proves, can be blown to the winds when emotional, idealistic
and practical movements storm the hearts of peoples. Fascism carries
over this anti-pacifist spirit even into the lives of individuals. The
proud motto of the *Squadrista*, "Me ne frego", written on the bandages
of a wound is an act of philosophy which is not only stoical, it is the
epitome of a doctrine that is not only political: it is education for combat,
the acceptance of the risks which it brings; it is a new way of life for
Italy. Thus the Fascist accepts and loves life, he knows nothing of
suicide and despises it; he looks on life as duty, ascent, conquest: life
which must be noble and full: lived for oneself, but above all for those
others near and far away, present and future.

4. The "demographic" policy of the regime follows from these
premises. Even the Fascist does in fact love his neighbour, but this
"neighbour" is not for him a vague and ill-defined concept; love for
one's neighbour does not exclude necessary educational severities, and
still less differentiations and distances. Fascism rejects universal concord,
and, since it lives in the community of civilized peoples, it keeps them
vigilantly and suspiciously before its eyes, it follows their states of
mind and the changes in their interests and it does not let itself be
deceived by temporary and fallacious appearances.

5. Such a conception of life makes Fascism the precise negation of
that doctrine which formed the basis of the so-called Scientific or
Marxian Socialism: the doctrine of historical Materialism, according to
which the history of human civilizations can be explained only as the
struggle of interest between the different social groups and as arising
out of change in the means and instruments of production. That
economic improvements—discoveries of raw materials, new methods
of work, scientific inventions—should have an importance of their
own, no one denies, but that they should suffice to explain human
history to the exclusion of all other factors is absurd: Fascism believes,
now and always, in holiness and in heroism, that is in acts in which no
economic motive—remote or immediate—plays a part. With this

negation of historical materialism, according to which men would be only by-products of history, who appear and disappear on the surface of the waves while in the depths the real directive forces are at work, there is also denied the immutable and irreparable "class struggle" which is the natural product of this economic conception of history, and above all it is denied that the class struggle can be the primary agent of social changes. Socialism, being thus wounded in these two primary tenets of its doctrine, nothing of it is left save the sentimental aspiration —old as humanity—towards a social order in which the sufferings and the pains of the humblest folk could be alleviated. But here Fascism rejects the concept of an economic "happiness" which would be realized socialistically and almost automatically at a given moment of economic evolution by assuring to all a maximum prosperity. Fascism denies the possibility of the materialistic conception of "happiness" and leaves it to the economists of the first half of the eighteenth century; it denies, that is, the equation of prosperity with happiness, which would transform men into animals with one sole preoccupation: that of being well-fed and fat, degraded in consequence to a merely physical existence.

6. After Socialism, Fascism attacks the whole complex of democratic ideologies and rejects them both in their theoretical premises and in their applications or practical manifestations. Fascism denies that the majority, through the mere fact of being a majority, can rule human societies; it denies that this majority can govern by means of a periodical consultation; it affirms the irremediable, fruitful and beneficent inequality of men, who cannot be levelled by such a mechanical and extrinsic fact as universal suffrage. By democratic regimes we mean those in which from time to time the people is given the illusion of being sovereign, while true effective sovereignty lies in other, perhaps irresponsible and secret, forces. Democracy is a regime without a king, but with very many kings, perhaps more exclusive, tyrannical and violent than one king even though a tyrant. This explains why Fascism, although before 1922 for reasons of expediency it made a gesture of republicanism, renounced it before the March on Rome, convinced that the question of the political forms of a State is not pre-eminent to-day, and that studying past and present monarchies, past and present Republics it becomes clear that monarchy and republic are not to be judged *sub specie aeternitatis*, but represent forms in which the political evolution, the history, the tradition, the psychology of a given country are manifested. Now Fascism overcomes the antithesis

between monarchy and republic which retarded the movements of democracy, burdening the former with every defect and defending the latter as the regime of perfection. Now it has been seen that there are inherently reactionary and absolutistic republics, and monarchies that welcome the most daring political and social innovations.

7. "Reason, Science", said Renan (who was inspired before Fascism existed) in one of his philosophical Meditations, "are products of humanity, but to expect reason directly from the people and through the people is a chimera. It is not necessary for the existence of reason that everybody should know it. In any case, if such an initiation should be made, it would not be made by means of base democracy, which apparently must lead to the extinction of every difficult culture, and every higher discipline. The principle that society exists only for the prosperity and the liberty of the individuals who compose it does not seem to conform with the plans of nature, plans in which the species alone is taken into consideration and the individual seems to be sacrificed. It is strongly to be feared lest the last word of democracy thus understood (I hasten to say that it can also be understood in other ways) would be a social state in which a degenerate mass would have no other care than to enjoy the ignoble pleasures of vulgar men."

Thus far Renan. Fascism rejects in democracy the absurd conventional lie of political equalitarianism clothed in the dress of collective irresponsibility and the myth of happiness and indefinite progress. But if democracy can be understood in other ways, that is, if democracy means not to relegate the people to the periphery of the State, then Fascism could be defined as an "organized, centralized, authoritarian democracy".

8. In face of Liberal doctrines, Fascism takes up an attitude of absolute opposition both in the field of politics and in that of economics. It is not necessary to exaggerate—merely for the purpose of present controversies—the importance of Liberalism in the past century, and to make of that which was one of the numerous doctrines sketched in that century a religion of humanity for all times, present and future. Liberalism flourished for no more than some fifteen years. It was born in 1830, as a reaction against the Holy Alliance that wished to drag Europe back to what it had been before 1789, and it had its year of splendour in 1848 when even Pius IX was a Liberal. Immediately afterwards the decay set in. If 1848 was a year of light and of poetry, 1849 was a year of darkness and of tragedy. The Republic of Rome

was destroyed by another Republic, that of France. In the same year
Marx launched the gospel of the religion of Socialism with the famous
Communist Manifesto. In 1851 Napoleon III carried out his unliberal
coup d'état and ruled over France until 1870, when he was dethroned by
a popular revolt, but as a consequence of a military defeat which ranks
among the most resounding that history can relate. The victor was
Bismarck, who never knew the home of the religion of liberty or who
were its prophets. It is symptomatic that a people of high culture like
the Germans should have been completely ignorant of the religion of
liberty during the whole of the nineteenth century. It was, there, no
more than a parenthesis, represented by what has been called the
"ridiculous Parliament of Frankfort" which lasted only a season.
Germany has achieved her national unity outside the doctrines of
Liberalism, against Liberalism, a doctrine which seems foreign to the
German soul, a soul essentially monarchical, whilst Liberalism is the
historical and logical beginning of anarchism. The stages of German
unity are the three wars of 1864, 1866 and 1870, conducted by
"Liberals" like Moltke and Bismarck. As for Italian unity, Liberalism
has had in it a part absolutely inferior to the share of Mazzini and of
Garibaldi, who were not Liberals. Without the intervention of the
unliberal Napoleon we should not have gained Lombardy, and without
the help of the unliberal Bismarck at Sadowa and Sedan, very probably
we should not have gained Venice in 1866; and in 1870 we should not
have entered Rome. From 1870–1915 there occurs the period in which
the very priests of the new creed had to confess the twilight of their
religion: defeated as it was by decadence in literature, by activism in
practice. Activism: that is to say, Nationalism, Futurism, Fascism.
The "Liberal" century, after having accumulated an infinity of Gordian
knots, tried to untie them by the hecatomb of the World War. Never
before has any religion imposed such a cruel sacrifice. Were the gods
of Liberalism thirsty for blood? Now Liberalism is about to close the
doors of its deserted temples because the peoples feel that its agnosticism
in economics, its indifferentism in politics and in morals, would lead,
as they have led, the States to certain ruin. In this way one can understand why all the political experiences of the contemporary world are
anti-Liberal, and it is supremely ridiculous to wish on that account to
class them outside of history; as if history were a hunting ground
reserved to Liberalism and its professors, as if Liberalism were the
definitive and no longer surpassable message of civilization.

9. But the Fascist repudiations of Socialism, Democracy, Liberalism must not make one think that Fascism wishes to make the world return to what it was before 1789, the year which has been indicated as the year of the beginning of the liberal-democratic age. One does not go backwards. The Fascist doctrine has not chosen De Maistre as its prophet. Monarchical absolutism is a thing of the past and so also is every theocracy. So also feudal privileges and division into impenetrable and isolated castes have had their day. The theory of Fascist authority has nothing to do with the police State. A party that governs a nation in a totalitarian way is a new fact in history. References and comparisons are not possible. Fascism takes over from the ruins of Liberal Socialistic democratic doctrines those elements which still have a living value. It preserves those that can be called the established facts of history, it rejects all the rest, that is to say the idea of a doctrine which holds good for all times and all peoples. If it is admitted that the nineteenth century has been the century of Socialism, Liberalism and Democracy, it does not follow that the twentieth must also be the century of Liberalism, Socialism and Democracy. Political doctrines pass; peoples remain. It is to be expected that this century may be that of authority, a century of the "Right", a Fascist century. If the nineteenth was the century of the individual (Liberalism means individualism) it may be expected that this one may be the century of "collectivism" and therefore the century of the State. That a new doctrine should use the still vital elements of other doctrines is perfectly logical. No doctrine is born quite new, shining, never before seen. No doctrine can boast of an absolute "originality". It is bound, even if only historically, to other doctrines that have been, and to develop into other doctrines that will be. Thus the scientific socialism of Marx is bound to the Utopian Socialism of the Fouriers, the Owens and the Saint-Simons; thus the Liberalism of the nineteenth century is connected with the whole "Enlightenment" of the eighteenth century. Thus the doctrines of democracy are bound to the *Encyclopédie*. Every doctrine tends to direct the activity of men towards a determined objective; but the activity of man reacts upon the doctrine, transforms it, adapts it to new necessities or transcends it. The doctrine itself, therefore, must be, not words, but an act of life. Hence, the pragmatic veins in Fascism, its will to power, its will to be, its attitude in the face of the fact of "violence" and of its own courage.

10. The keystone of Fascist doctrine is the conception of the State,

of its essence, of its tasks, of its ends. For Fascism the State is an absolute before which individuals and groups are relative. Individuals and groups are "thinkable" in so far as they are within the State. The Liberal State does not direct the interplay and the material and spiritual development of the groups, but limits itself to registering the results; the Fascist State has a consciousness of its own, a will of its own, on this account it is called an "ethical" State. In 1929, at the first quin-quennial assembly of the regime, I said: "For Fascism, the State is not the night-watchman who is concerned only with the personal security of the citizens; nor is it an organization for purely material ends, such as that of guaranteeing a certain degree of prosperity and a relatively peaceful social order, to achieve which a council of administration would be sufficient, nor is it a creation of mere politics with no contact with the material and complex reality of the lives of individuals and the life of peoples. The State, as conceived by Fascism and as it acts, is a spiritual and moral fact because it makes concrete the political, juridical, economic organization of the nation and such an organization is, in its origin and in its development, a manifestation of the spirit. The State is the guarantor of internal and external security, but it is also the guardian and the transmitter of the spirit of the people as it has been elaborated through the centuries in language, custom, faith. The State is not only present, it is also past, and above all future. It is the State which, transcending the brief limit of individual lives, represents the immanent conscience of the nation. The forms in which States express themselves change, but the necessity of the State remains. It is the State which educates citizens for civic virtue, makes them conscious of their mission, calls them to unity; harmonizes their interests in justice; hands on the achievements of thought in the sciences, the arts, in law, in human solidarity; it carries men from the elementary life of the tribe to the highest human expression of power which is Empire; it entrusts to the ages the names of those who died for its integrity or in obedience to its laws; it puts forward as an example and recommends to the generations that are to come the leaders who increased its territory and the men of genius who gave it glory. When the sense of the State declines and the disintegrating and centrifugal tendencies of individuals and groups prevail, national societies move to their decline."

11. From 1929 up to the present day these doctrinal positions have been strengthened by the whole economico-political evolution of the world. It is the State alone that grows in size, in power. It is the State

alone that can solve the dramatic contradictions of capitalism. What is called the crisis cannot be overcome except by the State, within the State. Where are the shades of the Jules Simons who, at the dawn of liberalism, proclaimed that "the State must strive to render itself unnecessary and to prepare for its demise"; of the MacCullochs who, in the second half of the last century, affirmed that the State must abstain from too much governing? And faced with the continual, necessary and inevitable interventions of the State in economic affairs what would the Englishman Bentham now say, according to whom industry should have asked of the State only to be left in peace? Or the German Humboldt, according to whom the "idle" State must be considered the best? It is true that the second generation of liberal economists was less extremist than the first, and already Smith himself opened, even though cautiously, the door to State intervention in economics. But when one says liberalism, one says the-individual; when one says Fascism, one says the State. But the Fascist State is unique; it is an original creation. It is not reactionary, but revolutionary in that it anticipates the solutions of certain universal problems. These problems are no longer seen in the same light: in the sphere of politics they are removed from party rivalries, from the supreme power of parliament, from the irresponsibility of assemblies; in the sphere of economics they are removed from the sphere of the syndicates' activities—activities that were ever widening their scope and increasing their power both on the workers' side and on the employers'—removed from their struggles and their designs; in the moral sphere they are divorced from ideas of the need for order, discipline and obedience, and lifted into the plane of the moral commandments of the fatherland. Fascism desires the State to be strong, organic and at the same time founded on a wide popular basis. The Fascist State has also claimed for itself the field of economics and, through the corporative, social and educational institutions which it has created, the meaning of the State reaches out to and includes the farthest off-shoots; and within the State, framed in their respective organizations, there revolve all the political, economic and spiritual forces of the nation. A State founded on millions of individuals who recognize it, feel it, are ready to serve it, is not the tyrannical State of the medieval lord. It has nothing in common with the absolutist States that existed either before or after 1789. In the Fascist State the individual is not suppressed, but rather multiplied, just as in a regiment a soldier is not weakened but multiplied by the number of his comrades. The Fascist State organizes the nation, but it leaves sufficient scope to individuals; it has limited useless or harmful liberties and has preserved those that are essential. It cannot be the individual who decides in this matter, but only the State.

12. The Fascist State does not remain indifferent to the fact of religion in general and to that particular positive religion which is Italian Catholicism. The State has no theology, but it has an ethic. In the Fascist State religion is looked upon as one of the deepest manifestations of the spirit; it is, therefore, not only respected, but defended and protected. The Fascist State does not create a "God" of its own, as Robespierre once, at the height of the Convention's foolishness, wished to do; nor does it vainly seek, like Bolshevism, to expel religion from the minds of men; Fascism respects the God of the ascetics, of the saints, of the heroes, and also God as seen and prayed to by the simple and primitive heart of the people.

13. The Fascist State is a will to power and to government. In it the tradition of Rome is an idea that has force. In the doctrine of Fascism Empire is not only a territorial, military or mercantile expression, but spiritual or moral. One can think of an empire, that is to say a nation that directly or indirectly leads other nations, without needing to conquer a single square kilometre of territory. For Fascism the tendency to Empire, that is to say, to the expansion of nations, is a manifestation of vitality; its opposite, staying at home, is a sign of decadence: peoples who rise or re-rise are imperialist, peoples who die are renunciatory. Fascism is the doctrine that is most fitted to represent the aims, the states of mind, of a people, like the Italian people, rising again after many centuries of abandonment or slavery to foreigners. But Empire calls for discipline, co-ordination of forces, duty and sacrifice; this explains many aspects of the practical working of the regime and the direction of many of the forces of the State and the necessary severity shown to those who would wish to oppose this spontaneous and destined impulse of the Italy of the twentieth century, to oppose it in the name of the superseded ideologies of the nineteenth, repudiated wherever great experiments of political and social transformation have been courageously attempted: especially where, as now, peoples thirst for authority, for leadership, for order. If every age has its own doctrine, it is apparent from a thousand signs that the doctrine of the present age is Fascism. That it is a doctrine of life is shown by the fact that it has resuscitated a faith. That this faith has conquered

minds is proved by the fact that Fascism has had its dead and its martyrs.

Fascism henceforward has in the world the universality of all those doctrines which, by fulfilling themselves, have significance in the history of the human spirit.

La Dottrina del Fascismo (1932)

§2. THE NATURE OF FASCISM

The National Fascist Party is a civil militia for the service of the nation. Its objective: to realize the greatness of the Italian people. From its beginnings, which are indistinguishable from the renaissance of the Italian conscience and the will to victory, until now, the party has always thought of itself as in a state of war, at first in order to combat those who were stifling the will of the nation, to-day and from henceforth to defend and increase the power of the Italian people. Fascism is not merely an Italian organization connected with a programme partly realized and partly still to be realized; it is above all a faith which has had its confessors, and under the impulse of which the new Italians work as soldiers, pledged to achieve victory in the struggle between the nation and its enemies. The Party is an essential part of this new organization, and its function is fundamental and indispensable to the vitality of the regime. In the hour of vigil, its organization was fixed according to the necessities of battle, and the people recognized the Duce by the marks of his will, his strength and his achievements. In the heat of the struggle, action took precedence of law. Every stage was marked by a conquest, and the assemblies were only gatherings of officers and men dominated by the memory of the dead. Without dogmatic formulas or rigid projects, Fascism knows that victory lies in the possibility of its own continuous renewal. Fascism lives to-day in terms of the future, and regards the new generations as forces destined to achieve the ends appointed by our will. Without order and hierarchy, there can be neither discipline nor effort nor education of the people, which must receive light and guidance from that high place where is to be found the complete vision of rewards, tasks, functions and merits, and where the only guidance is in the general interest.

From *The Preamble to the Statuto of 20 December* 1929

§3. THE FASCIST DECALOGUE

(i)

1. Know that the Fascist and in particular the soldier, must not believe in perpetual peace.

2. Days of imprisonment are always deserved.

3. The nation serves even as a sentinel over a can of petrol.

4. A companion must be a brother, first, because he lives with you, and secondly because he thinks like you.

5. The rifle and cartridge belt, and the rest, are confided to you not to rust in leisure, but to be preserved in war.

6. Do not ever say "The Government will pay . . ." because it is *you* who pay; and the Government is that which you willed to have, and for which you put on a uniform.

7. Discipline is the soul of armies; without it there are no soldiers, only confusion and defeat.

8. Mussolini is always right.

9. For a volunteer there are no extenuating circumstances when he is disobedient.

10. One thing must be dear to you above all: the life of the Duce.

1934

(ii)

1. Remember that those who fell for the revolution and for the empire march at the head of your columns.

2. Your comrade is your brother. He lives with you, thinks with you, and is at your side in the battle.

3. Service to Italy can be rendered at all times, in all places, and by every means. It can be paid with toil and also with blood.

4. The enemy of Fascism is your enemy. Give him no quarter.

5. Discipline is the sunshine of armies. It prepares and illuminates the victory.

6. He who advances to the attack with decision has victory already in his grasp.

7. Conscious and complete obedience is the virtue of the Legionary.

8. There do not exist things important and things unimportant. There is only duty.

9. The Fascist revolution has depended in the past and still depends on the bayonets of its Legionaries.

10. Mussolini is always right.

1938

§4. ON THE CONSTITUTION AND ATTRIBUTES OF THE FASCIST GRAND COUNCIL

I. The Fascist Grand Council is the supreme organ which co-ordinates and integrates all the activities of the regime sprung from the October revolution of 1922. It exercises the legislative function on the occasions specified by law, and it is bound furthermore, when consulted by the leader of the government, to advise on all other questions of national interest, whether political, economic or social.

II. The leader of the government, Prime Minister Secretary of State, is *ex officio* the President of the Fascist Grand Council. He calls it when he considers its meeting expedient, and he determines the agenda.

III. The secretary of the National Fascist Party is the secretary of the Grand Council.

The leader of the government is empowered to delegate to him the Presidency of the Grand Council if he himself should be prevented or absent, or when his office falls vacant.

IX. No member of the Grand Council may be arrested, unless caught *in flagrante delicto*, nor can penal procedure be proceeded with against him, nor police measures be taken, without the authorization of the Grand Council.

In the case of a member of the Grand Council, belonging to the National Fascist Party, no disciplinary measure can be taken against him without a deliberation of the Grand Council.

X. The functions of a member of the Grand Council are unpaid.

The State is not required to furnish the expenses of the functioning of the Grand Council.

The sittings of the Grand Council are secret. A private rule, approved by the Grand Council, shall govern all other measures concerned with its functioning.

XII. The advice of the Grand Council is to be taken on all questions with a constitutional bearing.

In every case, the decrees of the laws dealing with the following matters shall be considered to have a constitutional character:

(i) the succession to the throne, the attributes and prerogatives of the crown;

(ii) the formation and the functioning of the Grand Council, of the Senate of the kingdom and the Chamber of Deputies;

(iii) the attributes and the prerogatives of the leader of the government, Prime Minister Secretary of State;

(iv) the competence of the executive power to declare the juridical norms;

(v) syndical and corporative organization;

(vi) the relations between the State and the Holy See;

(vii) those international treaties involving either modifications of the territory of the State and the colonies, or limitations to the further acquisition of territory.

6. The charter (*statuto*) of the National Fascist Party shall be sanctioned by royal decree, on the recommendation of the leader of the government, Prime Minister Secretary of State, and (it is understood) of the Fascist Grand Council and the council of ministers.

7. The secretary of the National Fascist Party is appointed by royal decree, on the recommendation of the leader of the government, Prime Minister Secretary of State.

He is, *ex officio*, a member of the Supreme Committee of Defence, of the Higher Council of National Education, of the National Council of Corporations and of the Central Corporative Committee.

By royal decree or on the recommendation of the leader of the government, the secretary of the National Fascist Party may be called upon to participate and take his seat in the council of ministers.

8. The members of the National Directorate of the Fascist Party are appointed by a decree of the leader of the government, Prime Minister Secretary of State, on the recommendation of the secretary of the Party.

9. The secretary and the members of the National Directorate of the National Fascist Party remain in office for three years.

10. The federal secretaries of the National Fascist Party are nominated by decree of the leader of the government, Prime Minister

Secretary of State, on the recommendation of the secretary of the Party, and remain in office for one year.

From *The Law of* 9 *December* 1928 *as amended* 14 *December* 1929

§ 5. THE PRESS

All newspapers and periodicals shall have a responsible director.

If the director is a senator or a deputy he shall be one of the usual editors of the newspaper or periodical.

The name of the director or responsible editor shall be on the register of professional journalists.

The director or responsible editor should be approved by the magistrate of the Court in the jurisdiction of which the newspaper or periodical is licensed.

The magistrate may refuse to approve, or revoke his approval of anyone who has been twice convicted of a press offence. . . .

The publication of a newspaper or periodical shall not take place until the magistrate has approved of the person responsible for it.

Any newspaper or periodical which appears without the approval of the magistrate shall be suppressed.

At the same time as the request of the responsible person for recognition, the printer of the newspaper or periodical and the editor must present to the magistrate a declaration of all the names and occupations of all the proprietors of the newspaper or periodical, their domicile and their address. . . .

The proprietors of a newspaper share with the editor the civil responsibility for all sums due for damages or for the reparation of injuries, or for costs of actions brought for press offences. . . .

There shall be a roll of journalists in every town possessing a Court. This roll shall constitute the professional registers, which shall be deposited in the archives of the Court. Only the journalists who appear in these registers shall be permitted to exercise their profession.

The conditions governing registration shall be determined by a special rule.[1]

From *The Law of* 31 *December* 1925

---

[1] By a decree of 26 February 1928 the qualifications for admission to the Roll of Journalists are proof of good moral and political standing and the possession of a secondary school diploma or its equivalent. This means, in effect, for the future, satisfactory passage through the Young Fascist organizations.

§6. THE CHARTER OF LABOUR

(This is not a legislative act, but was approved and promulgated by the Fascist Grand Council, 21 April 1927, and is regarded in Italy as an "organic" law of regime.)

I. The Italian nation is an organic whole having life, purposes and means of action superior in power and duration to those of the individuals, single or associated, of which it is composed. It is a moral, political and economic unity, which is realized integrally in the Fascist State.

II. Work in all its forms—intellectual, technical or manual— whether organization or execution—is a social duty. And for this reason only it is regulated by the State. The process of production, from the national point of view, is a single whole; its aims are united and identified with the well-being of the producers and the promotion of national power.

III. Occupational or syndical organization is free; but only the juridically recognized syndicate which submits to the control of State has the right to represent legally the entire category of employers or workers for which it is constituted, in safeguarding its interests *vis-à-vis* the State and other occupational associations, in making collective contracts of work binding on all the members of the category, in levying contributions and exercising over its members functions delegated to it in the public interest.

IV. In the collective contract of work the solidarity of the various factors of production finds its concrete expression in the reconciliation of the conflicting interests of employers and employees and in their subordination to the superior interests of production.

V. The Labour Court is the organ by which the State intervenes in the settlement of labour disputes, whether they are concerned with the application of contracts or other existing regulations, or with the working out of new conditions of labour.

VI. Legally recognized occupational associations guarantee juridical equality between employers and employed, and maintain the discipline of production and work and promote the improvement of both. The Corporations constitute the unified organization of the forces of production and represent completely the interests of production. And on account of this integral representation, and because the interests of production are national interests, Corporations are recognized by law as organs of the State. As organs representing the unified interests of production, the corporation may make binding rules regulating the relations of labour on the co-ordination of production, whenever they receive the mandate of their affiliated associations.

VII. The Corporative State considers private enterprise in the domain of production to be the most efficient method and the most advantageous to the interests of the nation. Private enterprise in production, being an activity of national interest, the entrepreneur is responsible to the State for his organization. A reciprocity of rights and duties follows from the collaboration of the forces of production. The wage-earner, artisan, employee or labourer is an active collaborator in the economic enterprise, the direction of which belongs to the employer who also carries the responsibility.

VIII. Occupational associations of employers have the duty of using every means to increase and improve production and to reduce costs. The associations of those who pursue a liberal profession or an art, and the associations of employees and wage-earners in the public services, co-operate to safeguard the interests of art, science and letters, to improve production and to realize the moral ends of the corporative regime.

IX. The State intervenes in economic production only when private enterprise fails or is insufficient or when the political interests of the State are involved. Such intervention may take the form of control, encouragement or direct management.

X. In collective labour disputes judicial action shall be invoked only when the corporative organ has first made an attempt at conciliation. In individual disputes concerning the interpretation and application of collective contracts, the occupational associations have the power to offer their good offices as mediators. The competence to deal with such disputes lies with the ordinary courts, which act with the body of assessors appointed by the interested occupational associations.

XXVI. Provident insurance being an important manifestation of the principle of collaboration between the classes; both employers and workers should support it, bearing in proportion the expenses it involves. The State, through the medium of the corporative bodies and the occupational associations, exerts itself so far as is possible in co-ordinating and unifying the system and the various insurance institutions.

From *The Charter of Labour*, 21 April 1927

§ 7. LOCK-OUTS AND STRIKES

Lock-outs and strikes are forbidden.

Employers who, without justifiable cause, and solely for the purpose of obtaining from their employees modifications in the stringency of contracts of work, suspend work in their establishments, offices or workshops, shall be punished with a fine varying from 10,000 to 100,000 lira.

Employees or workmen who, to the number of three or more than three, by mutual consent without more ado stop work, or who carry on their work in such a manner as to endanger its continuity or its regularity, for the purpose of imposing on their employers a modification in the terms of their contract of work, shall be punished with a fine varying from 100 to 1000 lira. . . .

When the authors of the above-mentioned offences are more numerous, the principal instigators and organizers shall be punished by imprisonment for at least one year and at most two years, and by the fine stated in the preceding paragraphs.

Officials and employees in public services and those employed in enterprises involving the public interest, who, to the number of at least three, by mutual consent stop work, or carry on their work in such a manner as to endanger its continuity or its regularity, shall be punished by imprisonment for a period varying from one year to six months, with a prohibition on their filling a public office for six months. . . .

When the suspension of work by employers, or the negligence and irregularity in carrying on their work by employees, have for their purpose the exercise of pressure on the will, or the influencing of the decision of an institution of the State, the province or the commune, or of a public official, the leaders, instigators and organizers shall be punished with a term of imprisonment varying from three to seven years, with a permanent prohibition on their filling a public office.

From *The Law of* 3 *April* 1926. §§ 18, 19

BOOK LIST

A. Rocco. *The Political Doctrine of Fascism.* (*Bulletin of the Carnegie Endowment for International Peace.* No. 223. October 1926)

A. Lion. *The Pedigree of Fascism* (1927)

H. Finer. *Mussolini's Italy* (1935)

F. Pitigliani. *The Italian Corporative State* (1935)

V

NATIONAL SOCIALISM

If the Italian Fascists first drove to power, and only afterwards provided themselves with a philosophy, it was far otherwise with the National Socialists of Germany. As early as 1920—more than thirteen years before Hitler achieved the chancellorship, and at a time when the recently created *Nationalsozialistische deutsche Arbeiter Partei* hardly reached beyond the bounds of Bavaria—Gottfried Feder, upon whom Hitler leaned heavily for advice on economic matters, drew up, and the party in mass meeting adopted, the Twenty-five Points, very properly presented by Mr Oakeshott as his first selection in the group that follows. As a glance will reveal, the document is not a reasoned statement of political and social theory, but rather an enumeration of objectives—a program couched in the form of a series of categorical "We demands". From it, however, can be obtained a very good idea of basic National Socialist concepts. So firmly, indeed, was it grounded on the characteristic and enduring Nazi ideology that in 1926 it was declared unalterable; and notwithstanding its vagueness at numerous points, its manifest incongruities and inconsistencies, and the new twists imparted to it as the National Socialist movement advanced through later stages, the manifesto remains to this day the accepted official platform of the party.

Five years afterwards, Hitler, emerging from imprisonment in the fortress of Landsberg to which he had been condemned after the abortive Beer-hall *Putsch* of 1923, brought forth with him large portions of *Mein Kampf*, of which the first volume was published in 1925 and the second in 1927. In effect, the book was a commentary on the Twenty-five Points—the first in a long series of such commentaries by various writers, although, because of its authorship, by far the most important and influential. Mr Oakeshott found it impossible to secure permission to reproduce portions of the volume in his selections given below; hence he offers only (pp. 197–205) "some notes" undertaking to summarize the doctrines set forth. For English readers, however, an abridged translation, prepared by E. T. S. Dugdale, was published at London in 1933 under the title of *My Battle*; and, the volume growing in world-wide interest as the Nazi régime took on greater significance, in 1939 a "definitive and unexpurgated" annotated translation, under the editorial sponsorship of a group of capable

American scholars, was published at New York under the original title of *Mein Kampf* (Reynal and Hitchcock). This last-mentioned edition is easily available to American students, and every reader of the following section of the present book should resort to it.

Readers of *Mein Kampf* will, however, search the huge volume in vain for any systematic presentation of National Socialist doctrine. In his preface, Hitler, while acknowledging that "the basic elements of a doctrine" require to be "set down in some permanent form", disclaims intention to do more than describe "the object of our movement" and "draw a picture of its development"—from which, he adds, "more can be learned than from any purely doctrinary treatise." This intent of the author, together with his manifest lack of literary skill and his decidedly emotional bent, results in a loosely written, repetitious, bombastic book—"a propagandistic essay by a violent partisan", often distorting historical truth and sometimes ignoring it altogether. Persons who read German will find a far more orderly presentation of the National Socialist philosophy in the as yet untranslated *Der Mythus des 20. Jahrhunderts* of Alfred Rosenberg, who has been termed the high priest of Nazi ideology; and Mr Oakeshott presents a few significant quotations from that writer. It is from *Mein Kampf*, however, that millions of Germans and non-Germans alike have drawn most of what they know about National Socialist doctrine as expounded by its authors.

The remainder of Mr Oakeshott's materials are drawn chiefly from legislation emanating, under provision of the famous Enabling Act of March 24, 1933 (see pp. 224–225 below), from the *Reich* cabinet, and dealing with such important matters as racial relations, citizenship, labor, land tenure and inheritance, the administration of justice, the Hitler Youth, and the status of the party. For students of theory, the documents are valuable mainly as reflecting points of view, objectives, and approaches.

Further special references include: K. Heiden, *A History of National Socialism* (1936); F. L. Schuman, "The Political Theory of German Fascism", *Amer. Polit. Sci. Rev.*, Apr., 1934; L. Preuss, "Racial Theory and National Socialist Political Thought", *Southwestern Soc. Sci. Quar.*, Sept., 1934; and *The Nazi Primer* (1938).

V

The doctrine of National Socialism is many-sided rather than systematic; and although there is no lack of information, official and unofficial, on the subject, few of the authoritative documents have been translated into English. The extracts I have printed from the programme of the National Socialist German Workers' Party and from recent German legislation need no explanation; they illustrate most of the important aspects of National Socialist doctrine. But beyond these, there are two works of a different character which are essential to the understanding of National Socialism: Hitler's *Mein Kampf* (volume I, 1925; volume II, 1927) and Alfred Rosenberg's *Der Mythus des 20. Jahrhunderts* (1930). The second of these works has never been translated into English and in consequence we have a restricted understanding of National Socialism. But the author and publishers have given permission for the reproduction here of a few passages from it. These passages are not designed to give an impression of the work as a whole, which would be impossible in a short space (it is a long and intricate study), but merely to illustrate a particular aspect of National Socialist doctrine. Hitler's work has sold in Germany by the hundred thousand, and it is scarcely an exaggeration to say that no German home is complete without it. A greatly abridged and expurgated version of it has appeared in English, but this translation is bad and it contained none of the important statements of doctrine and consequently has been useless for my purpose. I had hoped to include a translation of the more important doctrinal passages from *Mein Kampf*,[1] but since, in the end, it has proved impossible to obtain permission for this, I have had to substitute a brief account in my own words of what appear to be Hitler's fundamental beliefs. This is a most regrettable departure from my plan of printing nothing but original and authoritative statements, but it is a departure which is unavoidable.

[1] Vol. I, ch. 11; vol. II, chs. 1, 2, 4.

§1. HITLER: THE TWENTY-FIVE POINTS[1]

The programme of the German Workers' Party is limited as to period. The leaders have no intention, once the aims announced in it have been achieved, of setting up fresh ones, so as to ensure the continued existence of the Party by the artificially increased discontent of the masses.

1. We demand, on the basis of the right of national self-determination, the union of all Germans to form one Great Germany.

2. We demand juridical equality for the German people in its dealings with other nations, and the abolition of the Peace Treaties of Versailles and St Germain.

3. We demand territory and soil (colonies) for the nourishment of our people and for settling our surplus population.

4. None but members of the nation may be citizens of the State. None but those of German blood, whatever their creed, may be members of the nation. No Jew, therefore, may be considered a member of the nation.

5. Anyone who is not a citizen of the State may live in Germany only as a guest and must be regarded as subject to the laws governing aliens.

6. The right to determine the leadership and laws of the State is to be enjoyed by the citizens of the State alone. We demand, therefore, that all official appointments of whatever kind, whether in the Reich, in the one or other of the federal states, or in the municipalities, shall be held by citizens of the State alone.

We oppose the corrupt Parliamentary custom of filling public offices merely with a view to party considerations, and without reference to character or capacity.

7. We demand that the State shall make it one of its chief duties to provide work and the means of livelihood for the citizens of the State. If it is not possible to provide for the entire population living within the confines of the State, foreign nationals (non-citizens of the State) must be excluded (expatriated).

[1] The National Socialist German Workers' Party announced their programme in these Twenty-Five Points at a mass-meeting of the Party in the Hofbrauhausfestsaal in Munich, on 25 February 1920.

8. All further non-German immigration must be prevented. We demand that all non-Germans who have entered Germany subsequently to 2 August 1914 shall be required forthwith to depart from the Reich.

9. All citizens of the State shall be equal as regards rights and duties.

10. It must be the first duty of every citizen of the State to work with his mind or with his body. The activities of the individual must not clash with the interests of the whole, but must be pursued within the framework of the national activity and must be for the general good.

11. We demand, therefore, the abolition of incomes unearned by work, and emancipation from the slavery of interest charges.

12. Because of the enormous sacrifice of life and property demanded of a nation by every war, personal profit through war must be regarded as a crime against the nation. We demand, therefore, the complete confiscation of all war profits.

13. We demand the nationalization of all business combines (trusts).

14. We demand that the great industries shall be organized on a profit-sharing basis.

15. We demand an extensive development of provision for old age.

16. We demand the creation and maintenance of a healthy middle class; the immediate communalization of the big department stores and the lease of the various departments at a low rate to small traders, and that the greatest consideration shall be shown to all small traders supplying goods to the State, the federal states or the municipalities.

17. We demand a programme of land reform suitable to our national requirements, the enactment of a law for confiscation without compensation of land for communal purposes, the abolition of ground rents, and the prohibition of all speculation in land.[1]

18. We demand a ruthless campaign against all whose activities are injurious to the common interest. Oppressors of the nation, usurers, profiteers, etc., must be punished with death, whatever their creed or race.

19. We demand that the Roman Code, which serves the materialistic world order, shall be replaced by a system of German Common Law.

[1] "It is necessary to reply to the false interpretation on the part of our opponents of Point 17 of the programme of the N.S.D.A.P. Since the N.S.D.A.P. admits the principle of private property, it is obvious that the expression 'confiscation without compensation' merely refers to possible legal powers to confiscate, if necessary, land illegally acquired, or not administered in accordance with the national welfare. It is directed in the first instance against Jewish companies which speculate in land." Adolf Hitler, Munich, 13 April 1928.

20. The State must undertake a thorough reconstruction of our national system of education, with the aim of giving to every capable and industrious German the benefits of a higher education and therewith the capacity to take his place in the leadership of the nation. The curricula of all educational establishments must be brought into line with the necessities of practical life. With the first dawn of intelligence, the schools must aim at teaching the pupil to know what the State stands for (instruction in citizenship). We demand educational facilities for specially gifted children of poor parents, whatever their class or occupation, at the expense of the State.

21. The State must concern itself with raising the standard of health in the nation by exercising its guardianship over mothers and infants, by prohibiting child labour, and by increasing bodily efficiency by legally obligatory gymnastics and sports, and by the extensive support of clubs engaged in the physical training of the young.

22. We demand the abolition of a paid army and the foundation of a national army.

23. We demand legal measures against intentional political lies and their dissemination in the Press. In order to facilitate the creation of a German national Press, we demand:

(a) that all editors of newspapers and all contributors, employing the German language, shall be members of the nation;

(b) that special permission from the State shall be necessary before non-German newspapers may appear. These must not be printed in the German language;

(c) that non-Germans shall be prohibited by law from participation financially in, or from influencing German newspapers, and that the penalty for contravention of this law shall be suppression of any such newspaper and the immediate deportation of the non-German concerned in it.

It must be forbidden to publish newspapers which do not conduce to the national welfare. We demand the legal prosecution of all tendencies in art and literature of a kind calculated to disintegrate our national life, and the suppression of institutions which militate against the above-mentioned requirements.

24. We demand liberty for all religious denominations in the State, in so far as they are not a danger to it and do not militate against the moral sense of the German race.

The Party, as such, stands for a positive Christianity,[1] but does not bind itself in the matter of creed to any particular confession. It is strenuously opposed to the Jewish-materialist spirit within and without the Party, and is convinced that our nation can only achieve permanent well-being from within on the principle of placing the common interests before self-interest.

25. That all the foregoing demands may be realized, we demand the creation of a strong central power of the Reich; the unconditional authority of the central Parliament over the entire Reich and its organization; the formation of Diets and vocational Chambers for the purpose of administering in the various federal States the general laws promulgated by the Reich.

The leaders of the Party swear to proceed regardless of consequences —if necessary to sacrifice their lives—in securing the fulfilment of the foregoing points.

Münich, 24 February 1920

§ 2. THE POLITICAL AND ECONOMIC PROGRAMME OF THE N.S.D.A.P.[2]

Questions of Programme do not concern the Council of Administration; the Programme is fixed and I shall never suffer changes in the principles of the movement as laid down in its Programme.

Hitler, 31 August 1927

Our aim is—Germany's rebirth in the German spirit to German liberty. The means to this end are:

I. The political axiom: The German Reich is the home of the Germans.

[1] Cp. the following passages from *Der Mythus des 20. Jahrhunderts*, by A. Rosenberg. "Goethe considered Christ's life important, not his death, and represented in this way the soul of the Germanic Occident, positive Christianity as opposed to the negative Christianity of the dominations of priests and of the belief in witches, both going back to Etrusco-Asiatic conceptions.... Negative Christianity (Roman Catholicism, and, in a lesser degree, Protestantism) emphasizes its Syriac-Etruscan tradition, abstract dogmas and old sacred customs, positive Christianity recalls to life the forces of the nordic blood." Pp. 78–79.

[2] "Our constitutional law is based upon the National Socialist *Weltanschauung* and is expressed in the general order of the Nation (*Volksordnung*). So far as this general order is formulated in propositions, legal principles or programmatical statements, the supreme constitutional foundation of the Third Reich is laid down in the Party programme." *Beamtenkalender*, 1937.

(a) *In foreign policy:*

    1. Formation of a closed national state, embracing all the German race.

    2. Energetic representation of German interests abroad.

(b) *In racial policy:*

    3. Dismissal of all Jews and non-Germans from all responsible positions in public life.

    4. Prevention of immigration of Eastern Jews and other parasitic foreigners. Undesirable aliens and Jews may be deported.

(c) *In internal policy:*

    5. None but Germans who profess entire community with the culture and destiny of Germany may exercise the rights of a citizen of the State.

    6. He who is not a German may live in the German State only as a guest and subject to the laws governing aliens.

    7. The rights of Germans shall have preference over those of citizens of foreign nations.

II. Our economic principle: The duty of the State is to provide the necessaries of life and not to secure the highest possible rate of interest for capital.

    8. National socialism recognizes private property in principle and gives it the protection of the State.

    9. The national welfare, however, demands that a limit shall be set to the amassing of wealth in the hands of individuals.

    10. All Germans form a working community for the promotion of the general welfare and culture.

    11. Within the limits of the obligation of every German to work, and the fundamental recognition of private property, every German is free to earn his living and to dispose of the results of his labour.

    12. The healthy combination of all forms of business, small and large, in every domain of economic life, including agriculture, shall be encouraged.

    13. All existing businesses which until now have been in the form of trusts shall be nationalized.

14. Usury and profiteering and personal enrichment at the expense of, or to the injury of the nation shall be punished with death.

15. Introduction of a year's obligation to work (for the State), incumbent upon all Germans.

III. Our financial principle: Finance shall exist for the benefit of the State; the financial magnates shall not form a state within the State. Hence our aim is to abolish the slavery of interest charges.

16. Relief of the State, and hence of the nation, from its indebtedness to the great financial houses which lend money on interest.

17. Nationalization of the Reichsbank and the issuing houses.

18. Provision of money for all great public objects (water-power, communications, etc.), not by means of loans, but by granting non-interest bearing State bonds.

19. Introduction of a fixed standard of currency on a secured basis.

20. Creation of a communal building and agricultural bank for granting non-interest bearing loans.

21. Fundamental remodelling of the system of taxation on social-economic principles. Relief of the consumer from the burden of indirect taxation, and of the producer from crippling taxation.

IV. Our social-political principle: The general welfare is the supreme law.

22. Development on a large scale of Old Age insurance by nationalizing the system of annuities. Every necessitous member of the German State shall be assured of an adequate income on attaining a certain age, or, if permanently disabled, before that age.

23. Participation by all engaged in production and value-creating enterprises in the profits of the enterprise, all being jointly responsible for the fulfilment of the national economic obligations of the enterprise.

24. Seizure of all profits made out of the War and the Revolution not due to honest work, and of the fortunes of usurers and money-grabbers, and their application to the extension of social services.

25. Relief of the housing shortage by extensive fresh construction of dwelling houses throughout the Reich by the means suggested in No. 20.

V. Cultural policy: Our highest cultural aim is that all the sciences and fine arts shall flourish on the basis of a politically free, economically healthy State. The means of achieving this will be:

26. Training of the young to become physically sound and intellectually free human beings, in accordance with the great traditions of German culture.
27. Complete liberty of creed and conscience.
28. Special protection for the Christian denominations.
29. Suppression and discouragement of dogmas which are opposed to the German moral sense and are injurious to the State and nation.
30. Suppression of all evil influences in the Press, in literature, on the stage, in the arts and in the picture theatres.
31. Liberty of instruction in the German secondary schools; and the formation of a class of leaders of men of high character.

VI. Military affairs:

32. To make the nation efficient in defence by granting every free German the right to bear arms.
33. Abolition of mercenary troops.
34. Creation of a national army for home defence under the command of a strictly disciplined corps of professional officers.

VII. Other reforms:

35. Press reform. Suppression of all printed matter which offends the dignity of the German people. Strict responsibility for all untruthful and intentionally distorted news.
36. Modification of the franchise so as to eliminate the demoralizing methods of electoral contests, and the irresponsibility (immunity) of those elected.
37. Formation of special Chambers for trades and professions.
38. Judicial reform as regards:
    (a) Land Laws. Recognition in principle of the rights of property in land; the owner may not borrow from private sources on the security of the land; the State to have the right

of pre-emption, especially in the case of land owned by foreigners and Jews; the State to be empowered to administer estates in the event of bad management on the part of the owner.

(*b*) Civil Law. Greatly increased protection for personal honour and health, as opposed to the one-sided legal protection of the rights of property, which at present predominates.

39. Constitutional reform. The form of the State most suited to the German character is sovereign control concentrated in a supreme head. Whether this central power shall be wielded by an elected monarch or a President must be left to the decision of the nation.

Federal character of the Reich. The constitution of the German nation, consisting as it does of a number of communities closely bound together by race and history, makes it necessary that each of the States shall enjoy the most comprehensive independence in internal affairs.

It is the function of the Reich to represent the German nation abroad, and to provide for passports and customs, and for the Army and Navy.

Drawn up for the Party by Gottfried Feder (1920)

§3. SOME NOTES ON THE DOCTRINES OF *MEIN KAMPF*

The most important statements of the fundamental National Socialist doctrine with regard to society and the state which appear in Hitler's work, *Mein Kampf*, are contained in four chapters devoted respectively to the exposition of (i) his conception of Race, (ii) his conception of *Volk* and *völkisch* as a political creed, (iii) his conception of society and the state, and (iv) his conception of individuality and leadership. Only Hitler's own words can give a true impression of both the force and the confusion of his ideas on these subjects. But since these ideas are the essence of National Socialism, and this book is (together with Alfred Rosenberg's work, *Der Mythus des 20. Jahrhunderts*) the only authoritative statement of the doctrine, some account of them must be attempted even if we are unable to reproduce extensively the words of the *Führer*.

(i) The whole doctrine of National Socialism appears, for Hitler, to be a superstructure built upon the foundation of what he calls the "iron logic of Nature". Others have sought to found National Socialism on the alleged chaos, political and economic, of contemporary Western Europe: they represent it as, primarily, an answer to a contemporary situation. But with Hitler this is not so; for him the true foundation is the law of Nature which decrees "the internal exclusiveness of the species of all living beings upon earth", which decrees that "each beast mates only with a companion of the same species". The argument by means of which we pass from this "obvious truth" to the more complex and sophisticated truths of National Socialist society is, in places, obscure; but it appears to run on these lines. Each beast normally mates with a companion of its own species; but when this is not so (in abnormal circumstances) Nature resists by endowing the offspring with inferior strength and inferior powers of reproduction. This observation leads to the conclusion that the purest stock is always the strongest, and the strongest always the most pure. Both the crossing of species and the mating of "two creatures of unequal stock" produce inferior offspring. But Nature's will is the continuous improvement of all life, and consequently her law is the continuous victory of the stronger species over the weaker species, the stronger elements of a stock over the weaker, the stronger race over the weaker race. All crossing of species, stocks or races results in weakness; so the law of Nature is against the contamination of species, stocks and races.

Out of this chaos of species, stocks and races rises the first principle of National Socialism: racial purity. The will of Nature is to preserve rigidly the distinction and differentiation of races; and the first duty of man is to co-operate with Nature, to behave in accordance with Nature's Will. The duty of man is not to try to conquer, change or moralize Nature, but simply to obey it.

The second principle and the second duty follow hard upon the first. The distinction of races does not imply the equality of races; indeed, there is no such equality. Some races are higher and others lower. And besides preserving the differentiation of races (their purity and exclusiveness) we are bound to promote the dominance in the world of the higher races, of the highest race, the Aryan race. The belief that the Aryan race is the highest and most valuable race of mankind appears, in Hitler's mind, to be founded upon the belief that "all we can see to-day in human culture, the achievement of art, science and technique, is almost exclusively the creative product of the Aryan". Everywhere the Aryan race, and that race alone, has been the creator and bearer of civilization. Having established the superiority of the Aryan race, the condition on which that superiority can be maintained is clear—the preservation of its purity. Its strength, like that of every race, lies in its purity; and since to mix it with other races is, *ex hypothesi*, to mix it with what is inferior, the offspring of such a mixture must be less and less able to carry on the civilizing mission of the Aryan race. The disappearance or degeneration of the Aryan race would "lower again the dark cloak of a cultureless age over the terrestrial globe"; the preservation of the Aryan race from contamination is the one way of preventing civilization and "the beauty of the world" from "sinking into the grave".

The root principles, then, of National Socialism, from which spring its rules of conduct, its laws and its institutions, are, first, the natural principle of the distinction of races and its corollary, the necessity of preserving the purity of each race; and secondly, the historical principle of the inequality of races and the superiority of the Aryan race over all others.

Of the many conclusions that are drawn from these principles we may notice two. First, it follows that the "pacifist-humanist" (liberal) ideal, the ideal which looked forward to the cessation of the struggle of man against man, class against class and people against people, is a false ideal. Not only does it hold out a false hope, the hope of peace not based upon conquest and force, but it rests upon a mistaken analysis of the fundamental conflicting elements in history. Its hope is false, because the law of nature is war and struggle and the victory of the strongest. Its analysis is mistaken because history is not composed of the struggle of class against class but of race against race. Liberalism is error because its thought lacks a racial orientation. And secondly, it follows that, just as for Communism the self-consciousness of the individual is essentially a class-consciousness, so for National Socialism the true consciousness of self is a race-consciousness. The foundation of personality is "racial sense and racial feeling".

It is, perhaps, worth noticing that these doctrines with regard to race are those which lie at the root of what Alfred Rosenberg calls the "religion" of the twentieth century. In Rosenberg's book, *Der Mythus des 20. Jahrhunderts*, they are explained with a lucidity and a wealth of historical and imaginative detail not to be found in *Mein*

Kampf. A few quotations will serve to show the tendency of the doctrine. First, the conception of race itself, and the new racial conception of history and civilization.

History and vocation no longer consist in struggle of class against class, church dogma against dogma, but in struggle between blood and blood, race and race, people and people. And this means: values of soul fight against values of soul. That history must be judged from the point of view of race is a truth that will soon be self-understood. . . . But the values of the *soul* of race, which are the motive powers behind the new philosophy, are not yet part of actual general knowledge. Now soul means race seen from within. Conversely, race is the outside of a soul. To call to life the soul of race is to recognize its supreme value and, under its guidance, to give the other values their organic position: in the state, art and religion. This is the task of our century: to create a new type of man out of a new myth of life. . . . (pp. 1–2.)

Each race has its soul, each soul its race, its own internal and external architecture. . . . Each race ultimately produces one supreme ideal only. If this ideal is altered or even dethroned by other systems of breeding, by a prevalent infiltration of foreign blood and foreign ideas, the consequence of this internal alteration comes to external expression in a chaos, in epochs of catastrophe. . . . (p. 116.)

And secondly, the superiority of the Aryan race.

However much may still be doubtful . . . the result of research will not alter this great fact that the "sense of the history of the world" went over the whole earth from the North, carried by a race with blond hair and blue eyes, a race which in several big waves determined the spiritual face of the world, determined it even where it had to perish. . . . (p. 28.)

To-day a new belief arises: the myth of blood, the belief that in defending blood we defend the divine nature of man; the belief, embodied in clearest knowledge, that nordic blood is that mysterium which has replaced and conquered the old sacraments. . . . Aryan India gave the world a metaphysics deeper than any other up to our time; Aryan Persia produced the religious myth on whose force we all feast even to-day; Doric Hellas dreamed a beauty in this world whose perfection, lying before us and resting in itself, was never again attained; Italian Rome showed us the formal state's discipline as an example of how a community menaced in its human values must frame and defend itself. And Germanic Europe gave the world the most wonderful idea of mankind, in the doctrine of the value of character as basis of all morals, in the hymn about the supreme values of nordic nature, the idea of freedom of conscience and honour. . . . (p. 114.)

In the midst of the most terrible collapse the old nordic soul of race wakes up to new, higher consciousness. It sees at last that different—of necessity mutually exclusive—supreme values must not co-exist with equal rights. . . . It sees that what is related to its soul and race may be fitted in, but that the foreign must be ruthlessly rejected and, if need be, fought down. Not because it is "wrong" or "bad" in itself, but because it is foreign to the kind and destroys the internal construction of our nature.... (p. 118.)

(ii) When these beliefs about race and civilization are put together they make what Hitler calls a *völkisch* philosophy of life; that is, a view of the world and human destiny governed by the notion of race and the belief in the superiority of the Aryan. It is admitted that the words *Volk* and *völkisch* are ill-defined, and the foreigner will have difficulty in discovering their precise meaning. In their place in the National Socialist doctrine they appear to combine the conceptions of race and nation: the *völkisch* philosophy is a racialist-nationalist philosophy; the nation conceived as a racial unit, the race conceived as an organized political entity and the individual conceived as a member of a racial, national community. But whatever difficulty there may be in this *völkisch* conception, the primary tenet of this philosophy of life is unambiguous: everything is a means to one end, "the preservation of the racial existence of man". The "racial existence of man" is Nature's primary concern, and it must be the primary concern of man in his rules of conduct, laws and institutions. The significance of man lies in his "racial fundamentals".

Now, this *völkisch* philosophy of life is opposed to the interpretation of the world and of the history of mankind current in Western Europe to-day. That interpretation fails to appreciate the "basic racial forces", denies or forgets that some races are higher and more valuable than others, and advocates a pacifist-internationalism in which the true values of life are lost or destroyed. This has resulted in an undermining of the security of human culture by the contamination and destruction of its bearers. National Socialism, then, with its *völkisch* philosophy, is a protest against the degeneration of the contemporary world. And since this degeneration is a fact and the interpretation of the world which has led to it is an organized doctrine with force and power behind it, the *völkisch* philosophy also must organize itself. A vague, indeterminate philosophy, whatever its truth, will perish if it lacks a "fighting representation". The first business of the believers in this philosophy is to formulate it definitely and in the simplest terms, so that it can be understood and believed by all; and their second business is to give it a "concrete organization", a "fighting representation". First it must be made the "dogma of a religious creed", and then it must be provided with "a fighting organization in the form of military power". These two services have been performed for the *völkisch* philosophy of life by the National Socialist German Workers' Party (N.S.D.A.P.). The programme of the party is the definite formulation of the philosophy, and the organization of the party is the "fighting representation" of the philosophy. "The National Socialist German Workers' Party takes over the essential characteristics of the fundamental train of thought of a general *völkisch* view of the world. From them, keeping in mind the practical reality of the time and of the actual human material, as well as of its weakness, it creates the precondition for the fight of this philosophy of life to a victorious conclusion." "Any philosophy of life, be it a thousand times right and of the highest utility to mankind, will remain without significance for the practical shaping of the life of a people so long as its principles do not become the banner of a fighting movement. This movement will in its turn be a party, so long as its activity has not fulfilled itself in the victory of its ideas, and will make the party-creed the new fundamental laws of the State created by the community of a people."

(iii) Since the "racial existence of man" is the only end valuable for its own sake, it follows that the social and political organization of a community is a means to this end and not something of intrinsic worth. It is impossible to enjoy the highest life without such social and political organization, without the State; but it is not, and cannot be the cause of the highest life—"the cause lies exclusively in the existence of a race qualified for civilization". Behind the State, behind the organized community, then, lies the racial existence of man, and these are the means by which it is preserved and advanced.

The first principle of the State must, therefore, be its racial unity. It belongs to the nature of a State, a politically and legally organized community, to be "a community of living beings, physically and mentally of the same species". And the primary task of preservation which falls to the State is the "maintenance of the racial characteristics" of the community. "States which do not serve this end are delusions, veritable abortions." It follows, then, that the excellence of a State is not to be determined simply by the level of its civilization or its power in the world, because it may happen that, at a given moment in history, a community careless of its racial integrity has reached a high level of civilization. This carelessness will, in the end, prove its ruin; but for the moment it is civilized and powerful. The excellence of a State must, rather, be judged by the thoroughness with which its organization is directed towards the preservation of the racial integrity of the community.

The German people (*Volkstum*), according to Hitler's view, no longer rests upon a uniform racial core. Its blood has been poisoned and its soul contaminated. This has led to a disintegration of the community, and has caused it to "lose the domination of the world". But for this there might exist in the world a true peace "founded upon the victorious sword of a ruling people, seizing the world in the interest of a higher civilization". But there is one great advantage in the failure of the mixture of races in Germany to form a satisfactory racial fusion— Germany to-day possesses "great quantities of racially-pure Nordic-German men and women". And this gives a foundation upon which to build a true State, a State according to the *völkisch* ideal. For "the highest end of the *völkisch* State is care for the preservation of those basic racial factors which, as bestowers of civilization, create the beauty and the dignity of a higher humanity".

(iv) The *völkisch* philosophy of life implies the recognition of the differing quality of different races and stocks. And just as it leads us to assign different values to different races, it leads us also to assign different values to different individuals within a race or a people (*Volksgemein-schaft*). Neither individuals nor races can be compared with one another on a basis of equal value. And it is characteristic, says Hitler, of the liberal philosophy to neglect both those principles: in the name of "humanity" it abolished the distinctions of quality between races; in the name of "democracy" it abolished the distinctions of quality between individuals.

A given race or a given community consists, then, of individuals of different values; and it is the first business of the *völkisch* State to recognize this and build it as a principle into the social and political structure of the community.

The first and most obvious consequence of the recognition of the differing value of individuals will be the provision of opportunity for the best elements in the community to "breed apart from the rest"— the best elements being those which are recognized as "especially valuable on racial grounds". But there is a more important consequence than this; it is the rejection of the whole democratic conception of a community and the substitution for it of an aristocratic conception. The earth must be given to the most excellent people (race), and further, to the most excellent individuals within that people. The principle of the *völkisch* State is the principle of "individuality" as against the principle of "majority".

Now this aristocratic principle of individuality is a "natural" principle; it is, indeed, a law of Nature which we forget at our peril. All change, all invention, all advance in living results from "the actions of specially clever individuals" and spreads from these to the race as a whole. "It is not the mass that invents nor the majority that organizes or thinks, but in all these activities always the single man, the individual." Consequently, a human society must be considered well organized only in so far as it is, in this matter, on the side of Nature, only in so far as it gives to the creative, inventive individual the scope that he needs, only in so far as it assists the emergence of creative individuals from the mass of men. Indeed, society is in its essence "the incorporation of the endeavour to set the individual above the mass and to organize the mass in subordination to the individual".

How can society assist nature in this matter? The relentless struggle for life itself is the principal agent for the selection of individuals who are specially valuable. But a society must be organized in such a way that the emergent individual shall be given his full value, shall be given what belongs to him, authority and responsibility. The model of such an organization is an army, where the idea of individuality is still supreme, of individual authority downwards and of responsibility to the superior individual upwards. The political community must abandon the false democratic principle of the majority for the great natural principle of individuality as exemplified in an army. And it is the work of the *völkisch* philosophy to recall the world to this neglected principle. For it, as for no other philosophy, "the best political constitution and the best kind of State is that which with the most natural certainty places the best individuals of the community in a position of leading importance and guiding influence". This principle of individuality must permeate the organization of the State from top to bottom. "The principle which in its time made the Prussian army the most wonderful instrument of the German people must at some future time be the decisive principle of the construction of our whole conception of the State: *authority of every leader downwards and responsibility upwards.*" Such a State requires an *élite* of Leaders; and this must be bred and educated. And just as the *völkisch* philosophy itself finds its first definite expression in the creed of a Party which is gradually extended to the community as a whole, so this principle of individuality and leadership finds its first expression in the organization of a Party and is later applied to the State itself.

§4. NATIONAL SOCIALIST LABOUR SERVICE

The government of the Reich has decided upon the following law, which is promulgated hereby:

Article 1

(1) The Reich Labour Service is a service of honour to the German nation.

(2) All young Germans of both sexes must serve their nation in the Reich Labour Service.

(3) The Reich Labour Service is created to educate the German youth in the spirit of National Socialism so that it may acquire a true national community feeling, a true conception of labour and above all a proper respect for manual labour.

(4) The Reich Labour Service is organized for the carrying out of public welfare works.

Article 2

(1) The Reich Labour Service is under the jurisdiction of the Reichs Minister of the Interior. Under him the Reichs Labour Leader exercises supreme authority in the Reich Labour Service.

(2) The Reichs Labour Leader is at the head of the Reich administration of the Labour Service. He determines the organization, supervises the distribution of work and directs training and education.

Article 3

(1) The *Führer* and Chancellor of the Reich determines the number of people to be called annually for service, and he determines also the length of service.

(2) Obligation for service begins with the completion of the eighteenth year and ends with the completion of the twenty-fifth year.

(3) Those liable for compulsory service will, generally, be called for Reich Labour Service in the calendar year in which they complete their nineteenth year. Voluntary enrolment in the Reich Labour Service at an earlier age is possible.

(4) These subject to compulsory service and those serving voluntarily are liable to imprisonment for not more than thirty days if they leave the Reich Labour Service in any ways other than those provided in Article 16.

Article 4

Those subject to compulsory service are drafted by the recruiting offices of the Reich Labour Service.

Article 5

(1) The following are excluded from Labour Service:

(a) Those who have been punished with penal servitude.

(b) Those who do not enjoy the rights of citizenship.

(c) Those subject to the measures for protection and reform set out in Article 42 (a) of the Criminal Code.

(d) Those who have been expelled from the National Socialist Labour Party because of dishonourable activities.

(e) Those who have been punished by court for treasonable activity.

(2) The Reichs Minister of the Interior may make exceptions to (c) and (e) of § 1.

(3) Those subject to compulsory service in the Labour Service who have been deprived of eligibility to hold public offices may be called for service only after the expiration of the period of sentence.

Article 6

(1) No persons shall be called for the Labour Service who are completely unfitted for the Reich Labour Service.

(2) Those subject to compulsory Labour Service who live abroad, or who desire to go abroad for a long period, may be relieved of the duty of labour service for up to two years, in exceptional cases permanently, and in all cases for the period of the residence abroad.

Article 7

(1) No one shall be permitted to serve in the Reich Labour Service who is of non-Aryan descent or who is married to a person of non-Aryan descent. . . .

(2) Non-Aryans who by Article 15 § 2 of the Army Law have been declared worthy of military service may also be allowed to serve in the Reich Labour Service. They may not, however, become leaders in the Reich Labour Service.

Article 9

The provisions for the Labour Service duties of young women are subject to separate legal regulations.

Article 10

(1) The Members of the Reich Labour Service are:

    (*a*) The permanent staff.

    (*b*) Those recruited for Labour Service.

    (*c*) Volunteers in the Labour Service.

(2) Persons may also be engaged by labour contracts for the performance of definite services.

Article 11

(1) The permanent staff consists of the regular leaders and officials and also candidates for these posts. The regular leaders and officials belong professionally to the Reich Labour Service.

(2) A candidate for the post of leader in the Reich Labour Service must, before he becomes a regular troop leader, give a written engagement to serve continuously for at least ten years and must supply proof of Aryan descent. He must also have completed his active service in the army.

(3) Regular leaders and officials are retired on the attainment of specific age limits.

(4) Officials of other departments who are transferred to the Reich Labour Service retain all the salary rights which they have already acquired.

(5) The *Führer* and Chancellor of the Reich appoints and dismisses all members of the Reich Labour Service from the rank of Work Leader upwards. All other members of the permanent staff are appointed and dismissed by the Reichs Minister of the Interior on the recommendation of the Reichs Labour Leader. He may devolve these powers upon the Reichs Labour Leader.

Article 12

(1) A regular leader or official may be dismissed from service at any time:

    (*a*) In reasonable cases on his own request.

    (*b*) If he no longer possesses the physical or intellectual powers necessary for the performance of his duties and if, in the view of the medical officer of the Labour Service, he cannot be expected to regain those powers within one year.

(c) If in the judgement of his superior leader he no longer possesses the capacity for the performance of his duties.

(2) Dismissal is compulsory if reasons barring membership of the Labour Service under Articles 5 or 7 are subsequently discovered.

Article 15

Members of the Reich Labour Service are subject to the discipline of the Reich Labour Service.

Article 17

(1) Members of the Reich Labour Service are not to engage in any active service in the National Socialist Labour Party or any of its affiliated organizations. This is not to prejudice their membership of the Party.

(2) Members of the Reich Labour Service must obtain permission before they solicit or exercise membership in organizations of any sort, as well as for the formation of organizations within or without the Reich Labour Service.

Article 18

Members of the Reich Labour Service must obtain permission before they marry.

Article 19

Members of the Reich Labour Service must obtain permission before they take over the direction of a business either for themselves or for the members of their family, as well as for accepting any additional occupation involving remuneration.

Article 20

(1) Members of the Reich Labour Service may refuse positions as guardian, co-guardian, trustee, adviser or any honorary activity in the Reich, state or municipality or in the party service.

(2) Permission must be obtained before such positions are assumed. Such permission may be denied only in exceptional cases.

Article 21

In case of sickness or accident members of the Reich Labour Service are entitled to free medical attention and nursing in accordance with separate regulations.

Article 22

Salaries of members of the Reich Labour Service are regulated by the salary decree of the Reich Labour Service.

Article 24

Pensions for persons injured in service, and for members of the permanent staff retiring after at least ten years' service and their survivors, are regulated by the Law of Pensions for the Reich Labour Service.

Article 25

(1) The *Führer* and Chancellor of the Reich, or any agent empowered by him, may permit retiring members of the Reich Labour Service to wear the uniform of the Reich Labour Service, subject to recall.

(2) This right may be granted only after honourable service of at least ten years.

From *The Law on Labour Service, 26 June* 1935

§5. RACE AND CITIZENSHIP

The Reichstag has unanimously adopted the following law which is hereby promulgated:

Article 1

(1) A subject of the State is he who belongs to the protective union of the German Reich and who, therefore, has specific obligations towards the Reich.

(2) The status of subject is acquired in accordance with the provisions of the Reich and State Law of Citizenship.

Article 2

(1) A citizen of the Reich is only that subject of the Reich who is of German or kindred blood and who, through his conduct, shows that he desires and is fit to serve faithfully the German people and the Reich.

(2) The right of citizenship is acquired by the granting of Reich citizenship papers.

(3) A citizen of the Reich alone enjoys full political rights in accordance with the laws.

Article 3

The Reichs Minister of the Interior, in conjunction with the Deputy of the *Führer*, will issue the necessary legal and administrative decrees for the carrying out and amplification of this law.

Reich Citizenship Law, 15 September 1935

Knowing that the purity of the German blood is the necessary condition of the continued existence of the German people, and inspired by the inflexible will to ensure the existence of the German people for all future times, the Reichstag has unanimously adopted the following law which is hereby promulgated:

Article 1

(1) Marriages between Jews and subjects of German or kindred blood are prohibited. Marriages contracted despite this law are invalid, even if they are concluded abroad in order to circumvent this law.

(2) Proceedings for annulment of marriages may be initiated only by the Public Prosecutor.

Article 2

Extra-marital relations between Jews and subjects of German or kindred blood are prohibited.

Article 3

Jews may not employ in domestic service female subjects of the Reich of German or kindred blood who are under the age of 45 years.

Article 4

(1) Jews are forbidden to display the Reich and national flag or to show the national colours.

(2) The display of the Jewish colours is permitted for them. The exercise of this right is protected by the State.

Article 5

(1) Whoever violates the provisions of *Article 1* shall be punished with penal servitude.

(2) The man who acts in violation of *Article 2* shall be punished with either imprisonment or penal servitude.

(3) Whoever acts in violation of *Articles* 3 *or* 4 shall be punished with imprisonment up to one year and with a fine or with either of these penalties.

From *The Law for the Protection of German Blood and
Honour,* 15 *September* 1935

On the basis of *Article* 3 of the Reich Citizenship Law of 15 *September* 1935, the following is hereby decreed:

Article 1

(1) Until further provisions regarding citizenship papers are made, all subjects of German or kindred blood who possessed the right to vote in the Reichstag elections at the time when the Law of Citizenship came into effect shall for the time being possess the rights of Reich citizens. The same rights shall be enjoyed by those upon whom the Reichs Minister of the Interior and the Deputy of the *Führer* shall bestow citizenship.

(2) The Reichs Minister of the Interior, in conjunction with the Deputy of the *Führer*, may revoke citizenship.

Article 2

(1) The provisions of *Article* 1 shall apply also to subjects who are of mixed Jewish blood.

(2) A person of mixed Jewish blood is one who has one or two grandparents who are racially full Jews, in so far as he does not count as a Jew under § 2 of *Article* 5. Jewish grandparents shall be considered to be full-blooded Jews if they belonged to the Jewish religious community.

Article 3

Only citizens of the Reich, as enjoying full political rights, may vote in political affairs and may hold public office....

Article 4

(1) A Jew cannot be a citizen of the Reich. He cannot exercise the right to vote; he cannot hold public office....

Article 5

(1) A Jew is anyone who is descended from at least three grand-parents who were racially full Jews....

(2) A Jew is also one who is descended from two full-blooded Jewish grandparents if:

    (a) He belonged to the Jewish religious community at the time when this law was decreed or joined the community subsequently.

    (b) At the time when this law was issued he was married to a Jew or has subsequently married a Jew.

    (c) He is the offspring of a marriage with a Jew in the sense of § 1, which was contracted after the coming into effect of the Law for the Protection of German Blood and Honour of 15 September 1935.

    (d) He is the offspring of an extra-marital relationship with a Jew according to § 1, and will be born out of wedlock after 31 July 1936.

Article 7

The *Führer* and Chancellor of the Reich is empowered to release anyone from the provisions of these administrative decrees.

From *The Decree of* 14 *November* 1935

§ 6. THE HITLER YOUTH

The future of the German people depends upon its youth. The whole German youth must therefore be prepared for the performance of its future duties. The Reich government has, therefore, decided upon the following law which is hereby decreed:

Article 1. The whole German youth within the territory of the Reich is unified in the Hitler Youth.

Article 2. The whole German youth, outside their homes and schools, is to be educated in the Hitler Youth organization physically, spiritually and morally in the spirit of National Socialism and for the service of the nation and community.

Article 3. The duty of educating the whole German youth within the Hitler Youth organization is entrusted to the Reichs Youth Leader of the National Socialist Labour Party. He hereby becomes Youth Leader of the German Reich. He is given the status of a chief Reichs Officer with his seat in Berlin, and he is immediately responsible to the *Führer* and Chancellor of the Reich.

Article 4. The legal decrees and administrative orders necessary for carrying out and amplifying this law will be issued by the *Führer* and Chancellor of the Reich.

Law of 1 *December* 1936

§ 7. THE LAW OF LABOUR

§ 1. In any business the employer as the Leader (*Führer*) of the business, and the employees and labourers as Followers (*Gefolgschaft*), work in common for the promotion of the aims of the business and the common good of the People and the State.

§ 2. (i) The Leader of the business, as opposed to the Followers, decides all matters relating to the business in so far as they are regulated by this law.

(ii) He shall care for the well-being of the Followers; who shall observe towards him the loyalty that is implied in their being members of the community of the business.

§ 3. (i) In the case of Corporations and unincorporated firms, the legal representatives are the Leaders of the businesses.

(ii) The employer, or in the case of corporations and unincorporated firms the legal representatives, may appoint as deputy a person responsibly associated with the control of the business; this must happen if they do not control the business personally. They may also appoint another person to deal with matters of lesser importance.

(iii) If the Leader of the business is disqualified from being Leader by a Court of Honour under § 38, and when the disqualification has taken effect, a different Leader shall be appointed.

§ 5. (i) In a business of generally not less than twenty employees the Leader shall be supported and advised by Spokesmen (*Vertrauensmänner*) of the Followers. They form with him and under his guidance the Council of Trust (*Vertrauensrat*) of the business.

(ii) Followers within the meaning of the provisions concerning the Council of Trust include workers who pursue some branch of industry in their own works, if in the main they work for the purpose and at the risk of the same business whether alone or with members of their families.

§ 6. (i) It is the duty of the Council of Trust to deepen the mutual confidence within the community of the business.

(ii) It is the task of the Council of Trust to consider all measures tending to improve the work done, the arrangement and observance of the general conditions of work, in particular the Rules and Regulations of the business, the observance and improvement of the safety precautions, the strengthening of the sense of loyalty of all members of the community of the business towards each other and towards the business itself and the welfare of all members of the community. The Council of Trust shall also endeavour to bring about a settlement of all disputes arising within the community of the business. It is to be heard before fines are imposed in accordance with the Rules and Regulations of the business.

(iii) The Council of Trust may delegate the execution of particular tasks to particular Spokesmen.

§ 8. A Spokesman must be a person who is at least twenty-five years old, who has belonged to the business or undertaking for at least one year, and who has been engaged for at least two years in the same or a related trade or branch of industry. He must possess civil rights, belong to the German Labour Front, be distinguished by exemplary qualities of character and be wholly dependable with regard to his willingness at all times unreservedly to uphold the national State. . . .

§ 9. (i) The Leader of the business, in consultation with the Head of the National Socialist Business Cell Organization, proposes in the March of each year a list of Spokesmen and their deputies. The Followers shall in due course express their opinion with regard to the list by a secret vote.

(ii) If the Leader of the business and the Head of the National Socialist Business Cell Organization do not reach agreement as to the Spokesmen and the deputies to be proposed, or if a Council of Trust fails to be formed for any other reason, in particular if the Followers do not approve of the list proposed, the Supervisor of Labour (*Treuhänder der Arbeit*) may appoint the requisite number of Spokesmen and deputies.

§ 10. (i) The members of the Council of Trust shall on National Labour Day (1st May) solemnly swear in the presence of the Followers that they will in the exercise of their offices subordinate selfish interests, serve only the welfare of the business and the community of the whole nation, and by their lives and the manner of their service afford examples to the members of the business.

§ 13. (i) The office of Spokesman is honorary and a remuneration for its exercise shall not be paid. The ordinary wage shall be paid for the loss of working-time involved in the execution of the necessary duties. Necessary expenses shall be paid by the management of the business.

(ii) The management of the business shall make the necessary arrangements and provide the necessary facilities for the Council of Trust to carry out its work properly. The Leader of the business is obliged to supply the Spokesman with such information as is necessary for carrying out their work.

§ 14. (i) The term of office of a Spokesman ceases, apart from voluntary resignation, with his leaving the business. The termination of a Spokesman's contract of work is inadmissible unless it is necessary because of the discontinuation of the business or of a department of the business, or takes place for a reason which justifies the termination of the contract of work without notice.

(ii) The Supervisor of Labour may remove a Spokesman on the ground of technical or personal unfitness. The term of office of a Spokesman who is removed shall cease with the written notification of the decision of the Supervisor of Labour to the Council of Trust.

(iii) The term of office of a Spokesman ceases also when sentences passed by a Court of Honour according to § 38 (2) to (5) take effect.

§ 16. The majority of the Council of Trust may immediately in writing appeal to the Supervisor of Labour against decisions made by the Leader of the business with regard to conditions of work, and in particular with regard to the Rules and Regulations of the business, if these decisions appear incompatible with the economic and social conditions of the business. The appeal shall not hinder the operation of the decisions of the Leader of the business.

§ 17. If several businesses, being economically or technically alike or in view of their objects connected, are under the control of one employer, he, or if he does not himself direct the enterprise, the Leader appointed by him, shall summon from the Councils of Trust of the several businesses an Advisory Council (*Beirat*), the purpose of which shall be to advise him in social matters.

§ 26. In every business in which normally not less than twenty employees and workmen are engaged the Leader shall issue in writing for the Followers the Rules and Regulations of the business (*Betriebs-ordnung*).

§ 27. (iii) The Rules and Regulations of the business may, apart from the provisions required by law, contain also provisions concerning the rate of pay or other regulations concerning work; they may also include rules regarding order in the business, the conduct of those engaged in it and for the avoidance of accidents.

§ 29. In so far as the Rules and Regulations of the business determine the wages payable to the workmen and employees, they shall contain minimum wage rates drawn up in such a way as to leave scope for the remuneration of individual members of the business according to the work done. Also generally speaking the possibility of a fitting reward to be given for special pieces of work is to be taken into account.

§ 30. The Rules and Regulations of the business shall be compulsory in the sense of providing minimum conditions for its members.

§ 32. (i) The Supervisor of Labour may, after consultation with a committee of experts (§ 23, (iii)), lay down guiding principles for the Rules and Regulations of businesses and individual labour contracts.

(ii) If it is necessary for the protection of those engaged in a group of businesses situated within the district controlled by a Supervisor of Labour that minimum conditions should be laid down with a view to regulating the conditions of work, the Supervisor of Labour may, after consultation with a committee of experts, in writing issue a scale of wages. . . . A scale of wages is compulsory as a minimum scale for the labour contracts which it covers. It shall override any provisions to the contrary in the Rules and Regulations of the businesses. . . .

(iii) The general principles and the scale of wages shall be published by the Supervisor of Labour.

§ 35. Every member of the community of a business shall be responsible for the conscientious fulfilment of the duties that belong to him by reason of his place in it. He shall by his conduct prove himself worthy of the respect which belongs to his place in the community of the business. In particular he should be constantly aware of his responsibility to devote his whole strength to the service of the business, and to subordinate himself to the common good.

§ 36. (i) Grave offences against the social duties implied in the community of a business shall be punished, as offences against social honour, by Courts of Honour. Offences of this character are committed if:

1. Employers, Leaders of businesses or other persons in authority by misuse of their superior position in the industry malevolently exploit the strength of the members of the Followers or offend their honour.

2. Members of the Followers endanger the peaceful relations obtaining in a business by malevolently inciting the Followers, in particular when Spokesmen knowingly and improperly interfere

with the control of the business or repeatedly and malevolently disturb the spirit of fellowship in the community of the business.

3. Members of the community of a business send repeatedly to the Supervisor of Labour ill-considered and unfounded complaints or requests, or persistently contravene his written instructions.

4. Members of the Council of Trust without authority reveal confidential information or industrial or business secrets which they have learned while fulfilling their special tasks and which they know to be secrets.

(iii) Civil Servants and Soldiers are not subject to the jurisdiction of the Courts of Honour.

§ 37. Prosecution by Courts of Honour of the offences against social honour described in § 36 is limited to a period of one year. This limitation commences from the day on which the offence was committed.

§ 38. The punishments that may be imposed by a Court of Honour are:

(1) Warning.

(2) Reprimand.

(3) A fine, up to R.M. 10,000.

(4) Disqualification from being Leader of a business or from holding the office of Spokesman.

(5) Removal from present occupation: the Court of Honour can in so doing prescribe a notice different from that required by law or by agreement.

§ 41. (i) Offences against social honour are tried, on the application of the Supervisor of Labour, by a Court of Honour which shall be established in each district controlled by a Supervisor of Labour.

(ii) The Court of Honour consists of a judicial officer, as President, who shall be appointed by the Reichs Minister of Justice in consultation with the Reichs Minister of Labour, a Leader of a business and Spokesmen as associates. Leaders of business and Spokesmen are to be chosen by the President of the Court of Honour from the list of nominees drawn up by the German Labour Front under § 23; they are to be chosen according to the order of the list, only in such a way that as far as possible persons shall be chosen who belong to the same kind of business as the accused.

§ 42. The associates before they undertake their duties shall swear before the President of the Court that they will conscientiously fulfil the obligations of their office.

§ 63. The provisions of Parts I to V [i.e. §§ 1 to 62] of this law shall not apply to employees and workmen of the State or of the Provinces in administration and business, of the State Bank, the State Railways, the enterprise of the *Reichsautobahnen*, municipalities and other corporations, establishments and other institutions coming under public law. As regards these, a special law will be enacted.

From *The Law for the Ordering of National Labour*,
20 *January* 1934

§8. BLUT AND BODEN

The Reichs Cabinet desire to preserve the peasantry as the source which keeps the blood of the German people vigorous, safeguarding at the same time old German usage in the matter of succession.

Farms shall be prevented from being encumbered with debts and split up in the course of succession, in order that they may remain constantly in the hands of free peasants as the inheritance of the clan.

A healthy distribution of free property is to be aimed at, since a great number of prosperous small and average-sized farms, spread over the whole country as evenly as possible, is the best guarantee of the healthiness of People and State.

The Reichs Cabinet therefore has decided on the following law. The principles of the law are:

Any rural property and forest of at least one field sufficient to afford a livelihood, and at most 309 acres, is a hereditary homestead if it belongs to a person qualified to be a Peasant.

The owner of the hereditary homestead is called Peasant.

A Peasant must be a German citizen, of German or closely related blood, and honourable.

The hereditary homestead passes to the principal heir undivided.

The rights of the co-heirs are confined to the remaining property of the Peasant. Descendants who are not principal heirs can obtain training and equipment in accordance with the means of the homestead; if they become destitute through no fault of their own, they will be given the shelter of the paternal roof.

The right of a principal heir cannot be set aside or restricted by will.

The hereditary homestead is essentially inalienable and unpledgeable.

The law is herewith published.

I. THE HEREDITARY HOMESTEAD

§ 1. *Definition*

(i) Any rural property and forest, used as such, is a hereditary homestead if in respect of its size it fulfils the requirements of §§ 2 and 3, and if a person qualified to be a peasant has the sole ownership.

(ii) Farms, the regular use of which consists in letting them on lease, are not hereditary homesteads.

§ 2. *Minimum size*

(i) The hereditary homestead must be at least the size of a field sufficient to provide a livelihood.

(ii) A field sufficient to afford a livelihood means that amount of land which is necessary to provide a family with their food and clothes independently of the market and the general economic situation, and for maintaining the economic life of the hereditary homestead.

§ 3. *Maximum limit*

(i) The hereditary homestead must not exceed 309 acres.

(ii) It must be possible to manage it from a farm-house without outworks.

§ 7. *The hereditary homestead*

(i) The hereditary homestead comprises all fields belonging to the Peasant which are regularly managed from the farm-house, and the accessories belonging to the Peasant.

(ii) Fields temporarily let on lease or temporarily used in a similar way, e.g. set aside for the parents, are not for this reason excluded from the homestead.

§ 8. *Accessories of the homestead in particular*

(i) The accessories of the homestead comprise in particular such cattle, farming and household utensils, including linen and beds, as are on the farm for its cultivation, the existing manure and the stock of agricultural products used for cultivation.

(ii) In addition the accessories comprise documents relating to the homestead, family letters dating from earlier generations, pictures valuable as mementoes, horns and similar memorials relating to the homestead and the family of Peasants settled there.

II. The Peasant

§ 11. *Definition*

(i) No one but the owner of a hereditary homestead is called Peasant.

(ii) The owner or holder of other rural property and forests is called a farmer.

(iii) All other descriptions of owners or holders of rural property and forests are inadmissible.

§ 12. *Requirement of German citizenship*

A Peasant must possess German citizenship.

§ 13. *Requirement of German or closely related blood*

(i) A Peasant must be of German or closely related blood.

(ii) He among whose paternal or maternal ancestors there is Jewish or coloured blood is not of German or closely related blood.

(iii) The day from which the requirements of section (i) must be fulfilled is 1 January 1800....

§ 14. *Exclusion through interdiction*

He who has been declared incapable of managing his affairs cannot be a Peasant, provided the appeal has been dismissed and the dismissal has taken effect or provided no appeal has been brought within the proper period.

§ 15. *The Peasant honourable and able*

(i) The Peasant must be honourable. He must be able to manage the homestead properly. Minority is no bar.

(ii) If the Peasant ceases to fulfil the requirements of section (i) or if he does not discharge his liabilities although with proper management this would be possible, the courts concerned with succession may, on the application of the provincial Leader of the Peasants, appoint the husband or wife of the Peasant or him who if the Peasant died would be the principal heir, permanently or temporarily to manage and use the hereditary homestead.

(iii) If there is no husband, wife or principal heir, or if they are not qualified to be Peasants, the court may, on the application of the Reichs Leader of the Peasants, transfer the ownership of the hereditary homestead to a person qualified to be a Peasant who shall be nominated by the Reichs Leader of the Peasants. The Reichs Leader shall, if there are suitable relatives of the Peasant, nominate one of these.

(iv) The ownership of the hereditary homestead passes as soon as the resolution to transfer it takes legal effect. . . .

§ 16. *Effect of the loss of qualification to be a Peasant*

If the Peasant ceases to be qualified to be a Peasant, he may no longer call himself Peasant. His ownership of the homestead and the character of the farm as hereditary homestead are not thereby affected, except for the case described in § 15.

§ 17. *Common ownership. Legal personalities*

A hereditary homestead cannot belong to the joint property of a married couple nor can it in any other way be owned by several persons in common.

§ 18. *Decision of the court concerned with the succession about qualifications of a Peasant*

If it is doubtful whether a person is qualified to be a Peasant, the court concerned with succession shall decide on his application or on the application of the district Leader of the Peasants.

III. SUCCESSION OF THE PRINCIPAL HEIR

§ 19. *Succession to the hereditary homestead*

(i) On the death of the Peasant the hereditary homestead, as regards the law of succession and the division of inheritance, forms a special part of the inheritance.

(ii) The hereditary homestead by law vests in the principal heir undivided.

§ 20. *Order of principal heirs*

These are qualified to be principal heirs, in the following order:

(1) the sons of the deceased; if a son is dead, his place is filled by his sons and grandsons;

(2) the father of the deceased;

(3) the brothers of the deceased; if a brother is dead, his place is filled by his sons and grandsons;

(4) the daughters of the deceased; if a daughter is dead, her place is filled by her sons and grandsons;

(5) the sisters of the deceased; if a sister is dead, her place is filled by her sons and grandsons;

(6) the female descendants of the deceased and their descendants, in so far as they do not come under (4). He who is nearer the male line of the deceased excludes him who is farther. Apart from that a male descendant shall be preferred to a female.

§ 21. *Particular provisions regarding the order of principal heirs*

(i) He who is not qualified to be a Peasant shall be discounted as principal heir. The hereditary homestead vests in that person who would have been principal heir at the time when the owner died, if the discounted one had not lived.

(ii) A relative does not succeed as principal heir so long as there is a relative of a higher order.

(iii) Within the same order the decision shall be based on the right of the eldest or the right of the youngest according to the custom obtaining in the region. If there is no established custom, the right of the youngest shall be the basis. If it is doubtful whether or which custom exists, the court concerned with succession decides on the application of a person interested.

(iv) Of sons, the sons of the first wife precede the other sons. Of brothers or sisters those of the same parents precede half-brothers and half-sisters.

(v) Children recognized by later marriage are on the same footing as legitimate children born in wedlock. Legitimized children of the father are preceded by legitimate children in the same order. Illegitimate children of the mother are in any case preceded by legitimate children.

(vi) Adoptive children cannot succeed as principal heirs.

§ 24. *Testaments*

(i) The owner of a hereditary homestead cannot set aside or restrict the right of a principal heir by will.

§ 27. *Bearing the name of the homestead*

The owner of a hereditary homestead may lay down that the principal heir shall bear, in addition to his name, the name of the farm.

§ 30. *Providing for the descendants of the Peasant.* *Shelter of the paternal roof*

(i) The descendants of the deceased Peasant, as far as they are co-heirs or entitled by law to a portion of the inheritance, are fittingly maintained and educated on the farm till they attain majority.

(ii) They shall also be trained for an occupation in keeping with the position of the farm and, when they become independent or in the case of female descendants also when they marry, shall be equipped as far as the means of the farm allow; the equipment may in particular consist in furnishing means for procuring a piece of land for settlement.

(iii) If they become destitute without fault of their own, they may even later take shelter on the farm and shall, in return, adequately help with the work: shelter of the paternal roof. This right belongs also to the parents of the deceased peasant, if they are co-heirs or entitled by law to a portion of the inheritance.

IV. Restriction Imposed on Alienation and Pledging of the Hereditary Homestead

§ 37. *Alienation and pledging of the hereditary homestead*

(i) The hereditary homestead is essentially inalienable and un-pledgeable. This rule does not apply to a disposition affecting accessories if it is made in the normal course of proper management.

§ 38. *Protection against execution*

(i) The hereditary homestead cannot be seized in the course of an execution taking place on account of a pecuniary debt.

V. The Authorities Dealing with Succession

§ 40. *Principle*

(i) In order to carry out the special tasks implied in this law there will be formed courts concerned with succession, courts concerned with hereditary homesteads and the Reichs Court concerned with hereditary homesteads.

§ 41. *The court concerned with succession*

(i) The courts concerned with succession are formed by the provincial board of justice, at each inferior court for its district. The provincial board of justice may fix the district in a different manner; it may in particular lay down that only one court concerned with succession shall be formed for several inferior courts.

(ii) The court concerned with succession consists of one judge as president, two more judges and two Peasants.

§ 44. *Appointments of Peasants as associates*

The Peasant-associates of the courts concerned with succession are nominated by the provincial Leader of the Peasants, the Peasant-

associates of the courts concerned with hereditary homesteads by the
Reichs Leader of the Peasants; both are appointed by the provincial
board of justice. In addition to the associates the requisite number of
deputies shall be appointed.

§ 47. *The Reichs Court concerned with hereditary homesteads*

The organization, procedure, and seat of the Reichs Court concerned
with hereditary homesteads are regulated by a decree of the Reichs
Minister of Justice and the Reichs Minister of Food and Agriculture. It
may be provided that the decisions of the Reichs Court concerned with
hereditary homesteads need confirmation by the Reichs Minister of Food
and Agriculture.

§ 57. *Immunity from estate duty and conveyance duty*

The principal heir need not pay any estate duty or conveyance duty
for the passing of the hereditary homestead.

§ 60. *Provincial laws*

This law having taken effect, the provincial laws relating to succession
are invalid.

From *The Reichs Law concerning Hereditary Homesteads,*

Berlin, 29 *September* 1933

[A commentary on this law is provided by R. W. Darré, *Neuadel
aus Blut und Boden,* 1934.]

§9. DICTATORSHIP AND PARTY

(i) LAW TO COMBAT THE MISERY OF THE PEOPLE
AND REICH

The Reichstag has enacted the following law...which is hereby
promulgated:

Article 1. National laws can be enacted by the Reichs cabinet as well
as in accordance with the procedure established in the constitution...

Article 2. The Reich laws enacted by the Reichs cabinet may deviate
from the constitution in so far as they do not affect the position of the
Reichstag and the Reichrat. The powers of the President remain undisturbed.

Article 3. The Reich laws enacted by the Reichs cabinet are prepared by the Chancellor and published in the *Reichsgesetzblatt....*

Article 4. Treaties of the Reich with foreign states which concern matters of national legislation do not require the consent of bodies participating in legislation. The Reichs cabinet is empowered to issue the necessary provisions for the execution of these treaties.

Berlin, 24 *March* 1933

(ii) LAW PROHIBITING THE FORMATION OF NEW POLITICAL PARTIES

Article 1. The National Socialist German Workers' Party is the only political party in Germany.

Article 2. Whoever undertakes to maintain the organisation of another political party, or to form a new political party, is to be punished with imprisonment in a penitentiary up to three years or with confinement in a jail from six months to three years unless the act is punishable by a higher penalty under other provisions.

Berlin, 14 *July* 1933

(iii) LAW SAFEGUARDING THE UNITY OF PARTY AND THE STATE

Article 1. (i) After the victory of the National Socialist Revolution the N.S.D.A.P. has become the keystone (*Trägerin*) of the government and is inseparably connected with the State.

(ii) It is a corporation in public law. Its constitution is determined by the *Führer*.

Article 2. To secure the closest co-operation of services of the party with the public authorities, the deputy leader is a member of the Reichs cabinet.

Article 3. (i) Members of the N.S.D.A.P. and of the Storm Troops (including affiliated organisations) have, as the leading and moving power of the National Socialist State, increased duties towards the people and the State.

(ii) For violation and neglect of these duties the members are subject to special party and Storm Troop jurisdiction.

(iii) The Leader may extend these regulations to the members of other organisations.

Article 6. Public authorities must, within their power, give assistance to party and Storm Troop officials who are vested with party and Storm Troop jurisdiction in rendering justice and legal redress.

Article 7. The law governing penal authority over members of the Storm Troops and the Special Guards (S.S.) of 28 April 1933, is declared inoperative.

Berlin, 2 December 1933

(iv) ADOLF HITLER

The idea of National Socialism is embodied in the organisation and structure of the Party. The Party stands for political appreciation, political conscience, political endeavour....

Since the Party is called upon to form an organization through which a political élite of the nation shall be continuously recruited to all eternity, the Party is also in duty bound to ensure that the State be led on the ground of a stable philosophy. In fulfilment of this historical imperative, the Party must create an organisation that assures the stability of the leadership of the State by the right selection, training, and orientation of the leaders of the State. The Party must, in this, act on the principle that all Germans should be brought up in the doctrine of National Socialism; that the best National Socialists become members of the Party; that the best members of the Party take the lead in the State. Thus shall the organization of the Party provide the German State in the future with a supreme general leadership; thus shall its educational activities provide a foundation for this National Socialist State in a National Socialist Nation.

From the *Speech at the Nuremberg Party Congress, September,* 1935.

§.10. CONSTITUTIONAL LAW AND JUSTICE

[The revolution in constitutional law and the administration of justice involved in the National Socialist doctrine is not the least important of its departures from Liberal Democratic principles. But it would have been difficult until recently to find any official account of these changes. The *Beamtenkalender* of 1937, however, gives a detailed description of the constitutional changes, and one important amendment of the Penal Code indicates the influence of National Socialist ideas on the administration of justice. By itself this amendment is, perhaps, not highly important; and certainly it has not so far been applied except in a manner more or less innocuous to the rule of law. But it represents a tendency in the National Socialist doctrine to depart from the principle of government by settled law; and in so far as it encourages a judge to judge the law and not merely to judge according to the law it may, in time, produce more sweeping changes. This is specially to be expected in courts, such as the German Peoples' Courts, in which a high proportion of the judges are laymen. This amendment of the Penal Code comes after a considerable use by the regime of *ex post facto* laws, and establishes as a principle what was previously only a subterfuge for getting rid of the enemies of the regime.]

(i)

In the National Socialist conception of the State the task is not that of protecting the individual against the State. National Socialism, on the contrary, undertakes to defend the people as a whole against the individual, when and wherever his interests are not in harmony with the common weal....

Since there is, in the National Socialist State, no difference, let alone opposition, between the State as a separate legal structure and the totality of citizens and the individual citizen; since the State consists here of the totality of citizens, united in a common destiny by common blood and a common philosophy of life and comprised in a single organisation, it is neither necessary nor possible to define a sphere of freedom for the individual citizen as against the State. Hence also it is neither necessary nor possible to protect 'subjective rights' derived from such a sphere of freedom by means of constitutional law....

Our constitutional law is based on the National Socialist philosophy of life and is expressed in the general order of the Nation. So far as this general order is formulated in propositions, legal principles or programmatical statements, the supreme constitutional foundation of the Third Reich is laid down in the Party Programme....In addition to the Party Programme the basis of the structure of the State is provided by those laws of signal importance which are termed 'fundamental state laws' because they aim at realising the essential tenets of the National Socialist philosophy of life....

It goes without saying that laws dealing with, for example, the purity of blood, health etc., and those dealing with compulsory military service and labour service are to be regarded as fundamental laws. The totality of fundamental laws of the State is what we mean by 'the constitution'.

From the *Beamtenkalender*, 1937

(ii) AMENDMENT OF THE PENAL CODE

§ 2. Whoever performs an act which the law declares punishable or which, according to the fundamental principle of a penal code and healthy popular sentiment, deserves punishment, shall be punished.

If no definite penal law is immediately applicable to the act, the act shall be punished under the law which, according to the fundamental principle, applies to it most nearly.

Berlin, 28 *June* 1935

BOOK LIST

G. FEDER. *Hitler's Official Programme* (1934)

W. SOMBART. *A New Social Philosophy* (1937)

H. LICHTENBERGER. *The Third Reich* (English translation, 1938)

S. H. ROBERTS. *The House that Hitler Built* (1937)

L. PREUSS. Germanic Law *v*. Roman Law in National Socialist Legal Theory (*Journal of Comparative Legislation and International Law*, vol. XVI, 1934)

L. PREUSS. La Théorie Raciale et la doctrine politique de National-Socialisme (*Revue générale de Droit International public*, vol. XLI, 1934)

MANKIEWICZ. *Le Nationalsocialisme Allemand; ses doctrines et leurs réalisations* (1937)

F. L. SCHUMAN. *Hitler and the Nazi Dictatorship* (2nd ed. 1936)

APPENDIX
REPRESENTATIVE DEMOCRACY

APPENDIX

Since the first publication of this book numerous improvements have occurred to me. To introduce all of them would involve changes of arrangement too great to be undertaken at present. But it would be foolish not to take the opportunity of a reprint to remedy some of the more serious defects of the first section. I find that I have failed in that section to represent what must be regarded as two of the most important elements of the Democratic tradition and doctrine—government by law (that is, government as the administration of justice and not as the discretion of a ruler), and nationality. To find passages from the literature of Democracy to represent these principles is not an easy task. But for the first I have taken the *Déclaration des Droits de l'Homme et du Citoyen* (1789), which in any case is a document of sufficient importance in the history of Democratic doctrine to deserve inclusion; and for the second, J. S. Mill's chapter on Nationality from the *Considerations on Representative Government* (1861).

§1. RIGHTS AND DUTIES

(i)

We hold these truths to be self-evident: that all men are created equal; that they are endowed by their Creator with inalienable rights; that among these rights are life, liberty, and the pursuit of happiness; that to secure those rights governments are instituted among men, deriving their just powers from the consent of the governed; that whenever any form of government becomes destructive of those ends, it is the right of the people to alter or abolish it, and to institute new government, laying its foundations on such principles, and organizing its powers in such form, as to them shall seem most likely to effect their safety and happiness.

From *The Declaration of Independence*, 4 *July* 1776

(ii)

The representatives of the people of France, formed into a National Assembly, considering that ignorance, neglect or contempt of human rights, are the sole causes of public misfortunes and corruptions of government, have resolved to set forth in a solemn declaration, these natural, sacred and inalienable rights: that this declaration being constantly present in the minds of the members of the community, they may be kept ever attentive of their rights and their duties; that the acts of the legislative and executive powers of government, being capable of being at all times compared with the end of political institutions, may be more respected; and also, that the future claims of citizens, being directed by simple and incontestable principles, may always tend to the maintenance of the Constitution and the general happiness.

For these reasons the National Assembly recognizes and declares, in the presence of the Supreme Being, and with the hope of his blessing and favour, the following sacred rights of men and citizens:

Article 1. Men are born and remain free and equal in respect of their rights. Civil distinctions, therefore, may be founded only on public utility.

Article 2. The end of all political association is the preservation of the natural and imprescriptible rights of man. These rights are liberty, property, security, and resistance of oppression.

Article 3. The source of all sovereignty resides essentially in the nation. No individual and no body of men is entitled to exercise any authority which is not expressly derived from it.

Article 4. Liberty consists in being able to do whatever does not injure another. Thus, the exercise of the natural rights of each man has no other limits than those that are necessary to secure the free exercise of the same rights by other members of the society. These limits may be determined only by law.

Article 5. The law ought to prohibit only actions hurtful to the society. What is not prohibited by law may not be hindered, and no one may be compelled to do that which the law does not require.

Article 6. Law is the expression of the will of the community. All citizens have a right to co-operate, either personally or through their representatives, in making it. It should be the same for all, whether it protects or punishes. All citizens, being equal in its sight, are equally eligible to all public honours, places and employments, according to their abilities, and without any other distinction than that created by their virtues and talents.

Article 7. No man may be accused, arrested or detained except in cases determined by law and according to the forms prescribed by law. All who solicit, promote, execute, or cause to be executed arbitrary decrees ought to be punished; but every citizen called upon, or apprehended by virtue of the law ought immediately to obey: he makes himself culpable by resistance.

Article 8. The law ought to impose only those penalties that are strictly and clearly necessary; and no one may be punished except under a law established and promulgated before the offence, and legally applied.

Article 9. Every man being presumed innocent until he has been convicted, should it be deemed necessary to arrest a man, all violence towards him beyond what is indispensable to apprehend him should be strictly repressed by the law.

Article 10. No man should be molested on account of his opinions, not even on account of his religious opinions, so long as his expression of them does not disturb the public order established by law.

Article 11. The free expression of thought and opinion is one of the most precious rights of man; every citizen may speak, write and publish freely, provided that he is responsible for the abuse of this liberty in cases determined by law.

Article 12. A public force is necessary to secure the rights of men and of citizens; this force is, consequently, instituted for the benefit of all and not for the particular advantage of those to whom it is entrusted.

Article 13. A common contribution is necessary for the maintenance of this force and for meeting the expenses of government; it should be levied equally on all citizens, in proportion to their means.

Article 14. All citizens have a right, either personally or by their representatives, to establish the need for the public contribution, to vote it freely, to appropriate it, to determine its amount, its mode of assessment, its collection and its duration.

Article 15. The community has a right to demand of every public servant an account of his administration.

Article 16. Every society in which the security of rights is not assured nor the separation of the powers of government established, lacks a constitution.

Article 17. Property being an inviolable and sacred right, no man may be deprived of his possessions, except in cases of evident and urgent public necessity established by law, and on condition of a just and previously determined indemnity.

Déclaration des Droits de l'Homme et du Citoyen, August, 1789

§2. NATIONALITY

JOHN STUART MILL

A portion of mankind may be said to constitute a Nationality if they are united among themselves by common sympathies which do not exist between them and any others—which make them co-operate with each other more willingly than with other people, desire to be under the same government, and desire that it should be government by themselves or a portion of themselves exclusively. This feeling of nationality may have been generated by various causes. Sometimes it is the effect of identity of race and descent. Community of language, and community of religion, greatly contribute to it. Geographical limits are one of its causes. But the strongest of all is identity of political antecedents; the possession of a national history, and consequent community of recollections; collective pride and humiliation, pleasure and regret, connected with the same incidents in the past. None of these circumstances, however, are either indispensable, or necessarily sufficient by themselves. Switzerland has a strong sentiment of nationality, though the cantons are of different races, different languages, and different religions. Sicily has, throughout history, felt itself quite distinct in nationality from Naples, notwithstanding identity of religion, almost identity of language, and a considerable amount of common historical antecedents. The Flemish and the Walloon provinces of Belgium, notwithstanding diversity of race and language, have a much greater feeling of common nationality than the former have with Holland, or the latter with France. Yet in general the national feeling is proportionally weakened by the failure of any of the causes which contribute to it. Identity of language, literature, and, to some extent, of race and recollections, have maintained the feeling of nationality in considerable strength among the different portions of the German name, though they have at no time been really united under the same government; but the feeling has never reached to making the separate states desire to get rid of their autonomy. Among Italians an identity far from complete, of language and literature, combined with a geographical position which separates them by a distinct line from other countries, and, perhaps more than everything else, the possession of a common name, which makes them all glory in the past achievements in arts, arms, politics, religious primacy, science, and literature, of any who share the same designation, give rise to an amount of national feeling in the population which, though still imperfect, has been sufficient to produce the great events now passing before us, notwithstanding a great mixture of races, and although they have never, in either ancient or modern history, been under the same government, except while that government extended or was extending itself over the greater part of the known world.

Where the sentiment of nationality exists in any force, there is a *prima facie* case for uniting all the members of the nationality under the same government, and a government to themselves apart. This is merely saying that the question of government ought to be decided by the governed. One hardly knows what any division of the human race should be free to do if not to determine with which of the various collective bodies of human beings they choose to associate themselves. But, when a people are ripe for free institutions, there is a still more vital consideration. Free institutions are next to impossible in a country made up of different nationalities. Among a people without fellow-feeling, especially if they read and speak different languages, the united public opinion, necessary to the working of representative government, cannot exist. The influences which form opinions and decide political acts are different in the different sections of the country. An altogether different set of leaders have the confidence of one part of the country and of another. The same books, newspapers, pamphlets, speeches, do not reach them. One section does not know what opinions, or what instigations, are circulating in another. The same incidents, the same acts, the same system of government, affect them in different ways; and each fears more injury to itself from the other nationalities than from the common arbiter, the state. Their mutual antipathies are generally much stronger than jealousy of the government. That any one of them feels aggrieved by the policy of the common ruler is sufficient to determine another to support that policy. Even if all are aggrieved, none feel that they can rely on the others for fidelity in a joint resistance; the strength of none is sufficient to resist alone, and each may reasonably think that it consults its own advantage most by bidding for the favour of the government against the rest. Above all, the grand and only effectual security in the last resort against the despotism of the government is in that case wanting: the sympathy of the army with the people. The military are the part of every community in whom, from the nature of the case, the distinction between their fellow-countrymen and foreigners is the deepest and strongest. To the rest of the people foreigners are merely strangers; to the soldier, they are men against whom he may be called, at a week's notice, to fight for life or death. The difference to him is that between friends and foes—we may almost say between fellow-men and another kind of animals: for as respects the enemy, the only law is that of force, and the only mitigation the same as in the case of other animals—that of simple humanity. Soldiers to whose feelings half or three-fourths of the subjects of the same government are foreigners will have no more scruple in mowing them down, and no more desire to ask the reason why, than they would have in doing the same thing against declared enemies. An army composed of various nationalities has no other patriotism than devotion to the flag. Such armies have been the executioners of liberty through the whole duration of modern history. The sole bond which holds them together is their officers and the government which they serve; and their only idea, if they have any, of public duty is obedience to orders. A government thus supported, by keeping its Hungarian regiments in Italy and its Italian in Hungary, can long continue to rule in both places with the iron rod of foreign conquerors.

If it be said that so broadly marked a distinction between what is due to a fellow-countryman and what is due merely to a human creature is more worthy of savages than of civilised beings, and ought, with the utmost energy, to be contended against, no one holds that opinion more strongly than myself. But this object, one of the worthiest to which human endeavour can be directed, can never, in the present state of civilisation, be promoted by keeping different nationalities of anything like equivalent strength under the same government. In a barbarous state of society the case is sometimes different. The government may then be interested in softening the antipathies of the races that peace may be preserved and the country more easily governed. But when there are either free institutions or a desire for them, in any of the peoples artificially tied together, the interest of the government lies in an exactly opposite direction. It is then interested in keeping up and envenoming their antipathies that they may be prevented from coalescing, and it may be enabled to use some of them as tools for the enslavement of others. The Austrian Court has now for a whole generation made these tactics its principal means of government; with what fatal success, at the time of the Vienna insurrection and the Hungarian contest, the world knows too well. Happily there are now signs that improvement is too far advanced to permit this policy to be any longer successful.

For the preceding reasons, it is in general a necessary condition of free institutions that the boundaries of governments should coincide in the main with those of nationalities. But several considerations are liable to conflict in practice with this general principle. In the first place, its application is often precluded by geographical hindrances. There are parts even of Europe in which different nationalities are so locally intermingled that it is not practicable for them to be under separate governments. The population of Hungary is composed of Magyars, Slovacks, Croats, Serbs, Roumans, and in some districts Germans, so mixed up as to be incapable of local separation; and there is no course open to them but to make a virtue of necessity, and reconcile themselves to living together under equal rights and laws. Their community of servitude, which dates only from the destruction of Hungarian independence in 1849, seems to be ripening and disposing them for such an equal union. The German colony of East Prussia is cut off from Germany by part of the ancient Poland, and being too weak to maintain separate independence, must, if geographical continuity is to be maintained, be either under a non-German government, or the intervening Polish territory must be under a German one. Another considerable region in which the dominant element of the population is German, the provinces of Courland, Esthonia, and Livonia, is condemned by its local situation to form part of a Slavonian state. In Eastern Germany itself there is a large Slavonic population: Bohemia is principally Slavonic, Silesia and other districts partially so. The most united country in Europe, France, is far from being homogeneous: independently of the fragments of foreign nationalities at its remote extremities, it consists, as language and history prove, of two portions, one occupied almost exclusively by a Gallo-Roman population, while in the other the Frankish, Burgundian, and other Teutonic races form a considerable ingredient.

When proper allowance has been made for geographical exigencies, another more purely moral and social consideration offers itself. Experience proves that it is possible for one nationality to merge and be absorbed in another: and when it was originally an inferior and more backward portion of the human race the absorption is greatly to its advantage. Nobody can suppose that it is not more beneficial to a Breton, or a Basque of French Navarre, to be brought into the current of the ideas and feelings of a highly civilised and cultivated people—to be a member of the French nationality, admitted on equal terms to all the privileges of French citizenship, sharing the advantages of French protection, and the dignity and prestige of French power—than to sulk on his own rocks, the half-savage relic of past times, revolving in his own little mental orbit, without participation or interest in the general movement of the world. The same remark applies to the Welshman or the Scottish Highlander as members of the British nation.

Whatever really tends to the admixture of nationalities, and the blending of their attributes and peculiarities in a common union, is a benefit to the human race. Not by extinguishing types, of which, in these cases, sufficient examples are sure to remain, but by softening their extreme forms, and filling up the intervals between them. The united people, like a crossed breed of animals (but in a still greater degree, because the influences in operation are moral as well as physical), inherits the special aptitudes and excellences of all its progenitors, protected by the admixture from being exaggerated into the neighbouring vices. But to render this admixture possible, there must be peculiar conditions. The combinations of circumstances which occur, and which effect the result, are various.

The nationalities brought together under the same government may be about equal in numbers and strength, or they may be very unequal. If unequal, the least numerous of the two may either be the superior in civilisation, or the inferior. Supposing it to be superior, it may either, through that superiority, be able to acquire ascendancy over the other, or it may be overcome by brute strength and reduced to subjection. This last is a sheer mischief to the human race, and one which civilised humanity with one accord should rise in arms to prevent. The absorption of Greece by Macedonia was one of the greatest misfortunes which ever happened to the world: that of any of the principal countries of Europe by Russia would be a similar one.

If the smaller nationality, supposed to be the more advanced in improvement, is able to overcome the greater, as the Macedonians, reinforced by the Greeks, did Asia, and the English India, there is often a gain to civilisation: but the conquerors and the conquered cannot in this case live together under the same free institutions. The absorption of the conquerors in the less advanced people would be an evil: these must be governed as subjects, and the state of things is either a benefit or a misfortune, according as the subjugated people have or have not reached the state in which it is an injury not to be under a free government, and according as the conquerors do or do not use their superiority in a manner calculated to fit the conquered for a higher stage of improvement. . . .

When the nationality which succeeds in overpowering the other is both the most numerous and the most improved; and especially if the subdued nationality is small, and has no hope of reasserting its independence; then, if it is governed with any tolerable justice, and if the members of the more powerful nationality are not made odious by being invested with exclusive privileges, the smaller nationality is gradually reconciled to its position, and becomes amalgamated with the larger. No Bas-Breton, nor even any Alsatian, has the smallest wish at the present day to be separated from France. If all Irishmen have not yet arrived at the same disposition towards England, it is partly because they are sufficiently numerous to be capable of constituting a respectable nationality by themselves; but principally because, until of late years, they had been so atrociously governed, that all their best feelings combined with their bad ones in rousing bitter resentment against the Saxon rule. This disgrace to England, and calamity to the whole empire, has, it may be truly said, completely ceased for nearly a generation. No Irishman is now less free than an Anglo-Saxon, nor has a less share of every benefit either to his country or to his individual fortunes than if he were sprung from any other portion of the British dominions. The only remaining real grievance of Ireland, that of the State Church, is one which half, or nearly half, the people of the larger island have in common with them. There is now next to nothing, except the memory of the past, and the difference in the predominant religion, to keep apart two races, perhaps the most fitted of any two in the world to be the completing counterpart of one another. The consciousness of being at last treated not only with equal justice but with equal consideration is making such rapid way in the Irish nation as to be wearing off all feelings that could make them insensible to the benefits which the less numerous and less wealthy people must necessarily derive from being fellow-citizens instead of foreigners to those who are not only their nearest neighbours, but the wealthiest, and one of the freest, as well as most civilised and powerful, nations of the earth.

The cases in which the greatest practical obstacles exist to the blending of nationalities are when the nationalities which have been bound together are nearly equal in numbers and in the other elements of power. In such cases, each, confiding in its strength, and feeling itself capable of maintaining an equal struggle with any of the others, is unwilling to be merged in it: each cultivates with party obstinacy its distinctive peculiarities; obsolete customs, and even declining languages, are revived to deepen the separation; each deems itself tyrannised over if any authority is exercised within itself by functionaries of a rival race; and whatever is given to one of the conflicting nationalities is considered to be taken from all the rest. When nations, thus divided, are under a despotic government which is a stranger to all of them, or which, though sprung from one, yet feeling greater interest in its own power than in any sympathies of nationality, assigns no privilege to either nation, and chooses its instruments indifferently from all; in the course of a few generations, identity of situation often produces harmony of feeling, and the different races come to feel towards each other as fellow-countrymen; particularly if they are dispersed over the same tract of country. But if the era of aspiration to free government arrives before this fusion has been effected, the opportunity has gone by for effecting it. From that time, if the unreconciled nationalities are geographically separate, and especially if their local position is such that there is no natural fitness or convenience in their being under the same government (as in the case of an Italian province under a French or German yoke), there is not only an obvious propriety, but, if either freedom or concord is cared for, a necessity, for breaking the connection altogether. There may be cases in which the provinces, after separation, might usefully remain united by a federal tie: but it generally happens that if they are willing to forgo complete independence, and become members of a federation, each of them has other neighbours with whom it would prefer to connect itself, having more sympathies in common, if not also greater community of interest.

From *Considerations on Representative Government* (1861)

SUBJECT INDEX

Date Due

466085